At Home in the World

Reflections of a Travel Addict

Matt Davis

For more information, or to book an event, contact:
(disastermatt1958@yahoo.com)
www.mattathomeintheworld.com

Cover design by Andrew Rainnie

ISBN: 978-1-962133-06-7

First Edition: September 2023

"Traveling – it leaves you speechless, then turns you into a storyteller."

— Ibn Battuta (14th Century Scholar and Traveler)

This book is dedicated to my mother, Carol.

Her independent spirit, curiosity about the world, strong faith, infectious laugh, appreciation for good food, and love of life continue to inspire me, even so long after she's been gone.

Contents

1. I Blame It All on My Mother

Like mother, like son! Monkey Jungle, Florida, 1974; Australia, 2003

I've devoted a significant chunk of my adult life to the field of psychology, first working my way through college and graduate school and then during my thirty-plus years as a psychology professor. Although I originally aspired to be a clinical psychologist or therapist, I recognized early on that I didn't have the patience to deal with patients, so I opted instead to teach and do research. Of course, throughout my career I was exposed to everything from the original writings of Dr.

Freud to the frightening array of pop psychology self-help books that abound in bookstores. A common theme in much of this work is the notion that whatever psychological issue you're dealing with, it's probably somehow your mother's fault. While I personally think mothers have too often been unfairly targeted as the root cause of our adult problems and neuroses, I can definitely say that my mother was to blame for the fact that I developed a very serious travel addiction by the time I reached adulthood.

I'm now almost 65 years old and at this point in my life, I've traveled to thirty-five foreign countries, visited every state in the U.S., and have made over fifty round-trip, coast to coast drives - including one that involved a detour to Alaska. I've already put 127,000 miles on my poor, four-year-old car, and I'm rarely happier than when I'm behind the wheel with my favorite music serving as a soundtrack, heading out on the road to anywhere. I often joke that when I die, forget the urn or the coffin; just bury me in my car in the driver's seat with my hands still on the wheel.

While some people might look at a long weekend as a chance to rest at home or take a short local trip, before I retired, I'd hop on a red-eye flight to make use of every bit of free time available, flying off to see friends and family across the country, enjoy my favorite restaurants, visit a national park, stroll a beach or play in the snow. I'd then catch an early morning flight back home, sometimes rushing directly from the airport to my university campus to teach a class or two that same day! A week-long Spring Break or Thanksgiving recess was a good excuse for me to run off to Maui or even to Italy. When friends or colleagues got wind of my plans, they'd scowl, asking incredulously, "Wait. You're going to Italy for a WEEK?" My answer was always the same: "Why not?"

One of the perks of being a professor was summer break, allowing me the freedom to take lengthier trips. There were many summers when I spent less than two weeks in my own apartment. Within hours of the graduation ceremonies at the university, I'd depart for a month-long trip abroad. I'd come home to do laundry, cook a couple of meals for myself, binge-watch all the TV shows I'd recorded while I was away and after a few days I'd experience that restless feeling again, ready to get in the car for a multi-week road trip across the country. Some might say I was out of control, and I sometimes wondered how I got to be this way.

Perhaps an early clue that I was on the road to a travel addiction later in life was that the very first word I uttered after "Mama" was "car." Although I raced my little Hot Wheels cars on artificial-looking, bright orange, racetracks in the house, I much preferred my more realistic Matchbox cars, creating scenic and winding "roads" in the dirt of my backyard and pretending I was driving them in some far-away place. While other kids gravitated toward the "dodgems" or "bumper cars" at local amusement parks, I hated getting stuck in "traffic" and being slowed down by idiots trying to slam into me. I preferred the ride where I simply got to drive a colorful motorized car along a winding track past flower beds, shrubs, and miniature buildings, imagining that I was actually going somewhere! It's obvious that my addiction had roots extending deep into early childhood development, but the answer to the question of what exactly caused or encouraged this now seems as clear as a bell and conforms with countless psychological explanations and theories about why we are who we are: I blame it all on my mother!

* * *

Carol Brown grew up in a working-class family in New Bedford, Massachusetts, an hour south of Boston. She married and became Carol Davis in 1951, and along came baby Matt seven years later. Unfortunately, my father moved out when I was six months old, ironically choosing Father's Day to inform my mother that he was having an affair. He soon left the area and didn't maintain contact, so I never knew him. I learned that he eventually moved to Florida and then North Carolina and became a long-haul truck driver. I wondered whether at least part of my wanderlust was genetically inherited from him; the nature vs. nurture debate so central to much of psychology rears its head in my own story as well.

My father's departure resulted in my mom having to move in with my grandparents; she worked as a payroll clerk and occasionally took on a second job as a waitress. We never had a lot of money, but I always joke that whenever she had an extra nickel or two, we were off on an adventure. Some of my earliest childhood memories are of her taking me on day trips to the zoo in Providence, Rhode Island or to the aquarium or science museum in Boston. The fact that she would even think of driving to Boston was noteworthy. Boston is a city that most people in southern New England regard as a terrifying, far-away place, spoken about in hushed whispers. Locals believe that those who value their own sanity or even their very life should avoid Boston at all costs for fear of becoming permanently lost in its maze of one-way streets, aggressive drivers, and formidable traffic, never to be seen or heard from again. Yet somehow Boston never seemed to scare my mother.

Her best friend, Norma and her two young daughters often piled into the car with us, my mother always behind the wheel, and we'd head off for a day or sometimes an overnight trip to Cape Cod, Connecticut's Mystic Seaport, or the wilds of Vermont or New Hampshire. One of my mother's favorite destinations was the coast of Maine, and on those outings, she'd generously allow me to order a lobster dinner just like she did. Though she did like to swim, my clearest memory is of her sitting on the beach reading a murder mystery by Agatha Christie while I floated happily, gradually turning blue after an hour or so in Maine's icy ocean waters. She often confided to me that she dreamed of living on the Maine coast near Kennebunkport someday and it wasn't until adulthood that I realized how unrealistic it was for a divorced woman supporting a young son to think about living in the same neighborhood as the Bush family's seaside compound. But my mother didn't seem to allow the reality of her financial situation or life circumstances to get in the way of her dreams or her passion to live life to its fullest, and she definitely passed that on to me.

Another vivid childhood memory I have was the occasional Saturday or Sunday when my mother announced that we were going for a drive, and when I'd ask where we were going, she'd smile mischievously and say, "We're taking a mystery ride." A "mystery ride" never ceased to induce excitement and curiosity in me. Typically, we'd drive what seemed to be a random route, while I tried to guess at every turn or fork in the road where we might be heading. My mother loved to drive, and we'd talk, look at the passing scenery, and listen to songs on the radio like "Sweet Pea," "Windy," or her favorite, "Mrs. Brown You've Got a

Lovely Daughter" by Herman's Hermits, which she must have felt was written just for her given her maiden name. In between songs I'd venture a guess as to where we might be going.

"A mystery ride? Yay!"

At a young age, I was really tuned in to my surroundings, so if we seemed to be heading toward Providence, I'd guess that we were going for a pony ride at Roger Williams Park. If we headed south or west, that could mean that we were going for clam cakes at Sakonnet Point or ice cream at Gray's in Tiverton, both on the Rhode Island coast. If we headed east or north it might be to visit a beach on Cape Cod or to explore Plymouth, where my mom's ancestors had arrived on the Mayflower in 1620. Perhaps she'd inherited her willingness to journey into the unknown from her Pilgrim heritage. At any rate, on these mystery rides it didn't really matter where we'd end up; the old cliché about the journey being more important than the destination definitely held true in this case.

Evidently, by the age of six or seven, I was showing an unusual aptitude for map-reading and directions. My mom's friend Pat has told me stories of how my mother might spontaneously call her on a Saturday morning and suggest that we all go on a "mystery ride" together. Pat marveled at how my mother never seemed afraid of anything and was willing to drive to places that Pat would never have gone on her own. But she also remembers a little redheaded boy in the back seat on these trips, avidly studying the maps and occasionally interrupting their adult conversation with an important proclamation: "Mama, you should have taken a left on Route 103 north back there. We're going the wrong way."

According to Pat, my mother would initially dismiss my advice and insist we were on the right track, only to quietly turn the car around a mile or two down the road and backtrack to Route 103. I'd be sitting in the back seat gloating, and my mother would playfully tell me to "Keep quiet back there!" when I'd giggle with satisfaction at having been right.

"I couldn't believe it! You were only seven years old, for God's sake, and you were ALWAYS right!" Pat reports.

Happy travelers: visiting New Hampshire and leaving for Illinois.

Around this time my mother shocked the family by announcing that she was using her two week summer vacation to drive to Illinois and visit my paternal grandparents, aunts, and uncles. Now, this was still a few years before TV role models like Mary Richards of the *Mary Tyler Moore Show* left her small hometown and drove off to Minneapolis to start a new life as a single woman, confident that she'd was going to "make it after all." A single woman with a seven-year-old boy traveling alone by car on a 2,500-mile road trip was unheard of back then – and is probably still pretty rare even today. There were heated arguments between my mother and my grandparents about undertaking this trip. Nevertheless, some weeks later we were packed and ready to head west on an adventure that introduced me to the feeling of freedom that only comes from cruising down an interstate highway or a scenic backroad. Along the way I saw exotic places like Niagara Falls, Chicago, and the Pennsylvania Dutch Country, not to mention learning about the strange aspects of life in rural Illinois where my relatives lived. I recall the horror and pity I felt when my cousins there informed me that they'd never even heard of coffee ice cream, which was always a staple in New England, and of course, amidst the endless fields of corn, clam chowder and lobster were nowhere to be found.

A few years later we made our first trip to Washington, DC, by car of course. We took in all the sights, and as we drove around the city by night, I was captivated by the beautifully illuminated buildings and monuments that adorn our nation's capital. I must have been particularly taken with the Lincoln Memorial, as I have a photo of myself sitting in a chair in our motel room imitating the pose captured in the president's statue. I learned an important lesson one evening as we dined at a Lebanese restaurant where I childishly mocked the way our Lebanese waiter pronounced the word "carrots" as "Cah-ROTS." This momentarily spoiled what had been a jovial mood; my mother sternly explained to me in no uncertain terms that it was rude to make fun of someone's accent. She rarely got angry, so her scolding definitely got my attention and I'd never dare to make such a mistake again.

In my early teens I took on a travel-related project that further confirmed that I was heading for a travel addiction. I decided to write letters to the chambers of commerce in a couple dozen American cities to request information on what there was to see and do in each one. My mother generously provided the stamps and for the life of me I have no idea how I got all those mailing addresses in an era when a Google search was not even a glimmer in anyone's eye. But I sent off all my handwritten requests, and for the next few weeks I raced home from school every day to see if I had mail. I can't describe the excitement I felt when a big envelope arrived, and out spilled colorful pamphlets adorned with photos of far-off skylines: Dallas, Seattle, Denver, Nashville, Las Vegas, Salt Lake City, Phoenix, New Orleans. I'd share them with my mom when she got home from work, and we'd talk about where we'd most like to go. I longed for the day when I'd be able to visit each and every one of them.

In 1973 we made a trip to Miami and the newly opened Walt Disney World in Orlando. My mom and I planned this trip for months and I found that sometimes the planning itself can be half the fun. I also learned about the disappointments that can happen when we travel. The beachfront Aztec Motor Lodge in Miami Beach, pictured in advertising pamphlets as a shimmering Mexican palace by the sea, turned out to be a tired, old motel with chipped paint. Though we'd reserved an oceanfront room, we'd been placed in a dark, dingy room facing the back parking lot. I behaved badly, pouting and almost on the verge of tears from such a let-down, and I remember Mama saying, "Please don't cry or I will too!" Now, as an adult, I can only imagine the disappointment she must have felt after saving so hard and planning this trip for so long; to this day I feel guilty for how I acted. Happily, the following day the mix-up was resolved, and we were relocated to a recently renovated oceanfront room with the sparkling Atlantic right outside the window.

It wasn't long after that Florida trip when my world changed forever; my mother was diagnosed with cancer. Despite several operations, radiation treatments and chemotherapy, it spread from her kidney to her brain over the next year and a half. There were multiple surgeries and week-long stays in Boston hospitals. By the time I was fifteen years old, I was often living out of a hotel room close to the hospital, visiting my mom during the day, and going back to the hotel to use the pool and do my homework at night. When I didn't get a ride from my mom's friend Norma, I'd take a bus back to New Bedford to attend school, get caught up on assignments, pack some fresh clothes, and head back to Boston for another few days. It was a strange, solitary existence and none of my friends could possibly relate to what my life was like at that time. I sometimes wonder how I was able to get through all this at such a young age, and yet I know this is another thing I can blame on my mother. She'd taught me how to be independent and how to handle so many of the logistics of travel. I knew how to order at a restaurant and how much to leave for a tip, I could check in at a hotel, and I knew how to consult a bus schedule and buy my ticket, so it was all second nature to me by this point.

As a distraction from what was happening in our lives, I kept myself busy with more travel planning. My mother had put aside a bit of money and we'd talked about taking what we considered THE dream trip: a visit to California. With the help of AAA guidebooks, I'd soon found great hotels in San Francisco and Los Angeles and had made a list of the must-see sites, from the San Diego Zoo to the Hollywood Walk of Fame and from the Big Sur Coast to the Redwood forests. I think that talking about these plans gave both of us a bit of hope and optimism about the future, despite the fact that my mom's situation was getting bleaker.

Unfortunately, my mother took the ultimate trip in January 1975, passing away at the brutally young age of forty-four. Much of that time is a foggy blur; I was totally numb. and I don't even recall details of her funeral. It's as though I repressed the memories and buried the emotions because it was all just too painful. I tried to carry on without her, aided to some extent by friends and family, but mainly relying on the inner strength she'd cultivated in me during our sixteen years together. I was now a junior in high school, living with my elderly grandmother and pretty much taking care both of her and myself.

My mom and I never managed to take our trip to California, but like someone motivated to complete an important spiritual pilgrimage, I knew that I needed to make the trip for us. Just as my mother had met with great resistance from the family about taking that road trip to Illinois, my aunts and uncles objected to me "running off to California" on my own, but I really didn't listen to any of their arguments. Aided by some insurance money that my mother left me, I marched into a local travel agency at the ripe old age of sixteen and booked a ten-day trip to California during April vacation, three months after my mother died. In retrospect, I've always wondered what the travel agents must have thought when this child walked into their office or why they even took me seriously, but I guess once my check cleared, they were totally in my corner.

Off I went to the Golden State, living the dream that my mom and I had created together. I spent five nights at the Holiday Inn Chinatown in San Francisco, with a room that looked out toward the Bay and Alcatraz. A wonderful young nurse who'd taken care of my mother at the hospital in Boston had stayed in touch with me, and she gave me the number of a friend of hers who lived in the Bay Area. He was a young fireman who lived across the Golden Gate Bridge in Marin County and was willing to spend some time showing me around. He made my day when he took me for an exciting tour to the redwood forests and

9

beaches of Marin on the back of his motorcycle. Because he worked part time at the exclusive San Francisco Yacht Club in Tiburon, he got me a table for lunch there one afternoon where I dined on an abalone steak as I stared across the bay at the San Francisco skyline. This was my first encounter with San Francisco, the city that would eventually become my home for thirty years. I sometimes fantasize about being able to go back in time and tell my younger self that one day he'd be living in San Francisco and teaching at a university just five miles up the road from that yacht club.

Dining in San Francisco, age 16; living in San Francisco, age 50.

On that same trip I took a night flight from San Francisco to Los Angeles and was in awe as the pilot pointed out a glow in the sky ahead of us, even though we'd just barely taken off. He told us that we were already seeing the lights of L.A., still 350 miles away. Again, I try to wrap my head around the idea of my teenaged self, landing at LAX at 11:00PM and taking a city bus to my hotel on the Sunset Strip in Hollywood. I can't believe I'd even thought of such details, but I'd asked in advance for a room with a view out over Los Angeles. Upon my arrival the desk clerk apologized and said that a room with a city view hadn't been available, but I noticed out of the corner of my eye that he exchanged a smile and a wink with the bellman who took my luggage and showed me to my room. When he opened the door, he didn't turn on the lights right away, but he didn't have to. My room was on one of the highest floors of the hotel and the lights of the entire L.A. Basin stretched out beneath me for miles, lighting the room in an orange glow. They call Los Angeles the "City of Angels." Looking back, I believe that on that night there was one very special angel beside me, smiling as she looked out at that view with me.

I was so taken with California that I returned that summer for a longer trip. Due to a cheap airfare deal that allowed travel to multiple cities, I added stops in Phoenix and Las Vegas, and then on to Illinois for a visit with my relatives there. The images of cities I'd seen in those Chamber of Commerce pamphlets a few years before came to life for me on this trip. Incredulously, I look back on these experiences: making reservations for dinner at San Francisco's famous Fairmont Hotel, booking a bus tour from Phoenix to the Grand Canyon, attending a comedy show featuring Bob Newhart at the Riviera Hotel in Vegas, getting to and from airports in San Francisco, L.A., Phoenix, Las Vegas, and Chicago all by myself and seemingly effortlessly. I wonder what my mother would have thought about all this.

The following year, after graduating from high school I made my first cross-country drive in my mom's car, camping out in a pup tent most of the time and exploring the country from the Blue Ridge and Smoky Mountains to the Rockies, to California and back. It took me another ten years before I made my first trip to Europe, but that opened up the world to me and from then on, there was no going back. Travel became as important a part of my life as eating and breathing. Well, perhaps not as important as eating, but I won't discuss my food addiction here!

I've been very fortunate to have been able to travel so extensively in my adult life, and it came as a nice reward after years of putting myself through college and graduate school and living like the proverbial "starving student" well into my early thirties. Aside from the generous vacation time that my career in academia provided, I was able to attend and make conference presentations in exciting destinations like Japan, New Zealand, Hawaii, Greece, and Italy. My university typically paid my expenses to travel to these conferences and then I'd tack on additional time to explore on my own. I also led many study abroad trips for students which involved teaching a class about the place we'd be trav-

11

eling to and then guiding them on a one or two week tour. Some of my most cherished memories are of those times when I could share my passion for travel with my students, bonding over an amazing meal at my favorite restaurant in Rome or hiking and watching an amazing sunset together on the Greek island of Santorini.

In order to earn promotions and tenure at the university, I was required to conduct research. My area of expertise revolved around how people living in dangerous places view their risk from natural disasters like earthquakes, volcanoes, and hurricanes and how to best encourage them to take precautions to prepare for such events. This earned me the nickname "Disasterman" on campus and led to collaborations with some Italian colleagues. I spent several months conducting surveys of the residents living close to Italy's famous volcano, Mt. Vesuvius. In short, I took every opportunity to turn my work-related responsibilities into travel opportunities, and I was pretty successful at it!

Getting a Big Mac in Pompei; my prized San Andreas Fault tie.

I must admit that my passion for travel has involved making certain sacrifices. While I benefitted from living in a relatively cheap, rent controlled apartment in San Francisco for thirty years, I spent much of my excess income on travel and as a result, I'll probably never be able to afford my own home and I may have created a more challenging future for myself by not putting more money away for retirement. I've never been able to have a pet, and I've lost many gorgeous plants and trees that either died of neglect while I was traveling or had to be given away because I was simply always on the go. I think that some of my personal relationships may also have suffered as a result of my tendency to spontaneously pick up and go or to be away from home so much. I don't regret the choices I've made; the experiences and memories I've had can never be taken away from me, but they have come at some cost.

Like my mother, I've tried to share my love of travel with friends and family, encouraging them to come along with me, whether for an afternoon mystery ride, a weekend trip around New England, a week-long road trip across the western states, or spending a few days in some European country. On many occasions my companions have mentioned that they feel a presence in the back seat of the car and are convinced that my mother is along for the ride, and I believe that too, with all my heart.

Many aspects of the man I am today can be blamed on my mother. She could find humor in almost any situation and her laugh was infectious. She truly enjoyed a good meal and was open to trying new or unfamiliar dishes. She taught me that we don't need lots of money to experience the world and that seemingly small things are worthy of our attention: an unusual cloud formation, a beautiful flower, a brazen bird invading our picnic lunch, or the sound of the waves at the beach. These were some of the gifts she passed on to me, and I think they're relevant whether you're traveling the world or just enjoying a quiet day at home. Probably the most important thing I learned from my mother is that we can't predict the future, so we need to live life to the fullest and shouldn't put things off until tomorrow. I know that may sound obvious or clichéd, but it's something we're all guilty of doing to one extent or another.

I've never lost sight of how fortunate I've been to have seen and experienced so much of the world. My travels have made me more confident, have resulted in friendships with people in far-flung states and countries, and have provided me with a feeling of being comfortable and "at home" in a dizzying array of places. My love of travel and desire to experience everything this amazing planet has to offer burns inside me constantly. I realize that some of you reading this may have little desire to travel as I have. Others may not have had the opportunity or resources to travel as much as they'd like, and some may be intimidated by the thought of venturing out on their own. And then there are those who've traveled to an even greater extent or to more exotic destinations than me. Whatever your background or your "relationship" with travel may be, I hope the stories I've shared in this book will at least amuse and entertain you and may perhaps even inspire you to follow your dreams and experience the world, whether that means wandering just fifty miles from home or traveling to far-off places on the other side of the globe.

And so, I'd like to invite you to come along with me on some of my most memorable adventures. I've selected tales from my international travels that were particularly noteworthy, funny, or somehow stood out against the backdrop of the many trips I've taken. Some chapters of this book started out as group e-mails that I sent back home to loved ones as I traveled. Thankfully, I sent them to myself too, saved them, and over the years edited them, adding or clarifying details, sharing thoughts and feelings I was having at the time, and including some of my favorite photos. I wanted to turn those memoirs that meant so much to me into something that might appeal to a wider audience, and I hope I've succeeded in that.

About twenty years ago during a visit with my Uncle Harry, my mom's older brother, and his wife, my Aunt Helena, I was both shocked and touched when Uncle Harry opened a desk drawer containing printed copies of every travel e-mail I'd ever written and every post card I'd ever sent them. He said, "By God, Matthew, if you don't turn all this into a book, I'll do it for you!" Though they're both gone now, their encouragement helped motivate me to finally tackle this project. Likewise, my mom's best friend Norma, now ninety-three years old, is one of my biggest cheerleaders, eager to see this book come to fruition and reassuring me of how proud my mom would be. But of course, most importantly, I want to dedicate this book to my dear mother, Carol. I can picture her laughing and shaking her head in disbelief if she could read these stories about the things I've done and places I've been and knowing that she'd started it all - that it was all her fault.

2. Crocodiles, Jellyfish and Killer Cassowaries, Oh My!

AUSTRALIA

Down under, literally and figuratively, Great Barrier Reef.

One of the greatest gifts of working in academia is being awarded a sabbatical. Every seven years, professors may apply for a sabbatical leave during which they are released from all their duties for a semester to work on some project or research. In Spring 2003 I received my first sabbatical, and while I spent much of that time conducting a survey of people living in volcanically active areas of Italy, I also used this opportunity to explore a new part of the world. I found an airline ticket that allowed me to fly in a circle around the Pacific Rim for several weeks, stopping as many times as I wanted as long as I didn't reverse direction. I started the trip in Thailand and then Bali, Indonesia. Both were incredible, filled with exotic sights, foods, customs, and some of the gentlest, kindest people on the planet. I rode an elephant, I fed monkeys, I watched dramatic dance performances at cliff-top temples, soaked in volcanic hot springs, and saw what back-breaking work it is to harvest rice, which made me vow never to waste another grain of it again. My third stop on the trip was Australia and by the time I'd arrived there, I was looking forward to spending some time in a more familiar western culture.

I always recommend that when planning a visit to a foreign country, it's important to do some reading and research about your destination to help you prepare and get the most out of your time there. In the months leading up to my Australian trip I read a lot about the "land down under" and I have to say that what I learned was somewhat unnerving. I'd watched enough Discovery Channel documentaries to know that Australia is home to some of the world's most venomous snakes and spiders, but unfortunately, that was only the tip of the iceberg. As someone who loves to swim in the ocean, I read with horror about box jellyfish, locally referred to as "stingers." They roam the warmer waters of the Australian coast from October to June. If stung badly enough, a person may stop breathing in under two minutes; death usually follows. I learned that during my February visit I could only enter the water at beaches protected by "stinger nets" which are used to rope off a small, safe area for swimming. Guidebooks also warned of dreaded cone shells at the beach; if stepped on they send a lethal dose of neurotoxins directly into the bloodstream. Note to self: wear sandals on the beach at all times.

But there was more! I also read that it wasn't terribly safe to walk in some of Australia's forests. I'd need to beware of "killer cassowaries" - huge ostrich-like birds that have been known to slice tourists with their huge claws. If you encounter one on a trail, guidebooks advise backing away slowly, being sure not to upset the animal. Of course, not being a cassowary expert, I had no idea what might upset these creatures, but I figured that to be safe, if I did encounter one, I'd keep the fact that I've eaten ostrich steaks in the past a secret and it would probably be a good idea not to mention that I'd had eggs for breakfast! The forests are also home to some plant species that, if brushed up against, cause excruciating pain due to a toxin on their leaves. I packed a pair of long pants made of thick material just for hiking, despite the fact that the weather conditions I'd be facing would be very hot and humid. And as if all of this weren't enough, Australia is also inhabited by dangerous crocodiles, both the salt and freshwater varieties, so I vowed to refrain from taking a dip in anything other than a swimming pool or an exceptionally crowded beach to reduce my odds of being on some rogue crocodile's dinner menu!

After this newly acquired knowledge, I was having some reservations about my visit, but I'm an optimist at heart. People travel to Australia all the time; how many of them are ravaged by cassowaries, eaten by crocs, killed by jellyfish, or burned by sap from some silly plant? I'm brave; I'm a seasoned traveler. I've watched every single season of *Survivor* and I've learned the show's mantra: "Outplay, outwit, outlast!" I was ready. Oz, here I come!

I flew into Melbourne, picked up a rental car, and after a few minutes of adjusting to shifting with my left hand and driving on the "wrong" side of the road, I headed west along the coast toward Adelaide, a distance of over 600 miles. I followed the famous Great Ocean Road that skirts the southern shoreline. The scenery was beautiful, and somewhat reminiscent of California's Big Sur Coast. Magnificent rock formations like the famous Twelve Apostles jutted out of the water, just begging to be photographed.

After spending the night outside Adelaide, I caught a morning ferry from Cape Jervis to Kangaroo Island, a popular tourist destination off Australia's south coast known for its large populations of koalas, kangaroos, seals, and penguins, as well as its inherent scenic beauty. It was quiet and rural, and as soon as I'd checked in at my hotel, I headed off to start exploring. Almost immediately I spied several wild koalas clinging to eucalyptus tree branches and munching on the leaves high above me. I'd read that koalas spend an average of twenty hours a day sleeping and the rest of their time eating eucalyptus; because this diet contains so few nutrients, they need an excessive amount of rest. Spending all day eating and sleeping did not sound unappealing. I think I could embrace my inner koala pretty easily, though I'd prefer pie or cookies to a "eucalyptus leaf salad."

My destination that afternoon was a wildlife sanctuary called Paul's Place where injured or orphaned animals were being cared for. Paul was a farmer with an accent and personality not unlike the now-deceased Steve Irwin, the Crocodile Hunter who had a popular TV show on Animal Planet. As I arrived, Paul was tossing a group of visiting children one by one several feet through the air and into huge bales of lamb's wool, where they landed seemingly unhurt, but rather dazed and dumbfounded. Minutes later he brought out an enormous python and draped it around a screaming woman's neck. This guy was a lunatic, but he was quite funny. I soon got to wear the python necklace myself, and given how heavy it was, I wondered if it had swallowed a stray child before I arrived. When it started to get a little too comfortable wrapping itself around my neck, I urgently got Paul's attention and asked him to come and collect his pet.

My visit to Paul's Place: anything but dull!

I then had the opportunity to hold and bottle-feed a baby kangaroo, and to feed sheep, emus, wallabies, and adult kangaroos. Of those, the nastiest by far were the sheep. They jumped up on me, almost knocking me over and plunging head-first into the food bucket. In contrast, the emus, despite being cousins of the dreaded cassowaries and standing almost six feet tall, were calm and polite and simply waited their turn. Suddenly Paul returned and before I could even react, he pushed me up against a tall picket fence and proceeded to pour a bucket of seeds over my head. He shouted something unintelligible and immediately a couple of giant emus appeared on the other side of the fence and began to peck the seeds off the top of my head, occasionally taking a few tufts of hair too, or at least that was how it felt! Amidst all of this, Paul somehow managed to take my camera and get pictures of this spectacle, so at least I had proof that this wasn't some crazy, down under dream I'd had. Eventually I got to cuddle a sleepy, domesticated koala bear. He was as heavy as lead; I'd never have imagined that one of these little buggers could get that heavy on a diet of eucalyptus leaves. I chuckled, thinking that if this guy could come and hang out with me at a bakery for a day or two, he'd have been impossible to lift.

As if my stay at Paul's Place wasn't enough excitement for one day, I went on a "Fairy Penguin Tour" that evening. As a resident of San Francisco, I was half-expecting to find a group of penguins with pink fur, marching in leather chaps and carrying gay pride flags. In reality they were simply very small penguins, barely a foot tall and weighing about two pounds, and they make a nightly routine of waddling ashore to sleep and tend their nests. They were absolutely adorable. I've since learned that shortly after my visit, it was decided that fairy penguins should be renamed over concern for offending the LGBTQ Community, which left me speechless. So now these animals are referred to by the much less colorful name, "Little Penguins." As they say down under, "Crikey!" You can't make this stuff up.

The next day I toured the Remarkable Rocks, jumbled, bizarrely sculpted formations that were created by erosion from both rain and ocean waves. I then took a tour of Seal Bay, where a ranger led me and two other people on a beach walk where we were able to get within ten feet of dozens of sea lions lounging in the sand and body surfing on the waves, virtually ignoring our presence. After Seal Bay, I explored many of the coves and beaches in the area and ended up at Admiral's Arch, within Flinders Chase National Park. Situated on cliffs at the southwest corner of the island, this is home to colonies of long-nosed or New Zealand fur seals. I could hear them barking at one another from a mile away, and after descending a long staircase down the cliff, I watched them leaping off rocks into the pristine waters below. At the end of the stairs was the dramatic Arch, its ceiling dripping with stalactites. The sun was getting low in the sky, creating intricate patterns of light on the water. Best of all, I was the only person there; I just sat and watched the seals for an hour or so in peaceful solitude.

It was dusk as I started the drive back to town along a rutted dirt road, so I wasn't able to go much faster than 25 MPH. Out of nowhere a very large kangaroo bounded from my left side and landed directly in front of the car! I had absolutely no time to stop. I hit the animal, which then bounced forward, and continued hopping off into the brush on the other side of the road. I got out of the car and tried to see if I could find it to see how badly hurt it might be. Guidebooks recommend trying to check the pouch of a kangaroo if you hit one, as there could be babies inside that might be saved. Unfortunately, I couldn't find the animal I'd hit, so I prayed that it hadn't been too badly hurt and had just kept going on its way. Meanwhile, the rental car's left front headlight had popped out of its socket, though nothing else seemed obviously broken, so I popped the light back in as best I could and headed on my way at an even painfully slower speed the rest of the way back to town.

I noticed an alarming number of animals dead along the roadsides: possums, wallabies, and especially kangaroos. They may be more dangerous than deer; although deer can quickly run out into the road, these animals simply hop from the bushes to the front of your car in one effortless leap and there is absolutely no way to see them coming. Of course, carnivore that I am, my feelings of guilt over hitting the kangaroo didn't keep me from ordering a kangaroo steak for dinner at the hotel restaurant that night. It was very, very good, and contrary to the old adage, it did not taste like chicken!

A wonderful perk of being in such a rural area was that the night sky was absolutely stunning. For those who've never traveled south of the equator, everything in the night sky is, from a Northern Hemisphere perspective, either backward or upside down. Here the moon moves from east to west across the northern, not the southern sky. The crescent of a new moon is open on the right side rather than the left. I noticed the constellation Orion, the hunter, but he looked funny, and it took me a minute to realize why: he was upside-down, his sword hanging upward instead of downward from his belt. Meanwhile, the Milky Way was unbelievably bright here, and the famous constellation of the Southern Cross that I'd heard so much about did not disappoint, just dazzling in the southern sky.

After a great couple of days on the island, I caught the ferry back to the mainland and started the long ride back to Melbourne. Taking the coastal route westbound had been almost 700 miles, so going back I took a shorter inland route, but it still took a long time. The highway passed through many congested towns with a lot of road construction. When I finally returned the rental car to the airport in Melbourne, they found damage to the undercarriage, as well as the headlight; they charged me a hefty insurance deductible before I was free to leave and catch a shuttle to my hotel in the city.

I spent the next two days exploring "Mel-bun" as the Aussies pronounce it and found it to be a very clean, safe city with flat topography and orderly, grid-like streets reminiscent of many big cities in the American mid-west. I stayed in a suburb at the beach south of town called St. Kilda and was glad I did. It's an area with a small, oceanside amusement park, and a couple of main streets, Acland and Fitzroy, jammed with interesting restaurants and cafes. I was also within walking distance of the main beach area. Thankfully, since the dreaded box jelly-fish are rarely found this far south, I was able to go for a refreshing swim, which was much needed given the extremely hot weather during my stay.

One morning I took a tram to Melbourne University to meet a renowned German researcher who taught there. He was an expert in the field of risk perception, and I'd read one of his books, so I was excited when he agreed to take time to meet me for lunch. He was an eccentric man who wore brilliant red socks, pants with legs a bit too short (maybe to show off the socks), and a festive, red button-down shirt with a Chinese dragon emblazoned across it. In his heavy German accent, he commended me for being so punctual for our meeting, complaining that the Australians seem to have no sense of time and are always late for appointments and classes. "Of course, I must be careful not to say too much about this issue, because then they accuse me of being a Nazi," he joked. We had lunch on campus while he looked over the survey I intended to use in Italy, giving me some valuable tips for ways to improve it.

From Melbourne I flew to Sydney and after an hour and a half on an airport shuttle that took a ridiculously circuitous route, I arrived at my downtown hotel. I checked in and got on the elevator to head up to my room when five Aussie "blokes" hopped in with me. They were loud, obnoxious, and though it was only 2PM, they seemed very, very drunk. One of them asked where I was from, and when I told him, one of the others yelled, "Wow, San Francisco! How's the pussy there? Must be great!" I was so caught off guard that all I could do was laugh. We stopped at one floor where two women wanted to get on the elevator, but there wasn't enough space for them. As the doors closed, one of these guys pointed at me and my luggage, "See that, mate, if you didn't have that bloody big bag of yours, we'd have had two ladies and six blokes in here! Them's good odds!" Again, all I could do was laugh and pray that we'd reach my floor soon! It was the longest elevator ride in history.

Despite my interesting encounter in the elevator, my overall first impression of Sydney was very positive. It's a vibrant, exciting, and sparklingly clean city surrounded by a dramatic backdrop of hills and inviting beaches. The beautiful harbor is alive with ferries chugging back and forth and is adorned with interesting bridges and the iconic Sydney Opera House. The city is also amazingly compact; I could walk almost anywhere within a half hour, though trains and buses were plentiful. It was considerably warmer than Melbourne and the foliage was far more tropical. The streets are tree-lined, and those trees are populated by a number of tropical birds that make beautiful music, though the little green parrots were singing rather loudly and a bit off-key. I took a stroll through the city's lush botanical gardens, unnerved by several trees filled with "flying foxes" - a cute nickname for bats! They were spooky even in the broad daylight. Sorry, but I'd have preferred to see cuddly koala bears hanging from those trees!

During my time in Sydney, I had to learn a few things about the culinary culture. Ordering coffee was a little daunting, as café menus offered no description of drinks with unfamiliar names. A coffee with milk is called a "flat white," an espresso is a "short black," and a large black coffee is, of course, a "tall black." Iced coffee, a favorite drink in my native New England, is unfortunately different here; they add a scoop of ice cream and loads of whipped cream into a tepid glass of coffee, so it's not the thirst-quencher that its American cousin is. Prices were not cheap and no refills on coffee were offered in restaurants, which put a huge dent in my caffeine addiction! I also found that there was a charge for a variety of condiments that we take for granted as being free in the U.S. If you want ketchup and tartare sauce for those fish and chips, or jam for your morning toast, it will cost you, significantly increasing the price of what may have started out as a relatively cheap meal.

Harbor Bridge from East Quay

My first night in Sydney I wanted to dine in an area called Circular Quay at a Chinese restaurant called East Quay. It had been strongly recommended by a friend who'd had a phenomenal dish of emu in black bean sauce there. I started walking toward the eastern side of the quay and spotted a Chinese place called The Quay. It was closed until 6 PM, but when I checked the menu in the window there was no emu. Drat! Could it have been a special of the day? Was it not emu season? Sighing heavily, I kept walking along the quay and soon saw another Chinese restaurant simply called East. I looked at their menu, and there it was: emu in black bean sauce, and the restaurant was open. I sat outside with a view of the Sydney Harbor Bridge while dining on emu and experiencing some guilty feelings given my happy times with the emus at Paul's Place. But the dish was indeed amazing, and I can again report that emu does not taste like chicken or any other poultry. Similar to ostrich steak, emu is more like lean, tender beef, and the Chinese preparation at East was wonderful.

Later that evening I decided to stop by the bar at the Oxford Hotel for a drink. As I attempted to enter, the doorman stopped me, carefully scrutinized me, and asked, "Sir, how much have you had to drink tonight?" I was so thrown off guard I laughed and answered truthfully that I hadn't had anything to drink at all. I thought he was joking, but with no humor in his voice whatsoever, he continued, "You look a bit out of it. Are you sure you haven't been drinking?" OK, I was a bit tired, and my contact lenses were dry, but damn, I didn't think I looked that bad! The situation reminded me of a famous psychology study: a researcher got himself admitted to a mental hospital to observe life from the inside, but then couldn't talk his way back out because everything he said, no matter how rational, was simply interpreted as evidence that he was crazy! Similarly, no matter what I said, the doorman seemed to use it as further proof of my drunkenness and ultimately refused me entry into the bar! I left, shaking my head in a mix of disbelief and disgust. This was all the more ironic because of the sheer number of loud, drunken people roaming the streets or the drunken fools I'd encountered in the elevator at my hotel that afternoon. But here I was, stone-cold sober and a bit tired and I couldn't even get into a bar to have a beer. Luckily, I found a place further up the block where apparently, I looked respectable enough to be admitted.

As much as I was falling in love with Sydney, I learned that it becomes a rather ugly place on Friday and Saturday nights. By day it's a very laid back and friendly city but literally transforms into a drunken horror show after dark. I made the mistake of taking a bus to Circular Quay one night. Little did I know that this bus route was frequented by hordes of college kids heading out for a night of debauchery after having apparently gotten a head start back in their dorms. Imagine a bus packed with a hundred people, many of them screaming to one another at the top of their lungs from one end of the bus to another, and the word "fuckin'" being the only adjective they seemed familiar with. We were caught in hellishly snarled traffic, and the trip to the Quay took forever. At every stop, another group of hellions was waiting to cram themselves into the packed bus, and those unable to squeeze in were banging on the sides of the bus as it lumbered away from the curb. One couple on the bus was having a domestic quarrel the likes of which you'd have only seen on the old *Jerry Springer Show*. The woman was shrieking, "Why don't you fuckin' take me home and fuck me tonight!? God knows it hasn't happened in fuckin' months, you fuckin' motherfucker!"

"Thanks for sharing!" I thought as I tried to ignore what was happening right beside me. I know there's a stereotype that Aussie men are rowdy and heavy drinkers; while there's some truth to that, I must tell you that in Sydney, the behavior of the "fairer sex" made the men look civilized by comparison. The young women I saw were dressed like something out of an MTV video, so over the top that it seemed like they were wearing a Halloween costume. Many of them were drunk out of their minds, dancing in the middle of traffic and screaming profanities at pitches that could damage the human ear. From the bus window I saw throngs of young people waiting in line to get into the many clubs along George Street but tucked away in back alleys I saw women vomiting as their girlfriends stood around holding their friends' hair up and out of the way. What a way to spend a weekend! I simply cannot comprehend it. I often say that I studied Psychology for forty years, but I will never understand people.

Sydney is far more appealing in the light of day. One afternoon I took a ferry to the beach at Manly, thirty minutes north of the city. The ocean water felt surprisingly cool, but the beaches were clean and beautiful. In fact, Sydney and Melbourne are both spotlessly clean and San

Francisco could take a lesson from them. It made me sad to see these pristine cities and remember that San Francisco looked like this when I first moved there, but has become a shabby, unsavory place where you want to throw your shoes away after walking the streets for a day.

An afternoon at Manly Beach.

I love good food and enjoy trying all sorts of local treats when I travel. I found a great brunch spot in the Surry Hills neighborhood where they served pancakes sprinkled with granulated sugar and lemon wedges, but without any syrup. At first, I thought that was odd, but after squeezing a bit of lemon juice over the cakes, wetting the sugar on top, it made the most delicious topping! I decided I'd have to try that back home. I went back there another day, and the staff remembered me, treating me like an old friend. When I ordered a flat white without any hesitation, one of them exclaimed, "Ah, look, he's embracing the culture!" I sat outside and dined on the corncakes they were known for, served with wonderful bacon, fresh avocado, and a salad. If I lived in Sydney, this would be my hang out.

Another day I took a bus to Bondi (pronounced BOND-EYE) Beach. I had brunch at a place called Brown Sugar, where my pancakes were literally buried under fresh kiwi, apples, grapes, and strawberries and topped with poached rhubarb and yogurt. I wandered the town, but it was very hot and crowded, so I found a shady place in a park near the beach. A border collie brought me a frisbee, dropping it at my feet and waiting for me to throw it so she could run off to catch it and bring it back to me. After a few rounds of this game of fetch, she took her frisbee to some other people, but eventually came back to me for a few more tosses. I guess she didn't want anyone to feel left out. Her owner watched all this with amusement and commented, "She's a very social dog."

I then decided it was time for a swim. The water was crystal clear and reminded me of Hawaii. I was probably out there for an hour, carefully dodging surfers and boogie boarders who occasionally seemed to aim themselves in my direction. Suddenly, a lifeguard in a jeep pulled up and announced over a bullhorn that swimmers needed to get away from the rocks on the south side of the beach. I noticed that there was a news crew there with a camera, and when I finally dragged myself ashore, I learned that some swimmers had gone missing near those rocks, and that there had been sightings of jellyfish swarms nearby. Good lord! I was glad I'd gotten my swimming in before I heard that scary news.

I dried off and walked a coastal trail connecting several beautiful beaches from Bondi to Coogee. Thankfully, clouds moved in, so it wasn't quite so hot. I have to say that Sydney gives Los Angeles a run for its money in terms of the sheer number of beautiful, athletic people jogging and surfing its beach areas. I sighed as I passed two amazingly well-built young men effortlessly doing chin-ups on a mini gym alongside the trail. "What would it be like to be that healthy?" I wondered. Alas, for me, the pull of a good pancake is too strong, so I will likely never know the answer to that question.

I'd have loved to have spent more time in Sydney, but the trip had to go on, and so after a few days, I said farewell, flying 1200 miles to Cairns, a city located in Queensland on the tropical northeastern coast of Australia. When I picked up my rental car, the woman in the office was hilariously funny and good-natured. She assigned me a new car with only ten kilometers on it, and when it came time to go over the little damage form you must sign to document any dents or scratches on the car, she said, "You needn't bother filling this out; the car's brand new. But by any chance, if you go out to the lot and find that it's been utterly destroyed, could you please come right back and complete the form?"

I drove up the coast about thirty minutes to my home for the next three nights: the Ellis Beach Oceanfront Bungalows. You couldn't be much closer to the ocean without actually being in it, and the place reminded me of the pristine, deserted beach from the Tom Hanks' movie *Cast Away* except that this one was lined with adorable little cottages and palm trees waving in the breeze. I could hear the surf from the bedroom and when the full moon rose that night, lighting up the clouds, making silhouettes of the palms and reflecting on the waters of the Coral Sea just outside my doorstep, I almost cried. What a place!

There was, however, trouble in paradise. It was stinger season, and this coast is often frequented by the deadly box jellyfish. The groundskeeper at my property told me that when he was a kid people weren't terribly aware of the threat of stingers and that they swam at all times of year. Sometimes, he said, someone just suddenly and mysteriously died in the water and people thought the cause was heart failure, but now they've come to the realization that it was probably a stinger! Crikey! Therefore, at this time of year swimming is only safe on beaches with stinger nets. But as I drove up and down the coast, I found that due to recent stormy seas, the stinger nets, which run through the water like a fine mesh volleyball net, were not sturdy and waves were washing right over them. This meant that the stingers could easily have gotten through the safety nets, so no ocean swimming was allowed at all. I was really disappointed, because the climate here felt like a muggy day on the planet Venus and the beaches were so beautiful and inviting. Strangely, these awful creatures do not like deeper ocean water and aren't commonly found on the Great Barrier Reef, only in shallower waters directly off the coast.

Speaking of the Barrier Reef, perhaps the biggest dilemma for tourists in this part of the country is deciding which tour operator to choose for a snorkeling trip to this amazing natural wonder. Unless you carefully shop around, you could end up on huge boats carrying 400 people at a time which dock outside the reef and shuttle their multi-tudes to snorkel spots in smaller motorboats, creating more traffic than I saw at rush hour in Sydney. This was not the experience I was looking for.

I finally settled on the forty passenger Poseidon for a full day trip that took us along the outer edge of Great Barrier Reef, stopping at three different dive sites. For people like me who had developed a phobia of box jellyfish, they offered "stinger suits" to wear while snorkeling, one-piece, blue suits with a hood and mittens. All that is left exposed to the water are your face and feet, and of course you wear flippers on your feet. The added bonus of the suits is that not only do they protect you from stingers, but they also keep you out of the sun, so there was no need for the twelve gallons of sunscreen I'd normally need to use! The bad news about stinger suits is that they are made of Lycra or Spandex. Of all the materials in the world, this has to be the least flattering for someone wanting to hide extra pounds. Still, if it came down to a choice between humiliation in a Lycra suit or death by stinger, I'd take the humiliation any time.

I was the first person on the boat to try on my suit, worried that it might not fit, and one of the comical Aussie mates who made up our crew asked me to show everyone how I looked once I'd gotten it on. There I stood in a full length, skin-tight, electric blue body suit with a hood and mittens! Coming up mischievously behind me he placed an upside-down coat hanger on top of my head and shouted, "Look every-one, it's Tinky Winky!" referring to one of the Teletubbies, those impish little characters from the British children's show. I just waved shyly and did my best impersonation of a Teletubby voice. Judging from the reac-tion of the other passengers, the crewmate and I could have gone out on the road and done the comedy club circuit with this routine.

The first two dive sites were ok, but the water was quite rough and truthfully, I'd seen many more fish in Hawaii. The third site was much calmer and here one of the crew took us on a snorkel safari where he'd dive under and find something interesting to bring to the surface for us to see, touch and hold. My favorites were the sea cucumbers, about one or two feet long, shaped like a very wide French baguette, and coming in various lengths, textures, and colors. Some had smooth, silky black bodies, others looked almost shaggy with hair, and some looked like a soggy loaf of bread. They could easily have passed for space creatures from an episode of *Star Trek*. They can shoot seawater several feet into the air if gently squeezed. I got to hold one of them and our guide had me put it on my head for a photo opportunity! I should have received a partial refund for my ticket given the comic relief I provided on this excursion.

Tinky Winky says hello; A sea baguette - er, cucumber.

Another thrill was seeing a couple of reef sharks, maybe two feet long, swimming very close to us. They look sleek and beautiful and not too threatening when they are that small. The coral here was just beautiful and came in every shape and color possible. All in all, it was a fantastic day; there were no jellyfish stings, I had no sunburn, and I got some precious photos to document it all.

From Cairns I drove up the coast to visit the rainforests at Daintree National Park. I hiked cautiously at a place called Mossman Gorge, ready to encounter a giant cassowary at every turn. I swam in a beautiful, fresh-water pool and waterfall area, keeping an eye open for a crocodile snout despite being told that this is one of the few places in all of Queensland where you can swim in fresh water without being at risk. Later in the day, however, I spotted dozens of crocodiles during a boat trip along the Daintree River, and I swear they were eyeing me as if I were the meal that got away.

Each night I drove into Cairns to have dinner, a pleasant city with pedestrian zones and streets lined with trees filled with tropical birds. I sampled the local fish delicacy, barramundi, a variety of Asian sea bass, and had more kangaroo steak, but the best meal was at Red Ochre Grill which served Italian gnocchi made from sweet potatoes and served with sundried tomatoes, caramelized onion, capers, smoked salmon, and a white wine cream sauce. It was some of the best pasta I have ever had outside Italy.

I spent my last day at Tjapukai Aboriginal Culture Park, which educated visitors about the history of the Aboriginal people of Australia and documented the struggles they faced to stay alive and maintain their culture once the first settlers came and began taking their land. I rode the Sky Rail, a sleek, silent gondola that took me up above the rainforest into the nearby mountains to an Aboriginal village called Kuranda. There I watched several interesting demonstrations of traditional dance, music, food preparation, medicine, and sports such as boomerang and spear-throwing. It was both moving and very entertaining, and I was sad to learn that this wonderful park closed in 2021, unable to overcome the effects that the COVID epidemic and travel restrictions had on international travel. What a great loss!

At one point during the day, I had to get parental; there were three children left alone in an amphitheater area, their parents nowhere in sight. One of the boys, maybe ten years old, was swatting at the air and throwing handfuls of sand and gravel while whirling around in a circle. At first, I thought it might be demonic possession, but then I realized that he was attacking the beautiful butterflies that were plentiful in this area. I shouted in my most authoritarian voice, "Hey! What do you think you're doing? Stop that! Stop it NOW!" He stared at me with no expression, and I added, " What is WRONG with you?" I suppose this example makes it obvious why I didn't pursue a career as a child psychologist. However, my scolding did stop him in his tracks, and he sat back down on the bench with his siblings until his parents returned. He kept looking back over his shoulder and glaring at me but didn't appear to tell his parents about our encounter. Later I saw this same family in a nearby village where there was an actual butterfly sanctuary that could be toured, and it took all my self-control not to run up to the parents and ask, "Have you toured the butterfly park yet? I have a hunch that your son would really get a lot out of it!"

At the end of my stay in Australia, I flew back to Sydney and spent a last glorious, sunny, picture-postcard-perfect day there. I took the bus out to Bondi Beach again to hike the cliff-walk, have a swim, and eat some great fish and chips. Back in the city that evening I was allowed into a bar without being accused of public drunkenness and watched in awe as people put away six or seven beers in the time it took me to drink one. The Aussies really seem to like their alcohol, and how they are able to be coherent after so many drinks is amazing to me. At the end of the evening, I took a ferry ride without really caring where I was going. I just hopped aboard and sat outside, enjoying the refreshing breezes as I watched the city lights, the flickering stars, and the sea gulls that followed the boat like a flock of angels. Their bodies were brilliantly white in the lights from the boat but then they'd almost vanish for a second as they flapped their dark gray wings, creating a strange strobe-like effect. I was hypnotized by the show they put on. It was a peaceful and intimate way to say goodbye to Australia, and I'd be leaving the next day with such vibrant memories of my time there.

I felt a little sense of victory too; despite all those ominous warnings in the guidebooks regarding the many ways I might meet my end down under, I'd survived and even thrived. Still, there was always the chance that a kangaroo could jump in front of my shuttle on the way to the airport, causing the vehicle to go off the road into a wooded area where I'd find myself at the mercy of killer cassowaries and hungry crocodiles, so I tried not to feel too cocky until I was safely on my flight and out of Australian airspace.

3. Even Farther Down Under

NEW ZEALAND

Magnificent mountain vista on New Zealand's South Island

If Australia is "The Land Down Under," then surely New Zealand should be known as, "The Land Even Farther Down Under." It was the next stop on my Circum-Pacific trip in 2003 and is over 1,000 miles southeast of Sydney. New Zealand is about as close as you can get to

Antarctica without actually being there, though I actually felt as if I was flying into Antarctica on my flight from Sydney to Christchurch, as the plane was ridiculously cold and there were no blankets to be had.

After clearing customs and picking up my rental car, I quickly warmed up under a blazing, late summer sun. I'd done less prior research on New Zealand compared to the other stops on this Pacific tour: Thailand, Bali, Australia and Tahiti. New Zealand, at least in my mind, seemed the least exciting or exotic of them all. Still, I knew that it was reputed to have amazing natural beauty and was a sparsely populated, uncrowded place with more sheep than people, two things that definitely sounded good to me. And New Zealand has volcanoes and earthquakes, which makes it a place that my Disasterman alter-ego would find appealing.

New Zealand is comprised of two islands: North and South. I began my visit on the South Island, leaving Christchurch and crossing the central mountains over to the west coast where I'd planned to spend the first night close to two big glaciers there. The center of the country was hotter and drier than I expected, and the golden hills reminded me a lot of California in summer. All that changed as I reached the coast where I found amazingly lush rainforests, with snow-capped mountains looming high above them. In some places, glaciers actually extended down the mountainsides to meet the forests.

The next day I explored Fiordland National Park on the remote southwestern coast. The fiords were originally valleys carved out by glaciers; as the glaciers receded, sea water flooded these valleys to create long, narrow inlets. I'd marveled at the fiords of Norway a few years prior, and my scenic cruise down New Zealand's Milford Sound did not disappoint. Misty and foggy, the Sound winds its way between stunning snowcapped mountains, and its walls are lined with myriad waterfalls.

I spent a couple of nights in the charming town of Te Anau, known as the "Gateway to Fiordland" and with that as a base, I did a bit of tramping. Get your minds out of the gutter; "tramping" is the New Zealand term for hiking. It was rather funny to see signs in places that said, "No tramping!" I was also amused by the term New Zealanders or "Kiwis" use for sheep herding: "sheep mustering." It brought to mind an image of someone playing reveille on a bugle and a regiment of fluffy sheep decked out in uniforms obediently lining up for a roll call!

The aptly named Mirror Lake; Falls along Milford Sound

Aside from learning a bit of new vocabulary, I had to adjust to the change from the Australian to the New Zealand accent. Superficially, the Kiwi accent is reminiscent of Australian, but the vowel sounds are much different and more extreme. For instance, there seems to be no short "e" sound; words such as bed, let, or red sound more like "bid", "lit", or "rid", or even ""beed," "leet" or "reed." When someone spoke my name, it sounded more like MET than Matt. Of course, I was always amused when I'd speak to someone, and they'd stare at me blankly because they couldn't understand MY accent! More than a few folks commented on how much they loved to hear American accents, so I suppose it's all a matter of perspective!

In addition to touring the fiords, my big plan while I was in this area was to try either hang-gliding or sky diving, activities that had been on my "bucket list" for a long time. New Zealand is the world capital for adventure sports, and in fact, bungee jumping originated here. I headed for the city of Queenstown, which seemed to be ground zero for adrenaline-junkies and made a reservation to do a tandem hang-gliding trip where I'd be accompanied by an instructor. I arrived at the tour company office all psyched up and ready to live my dream, launching off nearby Coronet Peak near Queenstown, and soaring over the area like a graceful bird.

My dream came crashing back to earth as the guy behind the counter at the hang-gliding office eyed me cautiously, looking me up and down for what seemed like an eternity before asking, "Er, so how much do you weigh, mate?" Unfortunately, my answer did not go over well, and he bluntly told me that I was about thirty pounds over the weight limit. This triggered a painful flashback to my childhood when my mom had taken me to a park in Rhode Island for a pony ride, a sort of annual tradition that I'd always looked forward to. However, that year the man operating the pony ride concession sized me up and proclaimed in a booming voice for all to hear, "You? You can't go on the ponies! You're too heavy to ride the ponies!" I was devastated, and my mother offered me a consolation prize by taking me out for ice cream, a pattern that may have at least partially contributed to the dilemma I was facing today!

Snapping back to the present, the guy behind the counter rubbed salt into my emotional wounds when he added, "If there'd been more wind today, we might have been able to risk it, but between the lack of wind and your weight, we'd have dropped out of the sky like a stone." Being fat-shamed in New Zealand had NOT been an item on my bucket list, so with a heavy sigh I got back in the car and headed on, looking for an ice cream shop. I didn't even inquire about the tandem sky-diving trip because if I was going to drop to earth too quickly in a hang-gliding situation, I could only imagine what free-falling from a plane at 12,000 feet might be like. Gravity was evidently not my friend!!

I finished my travels on the South Island by crossing its far southern tip, the Catlin Coast, a spectacularly beautiful region of rolling green farmland, low mountains, rainforests, and deserted beaches where sea lions lounged in the sand and barely noticed me as I walked past them. I stayed in wonderful little motels, reasonably priced and all with a full kitchen. An amusing custom here is that at every motel check-in, my host handed me the room key and asked, "Regular or trim?" Of course, I was mystified the first time I was confronted by this cryptic question, wondering whether it had anything to do with that sadistic hang-gliding operator phoning ahead to warn them that a man too fat to fly would soon be checking in! I learned that hotels provide a small container of milk for your morning coffee, and so you are invariably asked whether you prefer whole vs. non-fat. Still, it made me laugh as each motel clerk invariably said, "Oh, don't forget your milk. Regular or trim?" After being denied my hang-gliding experience, I always chose trim.

My final night on the South Island was in the very Scottish-influenced city of Dunedin, which is pronounced "Doo-KNEE-dun". I found a great little motel several minutes from downtown and had a one-bedroom apartment directly facing the beach for a very cheap rate. Yes, that included a choice of "regular or trim" too! At the end of the beach was a heated, salt-water pool which I visited that afternoon; it was very cool, gray and foggy, a lot like San Francisco in the summer, so a soak in a heated pool right at the beach felt great. I also had one of my best dinners there at a place called Palm Cafe, an informal but lovely place with high ceilings, candlelight, and a view toward a small park where I dined on a "lamb hotpot" - a stew of many vegetables and tender lamb poured over a flaky piecrust. It was absolutely delicious, but I must say that most of the meals I had in New Zealand were outstanding, particularly the lamb and venison dishes.

The next day I caught a short flight from Dunedin to Auckland on the North Island, got my rental car and was on the road again. Driving here, as in Australia, was not too difficult. I adjusted to driving on the left side of the road with little problem and the fact that there was virtually no traffic helped. However, I often turned on my windshield wipers when I wanted to use my turn signal, and I repeatedly caught myself trying to get into the car on the wrong side, since everything is on the opposite side from what I'm used to. I was sure that when people saw me going to the wrong door to get into the car, they immediately knew I was a tourist, so I tried to throw them off track by opening the passenger door and pretending to look for something in my backpack on that side of the car. Then I'd nonchalantly close that door and walk around to the driver's side as though nothing was amiss. I was probably not fooling anyone, but it made me feel like I maintained some semblance of my dignity!

Listening to the radio here was like taking a journey back to the 1970s. Two 1970s powerhouse musical artists, Olivia Newton-John and Fleetwood Mac had just released new albums that were getting a lot of airplay. Olivia in particular seemed never to have lost her popularity down under. I'd bought a rare compilation of her early material back in Sydney, and the young man working the register, who was likely not even alive when she was at the peak of her career, picked up the CD and exclaimed, "Oh don't you just love, Livvy? She's a bloody angel!" Of course, the Australians are also still crazy about ABBA and the Bee Gees, and they seemed popular here in New Zealand as well. Needless to say, since these are some of my favorite artists, I enjoyed pleasant 70s flash-backs as I drove the countryside.

Compared to the South Island, the North has a much smaller land-mass, yet about three-fourths of the nation's residents live here and it is noticeably more urban and built up than the South. I drove about three hours from Auckland to Rotorua, a lakefront town surrounded in all directions by volcanic hot springs, steam vents, and mud pools and I stayed at the Royal Geysers Hotel. My room overlooked a volcanic thermal park and there was literally a geyser and a rapidly boiling mud pool right beneath my balcony. Disasterman felt at home! The previous night I'd slept with the sound of the ocean out my window in Dunedin, but on this night, I had the sound of these mud pools lulling me to sleep. It sounded like someone had left a huge pot of stew furiously boiling on the stove. While I was in this area, I visited the hot springs and had my first mud bath ever at a place called Hell's Gate, which seemed an odd name for such a wonderfully relaxing place. Unfortu-nately, the weather was quite rainy and gray, but what better way to wait out the rain than to stay warm in volcanic hot springs and mud baths?

The next day I spent several hours touring a traditional Māori village built atop and amongst dozens of steam vents, geysers, boiling lakes, and mud pools. It was really interesting and reminded me of the Aboriginal Park I'd visited back in Australia, but this was less touristy. I'm embar-rassed to admit that before this trip I hadn't been aware that the Māori have a completely different history than the Aborigines of Australia.

While the Aborigines came to Australia from Southeast Asia, the Māori were Polynesian, distant cousins to the Hawaiians and Tahitians and there is much similarity among their languages. The word *wai* for example, which means "water" in Māori is the same in Hawaiian. The English word "taboo" meaning "forbidden" is actually derived from *tabu* in Tahitian, which becomes *tapu* in Māori and *kapu* in Hawaiian. The music and dance of the Māori also reminded me of Hawaiian hula, though it's more rigorous and less graceful than the hula.

I was also surprised by how much the Māori culture seems to mix with the prevailing Western culture here, especially on the North Island. In Australia, the Aborigines don't seem to be well-integrated into mainstream society, perhaps because the "colonization" of Australia was particularly brutal. In this way the situation in Australia reminded me of how marginalized Native American culture is in North America. In New Zealand, on the other hand, while there was the usual taking of native lands, it seems that the overall process was not nearly as violent and perhaps this is why Māori culture is more prevalent here.

In the village I visited, the Māori used separate pools for bathing, cooking, and laundry. My guide said that the pools contain a number of minerals that make the food they cook in them more nutritious. Many dishes are cooked in huge boxes placed atop steam vents. Their traditional *hangi* meal reminded me of a New England clambake minus the clams; potatoes, sweet potatoes, pumpkin, chicken, corned beef, stuffing, cabbage and onion are all cooked together in containers buried underground with heated rocks. The villagers served this delicious meal to visitors for lunch, along with sweet corn that had been boiled separately in the mineral pools.

They also hosted a music and dance concert and encouraged audience participation. I was chosen to help demonstrate Māori greetings, like shaking hands while simultaneously touching noses.

"Just touch noses, don't rub them together! We are not Eskimos!" said the helpful instructor. I had my picture taken with a Māori warrior, sticking out our tongues, eyes bulging in a traditional battle stance, though after my brief lesson, I'm not sure how convincingly I could ward off a potential attacker.

A mud bath in "hell"; Maori warrior training.

Between heavy rain and traffic, driving back to Auckland took a long time and the downtown area was a nightmare, as there was a huge rugby match and a Bruce Springsteen concert going on that night. Despite this I made my way to my hotel, and was pleasantly surprised by my luxurious room, again with a full kitchen... and milk. I spent my last day in New Zealand, wandering the city, which struck me as a smaller and more sedate version of Sydney. It was very clean, and enjoys a spectacular location overlooking a huge harbor, surrounded by many hills and even a lush, grassy volcanic cone. There seemed to be an endless number of restaurant cuisines to choose from, and one of my most memorable meals was a scrumptious breakfast at the cafe inside a downtown art gallery.

For dinner I had what was advertised as "The best fish and chips in Auckland." This claim made me laugh, as I had a friend in San Francisco who'd reflexively respond to anyone saying something like, "They make the best hamburgers in the world!" with a half-humorous retort, "How do you know? Have you tried all the hamburgers in the world?" I could just hear him challenging this restaurant's claim of having the best fish and chips in Auckland. Though I unfortunately wasn't able to sample all the fish and chips in town, I must say that this version was pretty damned good and featured *kumara* chips (sweet potato fries) rather than regular fries. I noted that the Kiwis dip their fries in sour cream instead of ketchup, but just as in Australia, you must pay extra for all condiments, whether it's sour cream, ketchup or tartare sauce. For dessert I visited a place called The Chocolate Cafe for some chocolate steamed pudding and an iced chocolate, which satisfied my cravings for a while. It was a memorable "last supper" in New Zealand, but as it turned out, it was not to be my last meal there after all.

* * *

It took me another seven years, but I happily returned to New Zealand in 2010 when I was awarded a second sabbatical leave from my university. I was asked to attend and speak at a workshop being held at Massey University in Wellington, New Zealand's capital city, by a colleague I'd collaborated with on some research projects. I didn't need to be asked twice and was thrilled to have a chance to return to New Zealand. The conference was attended by approximately forty city leaders and emergency management personnel from Australia and New Zealand; I was the only "Yank" in the bunch. The speakers were government officials, graduate students, professors, and emergency management experts. My presentation was scheduled for the final day of the week-long workshop, which I hated because I prefer to get things over with rather than having them hanging over my head.

The workshop had its entertaining moments. We did some group exercises, and I was elected to be the spokesperson for my group because, "Everyone likes hearing your American accent." We toured the disaster control center beneath the Houses of Parliament, where many of us made jokes about feeling like Jack Bauer from the TV series 24. We also participated in a disaster simulation exercise in which I convincingly played the role of a reporter from Radio New Zealand during a tsunami crisis. We also took a couple of field trips around the local area. Like San Francisco, Wellington is a very earthquake-prone city, and we walked through neighborhoods built directly atop the Wellington Earthquake Fault Zone and toured areas hit by a past tsunami. We stopped at beautiful look-out points along the coastline and then visited a park where we had a picnic lunch and I got to ride a zip-line or "flying fox" contraption that allowed me to briefly fly through the air. It wasn't quite like hang-gliding, but at least my weight didn't seem to be an issue.

I met some great people at the conference. Brenda (pronounced "Brinda" down here) was a graduate student from Christchurch whom I happened to sit next to at one of the presentations. We ended up passing sarcastic notes back and forth during some of the less stimulating presentations and tried not to laugh out loud. I noticed that many of the speakers loved using horrifyingly complicated flow charts in their presentations – dozens of little boxes connected by arrows going in twenty different directions. My mind simply could not make sense of them, and I shared my disdain for them with Brenda, who felt similarly. Every time one popped up on the screen, we'd try not to even make eye contact with one another for fear of an outburst of laughter. We became pals instantly, bonding over our mutual hatred of flow charts. Then there were Peter and Mike, two Aussie firemen who were fun to sit next to because they made lots of zany jokes and sarcastic comments during the boring presentations. One of the participants was acting like a know-it-all, interrupting anyone else who wanted to speak. Mike leaned over to me and whispered, "In Australia he's what we call a WANKER!"

I also met several kiwi graduate students who were great fun to hang out with. I noted that they often used an expression that made me laugh every time I heard it: They'd say that something was "Bigger than *Ben Hur*" (referring to the 1960s, Biblical epic starring Charlton Heston) as a way to describe anything that was exaggerated or an over-the-top spec-tacle. So, a speaker might say, "That tsunami warning they had up the coast caused a ruckus bigger than *Ben Hur*!" This all helped distract me from worrying about my upcoming conference presentation. I tried to reassure myself that I'd charm the audience with my American accent and hoped that my presentation would be bigger than *Ben Hur*. As it turned out, it went very well, and I got a lot of compliments. Brenda rated it a 10 out of 10, but I think she was biased: I hadn't included any flow charts in my presentation.

After the conference ended, I bid a fond farewell to my new friends, and headed north up Route 1. Despite being one of the main highways in the country, it is mostly a two-lane road with lots of roundabouts and lights, so travel was rather slow. When I reached the small city of

Taihape, I saw big signs saying, "Gumboot Day! March 20, 2010!" Gumboot Day? I shrugged it off, but when I parked the car and went to mail some postcards, I saw a "Gumboot Field" just off the main street. I finally asked a woman I passed on the street what this was all about, and she said, "Well, it's Gumboot Day here in Taihape! There's a gumboot throwing contest and everything!" I asked her what a gumboot was, and she looked at me as if I were from Mars. She explained that gumboots are rubber farmer's boots and the traditional way to celebrate Gumboot Day involves throwing them as far as possible. I really thought she was putting me on, but she pointed me in the direction of the field where the Gumboot Day festivities were taking place so, of course, I had to check it out.

Happy Gumboot Day!

What I found was a local fair with food, crafts, and live music - a rock band and a group of military men playing bagpipes at opposite ends of the field. There was a giant inflatable slide for kids shaped like, you guessed it, a gumboot! And then there was an area where the gumboot throwing contest was being held. People were competing to see how far they could throw a heavy rubber boot. Have these people never heard of horseshoes? It was all quite bizarre, but very funny! As I drove out of town I had to stop and take a picture of the enormous metal gumboot statue that welcomes drivers coming in from the north. It's right down the road from the Gumboot Manor Hotel. I imagined I could hear Rod Serling's iconic voice from the *Twilight Zone,* saying, "Submitted for your approval... an entire town whose reputation hinges upon residents' ability to toss a rubber boot as far as possible in a display of strength and stamina... you have just entered the Twilight Zone."

I drove a couple hours further north, listening to a compilation CD I'd made featuring a mix of Irish artists: the Cranberries, the Corrs, and Sinead O'Connor. It was upbeat music that seemed made for a pleasant drive. Well, OK, Sinead is not exactly upbeat; she sings a lot of mournful songs about dead babies, young Black men who die on mopeds, and a cheery little number called *You Cause as Much Sorrow Dead as You Did When You Were Alive.* But her melodies are very catchy and infectious! I also found a lot of native Māori music on the radio, which provided a more authentic soundtrack for the drive.

The weather was warm and clear as I drove around the impressive volcano, Ruapehu, which last erupted in 1995. I visited nearby hot springs and soaked awhile before finding a small motel near Lake Taupo, which is actually a submerged volcanic cone. The next day I stopped at a different hot springs area, this one a cold lake fed by two hot waterfalls which was unique and different. At one point I lost my glasses in the rushing waterfall and tried not to panic, but some guys nearby saw what happened and helped me find them. Crisis averted!

Then it was time to return to the South Island; I ended up staying in Dunedin at the same place as in 2003, since it had been one of my favorite stops. Of course, upon arrival I was faced with The Milk Question: Regular or Trim? I was happy to see that even seven years after my first visit to New Zealand, this custom had persisted like a strange welcome back greeting. However, this time things were more complicated; my host questioned whether there might already be milk in the fridge of my apartment, so he grabbed my trim milk back from me and said we'd have to see if I already had one! Good Lord, we're talking about a little cardboard container of milk like they give children before nap time in nursey school. Would it have been such a disaster to give me an extra carton by mistake? As it turned out, there was indeed already a carton of trim in my fridge, so my host took the extra one and left me to settle in. It really was a great apartment, set in an older, art deco building with gigantic windows that looked out at the hills to the north and west, and I could see the ocean from the bedroom window. It was also just one short block from a magnificent beach in an area of Dunedin called St. Clair.

Since man cannot live on one carton of trim milk alone, I headed into town to try a restaurant I'd heard about called Bell Pepper Blues, but it was closed, I assumed perhaps because it was Monday night. I headed further into town to the place I'd enjoyed seven years ago: The Palm Café; it too was closed and dark. Hmmm. I tried a third place called Plato and another joint known for venison burgers... both closed! I finally stopped an elderly couple on the street to ask what was going on and learned that it was some provincial holiday, the exact nature of which was lost to me as I couldn't decipher their thick kiwi accents. I just smiled and nodded but was pretty sure they hadn't mentioned Gumboot Day. They recommended an open restaurant, but unfortunately the meal was "not brilliant" as they say down here.

The Moeraki Boulders.

The next day was bright and sunny, and I decided to drive up the coast. I stopped at a savory pie shop and got a small apricot and chicken pot pie, a great combination and still warm from the oven. After about ninety minutes I reached the Moeraki Boulders, a place I'd read about in travel guides. The beach here was comfortably warm and the water a gorgeous shade of blue green. Beautiful, exotic-looking seabirds walked along beside me like loyal dogs, and then flew gracefully over my head. The beach was covered in colorful and delicate spiral shaped shells, and I relished the sound of the surf, the cries of the birds, and the feeling of the sun on my face. As for the boulders themselves, they were worth the trip. Perfectly round, they have odd linear markings on them making them appear to be cracking open like giant black eggs. They are truly bizarre and could pass for something out of a sci-fi movie.

Folks at the conference back in Wellington told me not to miss having seafood at "a restaurant near the boulders," but didn't know the name of it. I'd seen nothing along the coast road, but on a cliff above the rocks there was the Moeraki Boulders Cafe, so I checked it out. It was a cafeteria style affair but was clean and bright and offered sweeping views of the coast. I ordered a seafood platter, found a table out on the deck, and nothing could have prepared me for the feast they brought me.

Hands down, it was the most memorable meal of the whole trip: a heaping platter of fruit, seafood, and salad. There were two beautifully fried pieces of flakey white fish atop a pile of French fries, lightly breaded rings of calamari, prawns done two different ways, and several large fried oysters. Then there were a few chilled scallops and large clams that had been marinated in citrus, along with a large, chilled piece of marinated salmon. Surrounding this were grapes, lemon and orange slices, melon, and kiwi fruit, and under the fruit was a multi-colored salad of peppers, onions, and carrots. I'd lived in San Francisco for years and am a native New Englander, but I'm hard pressed to recall when I had such an amazing seafood meal. I also got to enjoy the 180-degree view of the beautiful South Pacific, the sun peeking in and out from behind majestic white clouds, and a warm breeze blowing. It was all just perfect.

It's times like this when I realize how good it feels to slow down and just enjoy the moment rather than filling the day with too many activities when I travel. I was reminded of those carefree mystery rides that my mom and I would take together, when there was no real goal or destination, just the joy of the journey itself; she would have loved this day. I made a mental note to myself to try and remember to do this a lot more often, not just when I'm traveling, but in everyday life as well.

I returned to Dunedin via the slower coastal road and had to keep stopping to take in the eye-popping views along the way. It's not surprising to me that it was the Scots who settled this area, as it really feels and looks a lot like Scotland, though with a somewhat warmer and sunnier climate. I headed back to St. Clair to have a swim in the heated saltwater pool at the end of the beach, a short walk from my apartment. Finally, despite my enormous "surf" lunch, I devoured a late "turf" dinner at the Palm Café that night, feasting on lamb medallions, mashed potatoes, and fresh vegetables.

Along the coastal road to Dunedin.

In the morning before departing from Dunedin, I revisited the little savory pie shop I'd discovered; this time I opted for a freshly baked pot pie of chicken, cranberry and brie. I'd love to have a place like this in my neighborhood back home. I then hit the road, climbing the steep hills south of St. Clair and taking a fond look back toward the beach before heading along the Otago coast road through Brighton. It was another warm, summery day and the beaches and coves I passed were beautiful.

As I gradually turned inland, blueberry, blackberry and strawberry stands began popping up and I had to sample all of them. I dug out a Fleetwood Mac CD and sang along at the top of my lungs with these old friends that I'd been listening to for thirty-five years. Along many of the roads I noticed that the highway department had gone above and beyond the call of duty with signs warning about the dangers of drunk driving or fatigue at the wheel. Every few miles there were ominous signs: "You fall asleep... people die. It's that simple." or "Drink, drive, die! It's that simple." Geez, I was just singing along to *Say You Love Me*, feasting on fresh strawberries and having a jolly afternoon and you are really bumming me out, people!

The land became drier and the hills browner as I headed inland. It seemed odd to see signs for harvest festivals and pumpkins for sale, but of course March is early autumn down here. Sheep started appearing more frequently, and as they stood in the fields munching grass, looking so sweet and innocent, I couldn't help but think how easily they could just end up on someone's dinner plate beside a heaping helping of garlic mashed potatoes. They were just standing out there like sitting ducks, or "sitting lambs." I imagined one of the road signs I'd been seeing targeted toward these lambs: "Eat, get fat, end up on the dinner table. It's that simple." I saw a T-shirt in a souvenir shop that made me laugh out loud; it featured lamb chops grilling on a barbecue with the caption, "Silence of the Lambs." I would have bought it if they'd had one in my size.

Not amused by T-shirt humor.

By the time I reached the road leading up toward Mt. Cook, New Zealand's highest peak, rain had set in, and the mountain was completely shrouded in mist, but there were lots of rainbows straddling the nearby hills. I finally reached my destination, Lake Tekapo, located in the mountainous interior of central South Island. I stayed at Pepper's Bluewater Resort, set right on the shore of the lake and though it was a little more expensive than I was comfortable with, when I opened the door to my room, I gasped. The resort was a modern, two-story building, but my Lakeview Studio was actually on a third floor, a single room sticking out from the roof of the building like a treehouse or a lighthouse. There were floor to ceiling windows on two sides and the view of the neon-turquoise colored Lake Tekapo with snowy mountains in the background was awesome. The lake gets its bizarre color from glacial run-off, which contains fine particles of silt that reflect sunlight, giving the lake a very bright, almost other-worldly aqua color. The view made me want to just sit and stare, but I dragged myself away to see a bit of the surrounding area. I visited the beautiful Church of the Good Shepherd, built on a promontory overlooking the lake. There was a spectacular sunset that evening, and I fully enjoyed the show before heading off to get dinner.

The stunning Lake Tekapo.

I ate at a nice steakhouse and of course ordered lamb, but I capped off the meal with a beautifully prepared pavlova, a dessert that both the

Aussies and the Kiwis claim they invented. Whoever was originally responsible is to be commended: pavlova is a meringue topped with passionfruit syrup and lots of fresh fruits. The version I had for my dessert was elegant, photogenic, and delicious. After dinner, I found that the town had a hot springs spa, so I went up there and enjoyed a fantastic soak in three giant pools, each a different temperature. There were very few lights, so the stars really put on a show, and I just laid back in the hot water and sent up a prayer of thanks for allowing me to experience this wonderful place. After the pools, I returned to my beautiful glassed-in house and watched the moon setting over the lake, the end to a perfect day.

A colorful Pavlova.

For my last day in New Zealand, I took my own advice and slowed down. I abandoned a plan to drive north to another hot springs resort that would have taken me hours out of the way. Instead, I enjoyed my room until check out, took a walk around the lake, had a delicious breakfast in the nearby village, and shopped for a souvenir t shirt. I finally found one I liked, which featured some cartoonish sheep and the caption, "Baa, baa, baa... Bar, Bar, Bar. That about sums it up: New Zealand." It wasn't as cute as "Silence of the Lambs," but it made me chuckle.

I made it back to Christchurch and spent the evening visiting my new friend Brenda from the conference. We had a nice stroll around the city center, a vibrant area of brick buildings, atmospheric restaurants and cafes with music spilling out onto the streets. We dined at a great Burmese place and had a fun evening, though Brenda was a bundle of nervous energy. She was facing a big career decision: whether to accept an offer to enter a prestigious doctoral program in Melbourne, Australia or to stay here in New Zealand working in disaster management with colleagues in Wellington. It sounded like an exciting choice either way, but of course it was a big decision to make.

As it turned out, Brenda chose the move to Australia; perhaps this was for the best. Six months after my visit and not long after she'd headed to Melbourne, Christchurch suffered an earthquake that produced dozens of aftershocks. The largest occurred in February 2011, causing 185 deaths and another 2,000 casualties. Buildings damaged in the original quake suffered a fatal blow during the aftershocks and just collapsed. Brenda told me that the entire downtown area of Christchurch where we'd walked and dined that night was left completely in rubble. It was a sobering reminder that San Francisco will one day face a similar fate, and it was another life lesson to me about enjoying each day to its fullest. We simply never know what tomorrow might have in store. Meanwhile, I'll always have a warm place in my heart for New Zealand, and I do hope that we haven't seen the last of one another yet.

4. A Little Magic, A Little Mystery
TAHITI

Flying into Paradise: Bora Bora, French Polynesia

"One visit to Tahiti will make you forget all about Hawaii!" How many times had I read such a proclamation? I'd first "discovered" Hawaii in 1994 and ever since, have been in love with the islands' majestic scenery, inviting waters, delicious food, and fascinating history, culture, and music scene. Despite my red hair, freckles, and an ancestry tracing back to the Pilgrims, I've always felt like an honorary Hawaiian. So, as I planned the itinerary for my 2003 trip around the Pacific Rim, I excitedly added Tahiti to the list, wanting to visit the place from which the Polynesians had migrated, crossing thousands of miles of the Pacific in outrigger canoes to eventually find and settle the Hawaiian Islands.

Tahiti was the last stop on the trip. I left New Zealand late on a Sunday afternoon and thanks to crossing the international dateline, I arrived in Pape'ete, Tahiti at 11:30 on the prior Saturday night. How often do we get to "re-live" a day? I had reservations at Hotel Matavai and had been instructed to call the hotel from the airport to have their shuttle pick me up. I located a Hotel Matavai phone just outside baggage claim, only to find that the cord had been ripped out of the wall. After another ten minutes of wandering the airport, I found an intercom on the wall labeled Hotel Matavai. I pressed the button, and after a few seconds, through static thick enough to make me think I was communicating with someone in another solar system, a far off, heavily accented voice asked, "EES THEESE MEESTER DAVESE?" I screamed that, yes, indeed it was, and heard the tinny voice say, "Look for bus, five minutes." A huge yellow bus arrived twenty minutes later, which seemed like overkill since I was its only passenger, and I finally arrived at the hotel at 1:00AM. It looked like a run-down Holiday Inn, but I was only there for one night, so I wasn't too worried. I asked the desk staff when the ferry departed for the island of Mo'orea in the morning, but they didn't know and advised me to come to the lobby to see the concierge at 7:00AM. So much for getting a full night's sleep!

I ended up "sleeping in" until 7:45, rushed to the lobby and learned that the ferry would be departing at 9:15. I caught a shuttle to the port and saw a bit of lovely downtown Pape'ete. Picture a cross between Fresno, California and Tijuana, Mexico, but with lots of chickens! There was a nice shopping area, but mostly the town was a muddy, messy little place. I couldn't wait to start my real Tahitian experience and sail off to the island of Mo'orea, which loomed on the horizon across the sea.

Once on Mo'orea, I had to catch that island's public transit system. Perhaps as a reminder that this is a French territory, it's called *Le Truck*. The *Le Trucks* are modified pick-up trucks, with bench seats in the truck bed and a covered roof. The ones I rode in seemingly had no shock absorbers. It took a half hour to reach Cook's Bay, a beautiful body of water, surrounded on three sides by tall green mountains which was where my hotel, the Club Bali Hai was located. I stayed in one of those stereotypical overwater bungalows, built on stilts over the bay; it was a roomy, pleasant little cottage with lots of windows, a porch, a cozy living area, separate bedroom, and an outdoor shower. This was no Hotel Matavai, and I was grateful for that!

I learned that Le Truck only runs immediately before or after scheduled ferry departures. Since there are only two ferries a day, there was no real form of public transportation on the island. Taxis were ridiculously expensive, and everything within the immediate vicinity of my hotel was closed on Sunday. I began to feel stranded in what was a beautiful, but deserted place, not unlike a contestant on *Survivor,* though thankfully, I didn't have to build my own shelter, collect grubs for dinner, or worry about being voted off the island. I ended up taking a nap, and then went for a swim at the beach, where I met Al, a sixty-ish year old guy from New Jersey. A former U.S. army officer, he now bills himself as an entertainer: "Al, Magician of Mystery." He said he was staying at the Hotel Kaveka, a mile down the road and was trying to convince the manager there to allow him to do a dinner show of magic (and mystery) in return for free lodgings and dinner. He was quite a character.

Since my hotel didn't serve dinner, I walked to the Kaveka that evening, which was a small, rather dark and depressing place. I sat on their outdoor terrace and ordered shrimp curry, rice, and a bottle of water; tap water is not drinkable here. My dinner was terribly expensive, as bland as it could be, and was served with ridiculously undercooked rice that was still crunchy. I soon spotted Al, lurking around looking for the hotel manager, who I'm certain was trying to hide from him. He joined me for dinner and entertained me with several magic tricks. A few were rather sad and pathetic, but some were impressive and truly stumped me, like smearing chocolate sauce into my right hand and having it magically appear on my left hand as well. However, when I gave that some thought, I realized that I'm able to do that little magic trick all by myself with very little effort when I'm eating an ice cream cone or a messy pastry. Al also did some interesting rope tricks, and I had no clue how he'd accomplished them. He was, however, quite mad, rambling almost incoherently about things that sounded like headlines from *The National Enquirer*. After dinner, he was off again in search of the manager, and I made a hasty retreat down the pitch-black road back to my hotel.

The next day, short on cash, I walked three miles into a "town" consisting of two restaurants, three banks, and a couple of souvenir shops. I went to an internet cafe and was horrified by the rates they were charging to use a computer. With nothing more to see, I ended up hitchhiking for the first time in my life, but I quickly got a ride back to my hotel from a friendly local family.

Club Bali Hai's tour director, Stefanie, had signed me up for a four-hour safari tour of the island in "a 4-wheel drive, air-conditioned van" scheduled to depart at 1PM. By 1:30 there was no van; Stefanie called and learned that because I was the only person who'd signed up, the tour had been cancelled. With determination, she got back on the phone and after four futile attempts to find a tour, got me a spot on "Ben Tours" - not Ben's Tours, but Ben Tours. They said they'd pick me up in front of the hotel within ten minutes, but sped past me as I waited out front. I had to run back into the hotel and tell Stefanie. She called them again; eventually they arrived, and my island safari began.

Unlike the original tour I'd booked, Ben Tours did not feature an air-conditioned van. We traveled in an open-air pick-up truck with planks for seats and a tarp slung across the top for a makeshift roof... a kind of mini Le Truck. Our driver and guide was Roger, pronounced the French way: "Ro-JAY", a Polynesian man who spoke fluent French and virtually no English. Two French couples were already in the truck and neither of them spoke English, so I had to rely on my incredibly rusty French to make pleasantries. Off we went to explore an agricultural area, a fruit juice distillery, a waterfall, and a scenic overlook, all stops on our island tour. We drove on terribly rutted, potholed, and muddy dirt roads, and had to hold on tightly to keep from bouncing off our plank seats. We entered the agricultural area and without leaving his seat or even slowing down, Roger began shouting fruit names, in French, out his driver's side window. It was hard to hear him with all the rattling and banging of the truck on the bad roads, and then of course, he only spoke French.

Friends tease me that the first things I learn when I study other languages, are food names, but that paid off here. "*Ananas!*" Roger screamed, and we all looked to the left to see a pineapple field. Then he shouted, "*Papaye!*" and we all turned to look at the papaya trees on the right. There were some avocados and bananas too. Roger continued his informative narrative: "*Ananas! Avocat! Ananas! Banane! Ananas!*" There were a LOT of *ananas*. I truly felt like I was in a comedy skit; it was so absurd I kept giggling but couldn't explain to my French friends why I found this all so amusing.

Ben Tours: NOT bigger than "Ben Hur"

We then drove fifteen minutes down even bumpier roads to the juice distillery. Free samples of tropical juice sounded good on this hot, sticky day, but alas, the distillery was closed. Why Roger didn't know this in advance is a mystery. We got to the scenic lookout, which might have been a nice photo opportunity if it hadn't been shrouded in clouds and rain, and then we stopped at a large structure made of huge, flat stones resembling a *heiau*, the ancient temples found throughout Hawaii. To my amazement, Roger actually got out of the truck here to give some explanation to the French tourists, and they all hopped out to have a look. Turning to me, all he said was, "ancient temple" which was a bit confusing, since a sign beside the structure had an English caption reading, "Ancient Archery Platform." Perhaps the Tahitians shot bows and arrows during their religious ceremonies? I'll never know, as Roger quickly herded us back into the truck for another grueling hour's drive.

Cars came flying up behind us, their drivers cursing Roger's slow speed, then zoomed past us at their first opportunity. I got into a fit of almost uncontrollable laughter as I started daydreaming that perhaps I should make a sign saying, "I've been kidnapped! Please send help!" and dangle it from the back of the truck. My French friends surely must have thought I was a complete lunatic by now. We finally stopped for a cold drink at a convenience store, the price of which was not included in the tour despite missing out on our fruit juice distillery visit. As we all got back into the truck, I noticed that one of the Frenchmen had purchased a beer and realized that this whole ordeal might have been a lot more fun if I'd been a little buzzed. I gestured to his beer and said, "*Bonne idee!*" (Good idea!) Holding up my juice, I added, "*Je suis stupide*" (I'm stupid), which got a hearty laugh from the French, who seemed every bit as bored as I was.

Finally, we got onto the dirt road leading to the waterfall, but halfway down, Roger stopped, got out of the truck, and pointed to a bare spot of rock on the hillside; the waterfall was completely dried up. Never fear. To make up for this sad state of affairs, Roger gathered several fruits whose French names I now knew by heart. We had *pamplemousse* (grapefruit), coco (coconut), and of course the ever-popular *ananas*. Taking a hygienically questionable knife from the glove compartment, he began slicing them all up for us to sample. I began laughing again as I imagined my germ-conscious, New England friend Carol being here, shaking her head and, saying definitively, "I'm not eating any of that fruit!" However, the fruit was tasty, and I lived to tell this story.

And that, *mes amis,* was my circle island safari. I can honestly say that other than a nice view here or there, I saw nothing on the island to warrant further exploration. There were widely scattered hotels, a restaurant or a small general store here and there, and little else. The Shania Twain song, *That Don't Impress Me Much*, came to mind and I found myself making up my own lyrics in my head as we drove: *So, you've got a closed juice distillery? So, you've got a dry waterfall? That don't impress me much!*

Things improved that night. At 5:30 each evening, an American guy named Muk – I have no idea why he's called Muk - who'd founded the Club Bali Hai in the 1960s holds a get together around the pool. All the guests attend, have a drink and talk. It was actually fun, and I got the scoop on where to eat. A couple from New Zealand, Kevin and Anne invited me to join them for dinner at a tiny place called *Chez Michelle*, run by a single French woman whose name I'm assuming was Michelle. Evidently, she closes by 7:30 if no one shows up for dinner. We were her only customers that night, but for $15 she made us a stupendous dinner of fresh fish, vegetables, fluffy rice, and some of the best ice cream I've ever tasted. *Merci, Michelle!*

The next day I'd signed up for a shark and stingray feeding expedition. According to Stefanie, whom I should never have trusted after sending me on the safari from hell, this trip included full snorkel gear. However, once we'd anchored out in the bay and the captain started feeding dead fish to some black-tipped reef sharks, the crew told us that no snorkel gear was available. When half the boat almost mutinied, the crew "found" a few stray masks with no snorkel attached, many with broken straps. We were told to just press the mask to our faces, hold our breath and stick our heads underwater for as long as we could. With this deluxe equipment and expert preparation, I hopped off the boat into the water, trying to hold my mask against my face with one hand while trying to grip a rope that we were supposed to hang onto with the other. The water was very choppy, and it was hard to balance. I held onto the rope, but occasionally someone yanked on it, pulling me under for a huge drink of sea water. Then someone else would panic and cling to me for support, either pushing or pulling me underwater again. It was a nightmare, and all I got were a few quick glimpses of the six foot long, golden reef sharks with black-tipped fins. Had they decided to attack, at least I wouldn't have had to watch the carnage, as my eyes were stinging from repeated dunks in the salt water.

Thankfully, the stingray feeding part of the trip was a whole different kettle of fish, so to speak. We anchored in much calmer and shallower water, and as soon as we got out of the boat we were surrounded by dozens of these creatures, deep gray with white underbellies, four to five feet across and sporting four-foot-long stingers. They were gentle and curious animals and came right to us, sliding up onto our bodies like playful puppies until the front of their head was out of the water. They had very human-looking eyes that looked right into mine, and we were able to pet them and feed them fish. It was a wonderful experience. Toward the end, several black-tipped sharks started to gather around us looking for scraps, and though some of them were swimming only ten feet from me, it wasn't scary, though perhaps it should have been. At least my stay on Mo'orea ended on a positive note.

Greeting a stingray.

The following day I caught the ferry back to Papae'ete, then headed to the airport for my flight to Bora Bora. Of all the exotic place names in the world, Bora Bora has to be near the top of the list. Although my Tahitian experience had not been quite what I'd imagined it would be, the idea of boarding a tiny prop plane and flying off to the island of Bora Bora stirred the traveler's heart that beats within me. The flight took forty-five minutes, and despite a lot of cloud cover, during the descent, we were treated to one of the most magnificent sights I've ever seen: a spectacular aerial view of the island and its surrounding lagoon and *motu*. A *motu*, I'd learned years ago from yes, watching *Survivor*, is a narrow barrier island of coral and sand that rings the main island and protects the lagoon. The airport was located on a *motu*, and was open-air, fronting a beautiful beach with a view toward the main island. A small boat from my hotel was waiting to greet me, and I was taken across the lagoon to my hotel, the Eden Beach, located on another very long, skinny *motu* on the east side of the island.

I can truthfully say that as the boat docked at the Eden's pier, I felt as if I'd arrived on *Fantasy Island*. The lagoon is an indescribable shade of blue - green, and the white, coral sand beach was blinding in the sunlight. Palms trees lined the beach and the pool area offered stunning views of the lagoon and the main island of Bora Bora and its craggy green mountains. The hotel had a dozen units, and I learned that only four were occupied the day I arrived, so it was very quiet. I checked in and was shown to my beachfront bungalow, which shared this same view. This was the most expensive place I've ever stayed in, yet it represented a "bargain" at a mere $350 a night compared to other properties I'd looked at that were going for as much as $800 a night. My bungalow had no refrigerator and few amenities, but was clean, comfortable and in a spectacular locale. However, other than the hotel, there was absolutely nothing else here, not so much as a convenience store or cafe. If you wanted anything else, a free shuttle boat was available to take you to the main island, but it left and returned only four times each day.

My first stop was the hotel's restaurant for lunch. To my surprise I realized that of the three waitresses who seemed to be running everything, two were actually either transvestites or transsexuals. After later doing some research, I learned that such people are referred to here as *mahu*. In Hawaii this is a derogatory term for gay men; in Polynesian tradition it's used to describe individuals who have a mix of both masculine and feminine traits: a "third sex." Mahu typically dress and live as women out of a natural orientation, but in some cases, especially in the past, boys who were born into a large family with many male siblings might be chosen to be raised as mahu from birth. Mahu are regarded with a very special, gifted status in this culture, but may find life very difficult if they move to places like New Zealand or Australia, where they're subjected to prejudices and violence, much like transgendered people are in the west.

The view from Eden Beach.

After lunch I decided to take the shuttle over to the main island, but by the time I reached the other side, it was raining and I discovered that there was nothing there except for a car and bike rental agency, which was closed. There were no stores, no restaurants, nothing! Evidently the only substantial town was on the other side of the island and there was no public transportation. At that point I decided to catch a shuttle boat over to the Meridien Hotel, located back out on the motu. I figured I could just walk back to my own hotel from there. The Meridien was a beautiful, five-star property, but other than lovely grounds, there wasn't much in the way of shops or anything to see, so with a sigh I began the walk back to my hotel.

After several minutes of walking northward, the paved paths

vanished and I followed what appeared to be an established trail, but the farther I walked, the less developed the trail became. Rain started again with a vengeance. I headed east across the *motu* to the ocean side and followed a gravel path for a while, but that soon gave way to a rough coral path that was difficult to walk on, with little cover from trees to keep the rain off. I went west again, back to the lagoon side and the trail got still rougher, at some points vanishing entirely. I had no option but to walk into the warm lagoon and wade in hip-deep water for many yards, my backpack over my head to keep it out of the water. Soon, small shacks cropped up in the dense foliage around me that seemed abandoned and looked like temporary quarters used by local fisherman. Signs saying, "*Tabu*!" (Keep Out!) were plentiful, but by now I'd been walking almost an hour and figured my hotel couldn't be too much farther away. Some shacks were guarded by barking dogs, so, back into the lagoon I went, giving the dogs a wide berth until it felt safe to come ashore again.

Several times I was startled by things moving in the brush, and knowing there are no snakes on the *motu*, I wondered what they were. Finally, I got a good look at one: it was a huge crab, the size of an Alaskan king crab! There were also plants covered in tiny, sharp-tipped seeds that clung to both clothes and skin. Some of them got on my leg, and I thoughtlessly tried to sweep them off with my hand, only to have one embed itself in my thumb causing much pain and considerable bleeding! As if this weren't exciting enough, two enormous explosions could be heard in the distance, but this didn't sound like thunder. The way my luck was going, I wondered whether France had decided to choose this day to resume the nuclear bomb tests it had conducted in Polynesia in the 1960s and 1970s. There was a popular bumper sticker I recall from years ago, "One nuclear bomb can ruin your whole day." Yeah, that would have been the perfect ending to this ill-fated excursion!

After about ninety minutes I made it back to the Eden Beach, soaking wet, bloody, and exhausted. I showered and napped, and then went to the restaurant for what turned out to be a lousy and very expensive dinner. One of the waitresses, Anastasia, urged me to return at 9PM for the Polynesian dance show that she and her "girlfriend" were doing, but I reclusively hid in my bungalow, watching the rain from my porch. I've seldom felt so completely isolated: a rather offbeat hotel staff, a handful of solely French speaking guests, no easy way off the motu and nowhere to go even if I could leave. My imagination wandered from *Survivor* to the silver screen as I went out on the beach and stole a scene from the film *Cast Away*, playfully screaming, "Wilson!" several times. If you've never seen the film, Wilson was a volleyball that served as Tom Hanks' character's only companion during his time on a deserted tropical island. He talked to Wilson as if the volleyball were a real person – until Wilson came loose from the escape raft and floated away. Well, at this point in my trip, I could really have used a Wilson.

The next day I decided I'd go to the main island and rent a bike for the day. I caught the 8:30 shuttle, but as the boat approached the shore, rain poured from the skies, so I rented a car instead. It cost about $100 for eight hours, had no air conditioning, a manual transmission, and no radio, but I was desperate. As I signed the contract, I saw that if I were to have an accident there was a $2,000 deductible; when I asked if I could purchase additional insurance coverage to reduce my liability, I was told that wasn't an option. Risk taker that I am, I rented the car anyway, but ended up returning it two hours early. I circled the whole island twice and there was simply nothing else to see! There were a couple of nice views, many exclusive hotels that allowed no public access, and very few shops or galleries. For such a popular tourist destination, I was stunned by how little it had to offer.

I did have the good fortune to bump into American newlyweds John and Erica, whom I'd met back on Mo'orea, and we decided to meet for dinner at a famous restaurant called Bloody Mary's that evening. I was happy to know I'd have some companionship and I could thoroughly enjoy my night out without being limited by the shuttle schedule, as the restaurant provides a free shuttle to its customers. Before leaving the main island that afternoon, I stopped at a general store and stocked up on some snacks for the next day. I'd decided to try and make the most of things and spend the next day at the hotel, taking advantage of the lagoon, the beach and the solitude.

Back at Eden Beach that afternoon I chatted a bit with the French woman who managed the property. She seemed bitter and disgruntled, and it became quite obvious that she hated being on Bora Bora, which is all the more interesting when I learned that her previous hotel job was in

Nigeria! She had a look in her eyes that said, "Get me off this rock!" and complained that there was nothing to do and no reliable phone or e-mail service. I almost laughed when I asked how long she'd been there: only eight months! I tried to offer her comfort, "Well, it's a beautiful place," and she replied, "It has the lagoon... that is all". I half-expected her to break into a chorus of Shania Twain's song: "So you've got a lagoon? That don't impress me much!"

The multi-hued lagoon of Bora Bora.

My evening at Bloody Mary's was fun and I was excited to be "going out" for dinner, though Anastasia back at the Eden Beach seemed disappointed that I'd be missing her show. Bloody Mary's is frequented by many celebrities, and the fresh fish is cooked to order on a grill. My calamari steak and ahi tuna were amazingly good, though very expensive. John and Erica were fun company, though that woman never let him get a word in edgewise. Poor John. They'd been married only a few weeks and as I imagined listening to Erica's voice for the rest of my lifetime, a feeling of deep sadness swept over me. I got back to the hotel at 10PM, with my shuttle boat driver taking me across the dark and treacherously shallow lagoon holding only a flashlight in front of him for navigation amidst driving rain and strong gusts of wind.

It was still raining hard when I woke up, so I stayed in bed until almost noon when it finally stopped. I ordered a picnic lunch to go from Anastasia, and then went hiking along the outer edge of the *motu*. The open ocean with a couple of islands visible in the distance was beautiful and I made a bit of peace with this place. After my picnic I went back to the hotel and took a sea kayak out on the lagoon for several hours. The water was so shallow here that you could easily walk a half-mile out and still be in water up to your knees, making swimming impossible. But the sea was flat and calm, it was easy to paddle the kayak and I had a nice time exploring the coast, eventually paddling out to water deep enough to allow me to hop in for a real swim.

For my final evening I arranged a shuttle to the Meridien to attend a Polynesian buffet and dinner show. The food was only fair, but the show, which was put on by several local families, was charming. However, I missed a lot due to people with video cameras jumping in front of me and blocking the view. It amazes me how people are so busy trying to record an event that they miss out on the actual experience. I inevitably got recruited to dance with one of the young Tahitian girls for a number that involved me taking on a surfing posture and clacking my knees together in time with the beat of the music. Luckily, as far as I know, no one got a video of that! I'd heard Tahitian music in Hawaii, and both the music and the dancing are a bit different from their Hawaiian counterparts. In Tahitian music there is far more reliance on drums and rhythm, and this is reflected in the more energetic style of Tahitian dance. Hawaiian music is generally more soothing and more melodic, and hula movements are subtler and depend more on hip motions and the hands. I was also amused to hear semi-Tahitian versions of Cher's *Believe*, and the old Bee Gees' song, *Massachusetts* performed by local artists at the Meridien. It truly is a small world after all!

I returned to my hotel around 11PM, and it was a beautiful night with no rain. Everyone was asleep, but I got my Walkman and one of my favorite Hawaiian music CDs and dragged a lounge chair to the lagoon's edge, my feet dangling in the water. I listened to my music and watched the sky as clouds parted and exposed a brilliant star or two before hiding them once again. I watched shells on the beach moving all around me: tiny crabs lugging them around on their backs. It was surreal to see dozens of shells moving in chaotic patterns all around me: Mother Nature playing her own version of The Shell Game. After almost an hour, lightning started in the distance, and I watched as the storm came gradually closer. I could see the beautiful central peak of Bora Bora's main island illuminated for an instant against the lightning flashes. This was what I'd dreamed about when I decided to come to Tahiti, and I'd finally managed to find it on my last night. Still, the Hawaiian music made me long to return to my beloved islands again. I thought about how the ancient Tahitians had set out from Bora Bora and found their way to Hawaii. I wanted to follow their path, but decided that a plane flight would be preferable to weeks in an outrigger canoe on the open ocean. I laughed out loud thinking of people who'd told me that once I visited Tahiti, I'd forget all about Hawaii. Don't worry, my beloved islands, you have nothing to worry about!

Perhaps because I dared to crown Hawaii the winner of the little popularity contest I was having in my mind, Tahiti had one last parting shot, one more trick up its sleeve for me. The next day, back at the stuffy, humid little airport in Papae'ete I wondered how I'd survive a boring, four-hour layover. As I finished checking my bag, I heard a booming voice shouting from across the terminal, "Matt! How was Bora Bora?" And there he was, Al – Magician of Mystery. Just like the chocolate sauce smear he'd made appear on my left hand, Al had materialized seemingly out of nowhere, and I knew that my layover would be anything but boring.

5. Attack of the Killer Sumo Bee and Other Adventures

JAPAN

Hanging out with the geisha in Kyoto.

Like many of my international trips, visiting Japan in 2007 centered around attending a conference on volcanoes being held in the town of Shimabara on the island of Kyushu. Since I'd never been to Japan, I arranged to tour some of the country before and after the conference.

Like an experienced contestant on TV's Amazing Race, I limped off my twelve-hour flight from San Francisco, exhausted and jet-lagged, but quickly found a train from the airport to the city of Kyoto. Cursing the fact that my luggage was too heavy and that I was carrying a four-foot-long, laminated poster for the conference in a canister over my shoulder, I made my way through the crowded train stations and city streets and found my hotel.

Other than a few important words like *sushi, sashimi, tempura* and *tsunami*, I don't speak Japanese, and despite being a very well-seasoned world traveler, I found that language was going to be an issue right from the start, even in such a heavily touristed city as Kyoto. Finding my first night's dinner was rough; none of the restaurants had an English menu, and the Japanese menus didn't list prices, which made me nervous. I was turned away from several places because they were closing at 8:30PM. Finally, I found a place called Omen which evidently has a sister restaurant in New York City. There was an English menu, and I ordered a reasonably priced, fixed menu that included sea bream sushi, vegetable tempura, deep fried lotus root balls, turnip in miso sauce, deep fried sweet potatoes in a crab sauce, udon noodles, and a broth with all kinds of fresh, but unidentifiable vegetables. It was all delicious, but I had no idea of the logistics of how to eat various things. At one point I motioned to a nearby patron, asking her in mime-like fashion if I was supposed to be putting my noodles into the broth with all the veggies. She gave me the "OK" sign, so either she was telling me I was correct, or she was saying "Do whatever you like, crazy man!" I'll never know which and as a tsunami of jet lag and fatigue washed over me, I honestly didn't care.

After a good rest, I set out on a brisk, sunny autumn morning to the Gion district. The bus took forever to get there, and I could have easily gotten there faster by walking because of the dense traffic. I'd read in travel guides that Kyoto's Gion neighborhood is an area frequented by the famous, white-faced geisha, professional female entertainers and hostesses who dance, sing, and perform in clubs and theaters. Kyoto is where this tradition originated. Almost immediately I came upon a group of professional photographers taking pictures of three geisha dressed in colorful kimonos. I tried to unobtrusively sneak a couple of photos but wasn't able to get any good shots. As they started to pack up, a bystander who'd evidently been watching me from a distance approached me and in heavily accented English asked if I wanted to have my photo taken with the geisha. I was embarrassed and didn't want to bother the group, but this sweet little man went over to talk with them and in a flash my new friend was snapping a number of well-choreographed photos of me standing with the geisha. Once the group left, the man and I chatted awhile, and I learned he had a son studying economics at the University of Michigan. He shook my hand vigorously, saying, "Japan and America, we are good friends! God speed!" As he walked away, he turned and waved vigorously several times. I continued walking along the river under trees bursting with fall color and feeling chilled from the autumn air, but nevertheless warmed by thoughts of such generous hospitality and friendliness.

I climbed to a famous hilltop temple called Kiyomizu, a wonderful, deep shade of orange almost camouflaged amidst the fall foliage. From the temple there were panoramic views over the city and the streets leading to the temple were lined with shops, most of which were selling food and giving away free samples. There were delicious candies called *nama yatsuhashi,* shaped like uncooked ravioli and stuffed with chocolate, cinnamon, and bean paste. Another place gave out sample cups of green tea, while others had several kinds of pickled vegetables to try. I stopped at one place and ordered a giant fritter filled with pumpkin, sweet potato, and carrot, three of my favorite vegetables and all in my favorite color. I also tried a delicious bun filled with a sweet pumpkin paste and herbs. Basically, I just ate my way down the length of the street, not unlike Godzilla plundering a small Japanese village in a bad 1950s movie. I then burned a few calories by walking to Kinkaku-ji, or the Golden Temple, a three-story Zen Buddhist shrine covered in gold leaf from top to bottom. There were hundreds of people there, but the walk through the red and gold trees along the shore of a pond and the view of this magnificent temple reflected in the water was completely calming and serene.

As a social psychologist and someone who likes to have at least some understanding of the culture of places I visit, I'd read a lot about Japanese etiquette and customs before I left home. I learned that perhaps the worst thing one can do is to blow his or her nose in public. One guidebook I'd consulted stated: "Among the *faux pas* considered nearly unpardonable, perhaps the worst is blowing your nose." In another place it said, "Never blow your nose in public. Seriously." After only a couple of days in the country, I decided that this was one cultural norm I'd like to change. People beside me on planes and trains sniffled and snorted and made sounds that, at least in this humble American's opinion, were far more disturbing to me than a good, solid nose blow!

A more pleasant custom here is that there is absolutely no pushing or jockeying for position in lines. Everyone boards a bus or train in the order in which they'd lined up and it just amazes me. This politeness is also reflected in the custom of bowing. Before the official who walks through the train car to check your ticket leaves, he turns and makes a full bow to the passengers before proceeding to the next car. People on the street do quick little bows as you pass them, which can get a bit tedious in a crowded area, but I endeavored to return the gesture. Sometimes it was fun to initiate the bow because the people you're passing, no matter how much of a hurry they are in, must reflexively return the bow.

My next destination was the city of Hiroshima, and on the train ride from Kyoto an elderly man shyly approached me and asked where I was from. We had an extremely long conversation, chatting about Social Psychology, Faulkner novels, the American Civil War, and World War II. Of course, the last topic was more than a little awkward given that we were bound for Hiroshima, site of the first atomic bomb blast in 1945. However, my new friend surprised me when, with a constant, easygoing smile, he insisted that Japan "deserved" to be hit with the atomic bomb because it was the only way to stop the war. However, he added that the Americans "went too far" when they firebombed Tokyo!

I reached Hiroshima just as it was getting dark and was surprised by how much colder it was here than in Kyoto. I took a streetcar to the A-Bomb Dome, which sounds like a sports stadium with a very twisted name but is actually the wreckage of the only building still standing after the atomic bomb leveled the city. It was dark, but the ruins were floodlit and surrounded by a lush and beautiful park along the river. I sat on a bench there for a while, getting teary-eyed thinking about what had happened here and of all the hell of World War II that led up to it. As often happens to me when I'm in Europe, I struggle to imagine the horrors that went on just a few years ago and marvel at how people and nations are often able to heal those wounds and reach out to one another again in friendship.

Hiroshima's A-Bomb Dome; Kyoto's graceful Golden Temple.

As I walked back toward my hotel, I entered a pedestrian-only area lit by neon signs and Christmas lights. Yes, Christmas appears to be a big deal here: "Merry Christmas!" banners were everywhere, with beautifully lit and decorated trees. It's so strange, as I didn't think it would be such a big event in a country where almost eighty percent of the citizens are either Buddhist or Shinto. Some streets were lit up like the Vegas Strip or New York's Times Square. There was a street fair going on, with dozens of food booths, a good rock band, and a troupe of drum players who put on a wonderfully energetic show. It was a jolting contrast to have been sitting in contemplative silence at the A-Bomb Dome minutes before, and now caught up in festivities that demonstrated just how alive and vital this city is.

From Hiroshima my next stop was the conference at Shimabara, which lies precariously close to Mt. Unzen, a volcano that erupted in 1993 killing about forty people and laying waste to large areas close to its summit. The arena in which the conference was being held was built atop a volcanic debris flow. I stayed in a *ryokan*, a Japanese style hotel characterized by rooms with very little furniture and floors covered in straw mats. My tenth-floor room provided a nice view of the coast and nearby islands and was enormous, but spartanly furnished; there was a long, low table with a tea set, a single seat cushion to sit on, and a futon mattress placed directly on the floor. It was a little hard on me getting up and down off the floor, but otherwise it was quite comfortable.

Sashimi for seven?

After settling in, I walked around town for over an hour, hoping to see some of my conference colleagues and find a place to eat, but there weren't many options. Eventually, I was so tired and hungry I took a chance and entered a very small establishment. I was seated at a bar-like area surrounding the chef's station, so I could watch as he worked. The husband-and-wife team running the place were very friendly but spoke no English and I spent several uncomfortable moments trying to communicate. Finally, my host raised an eyebrow and asked, *"Sashimi?"*

At last, a word I knew! I excitedly replied, *"Hai!"*, which is Japanese for yes, feeling like I'd just mastered the language. He smiled with relief, left his post, and went over to a large fountain pool by the door that I'd thought was merely decorative. Suddenly he reached in and grabbed a live fish, easily ten inches long, and brought it back to the bar as it struggled and thrashed violently. Before I even had time to react, he chopped its head off and within a couple of minutes placed a platter of uncomfortably fresh sashimi in front of me. I really enjoy sushi, but the shock of seeing my appetizer killed in front of me made me a bit uneasy. My guilt over the slain fish, coupled with my desire not to offend, made me dig in; It really was quite tasty; I was just thankful I hadn't ordered beef!

My host then brought out a strange instrument that looked like a calculator, typed something into it and showed me the screen. It was an instant language translator, and the word "blowfish" was displayed as he pointed to my plate. It was interesting to know what I'd eaten, but I've since read that while blowfish is a popular sashimi in Japan, the liver and skin contain a toxin for which there is no antidote. These parts must be removed by a specially trained person; since I'm still alive, I assume that thankfully, my host was such a person!

I followed the sashimi with a safer and delicious shrimp and vegetable tempura, but then my host brought me a small dish of strange, brown, meaty looking things that he indicated were eel. I ate them with difficulty and smiled, though I honestly wasn't a big fan. What helped immensely was that I'd ordered a small pitcher of hot *sake*, Japanese rice wine, and after three small but potent glasses of that, I was almost ready to go catch and kill my own dinner! Before long a group of three Japanese men wearing conference badges came in and sat next to me at the bar. They spoke no English, but they soon ordered *sake* and offered me some. I'd read in my guidebook that it's a big offense to turn down an offer of a drink in Japan, so I gratefully accepted and left feeling quite jovial. It was a one of those crazy evenings that make travel so exciting.

After dinner I retreated to the *onsen,* the hotel's outdoor spa. This became my nightly ritual, and it really is a ritual. In my room, I put on the long, just-barely-wide-enough kimono supplied by the hotel, some way-too-small slippers that left half of my foot hanging off the back, and carefully shuffled down to the onsen. There you need to strip naked, grab a plastic bucket and seat yourself in front of a small shower where liquid soap and shampoo are supplied. You must be squeaky clean, taking your time to avoid the glares of other folks, lest they think you finished washing too quickly. Then you take your tiny hand towel, place it over yourself in a modest, fig leaf-bearing pose, and walk to the pool. Baths are separate for the men and women, and everyone is nude. While bathing, the men wear their little towel on top of their head to keep it dry, but when they get out of the water the towel is again used to cover their private parts. I was happy to follow any and all of these norms, because to me, being outside on a briskly cold night and soaking my bones in hot water is a little piece of Heaven.

The next day I went on a conference field trip to explore Mt. Unzen and the damage it caused in 1993. We saw the lovely natural scenery that any volcanic area provides (Hawaii, the Pacific Northwest, and New Zealand), but also toured Pompeii-like ruins of buildings covered in ash or blown apart by powerful volcanic explosions. At one site, as we were donning our hard hats to walk through the area, the most amazing bug started to hover over our group. It was a bee, with classic black and yellow stripes and a huge stinger, but what got our attention was the sheer size of it: perhaps five inches long! This thing was huge! Its face was flat and had markings that almost made it look like one of those bright yellow "Have a Nice Day" smiley face buttons! It was bizarre, and all I could think of was Mothra, the giant flying caterpillar from one of those low-budget 1950s Japanese monster movies. The bee tried to land in one man's hair, diving with the sound of a small helicopter, and our tour guide looked alarmed. Everyone was screaming and ducking; I actually found it hilarious as long as it was far enough away from me! Finally, the monster backed off and flew away, but everyone was disheveled and agitated by now. I brought the house down when I exclaimed, "What was that? A Sumo Bee?" in reference to the gigantic sumo wrestlers that seem to always be on TV here. Later I wondered if "Bee-Zilla" would have been funnier. Anyway, I felt I'd witnessed the discovery of what seemed to be an entirely new life form.

The highlight of the day was a visit to an elementary school. As we walked to the auditorium where students were putting on a show for us, we faced a reception line of at least one-hundred adorable kids. Each one greeted us and seemed to want to practice his or her English. With beaming grins, they shouted "Hello!", which invariably sounded more like "*Herro!*" With dozens of enthusiastic *herros* still ringing in my ears, I scored a front row seat for the show.

The students put on a play about the 1993 eruption, acting out the event and aided by a slide presentation in the background showing actual footage. One little girl played a journalist, and armed with a microphone as a prop, she interviewed kids dressed as townspeople about the aftermath of the eruption. She had it down, handling that mic like a Japanese Katie Couric or Oprah. Finally, the class joined together for a concert, playing xylophones, flutes, giant drums – all quite well – and singing a song about the eruption. They passed out English lyrics so we could follow along, and my favorite verse had to be this one:

At the elementary school in Shimabara.

"I heard that the hot air came down to Kamiori Bridge and caused bad burns on the cows, their breasts melted, and their eyes popped out. I felt very sorry for the cows." It certainly painted a vivid picture! They should do a follow-up about the attack of the Killer Sumo Bee!

After the show, the kids swarmed around us, wanting to shake or just hold our hands. They seemed particularly fascinated with me, I guess because of my freckles and red hair. Several of them were petting my hands and arms as if I were an Irish setter. At one point I asked a colleague to take a picture of me with a few of the kids, and by the time I'd knelt amongst them, a veritable tsunami of other children almost knocked me over, wanting to be in the picture too. It's one of my most treasured photos.

As we returned to Shimabara, we noticed an army of local people in lime green jackets stationed at the conference center and on some city streets to aid conference attendees. Most didn't really speak English very well, but they made up for it with their boundless enthusiasm and desire to do whatever they could to help. My favorite was Miyashi, a young woman I befriended and nicknamed "Raggedy Ann," as her hair was dyed an odd shade of red, and she wore it in two thick pigtails. She insisted I attend a party being held in the city for the conference-goers that night and I couldn't say no. However, later in the day there was great confusion regarding transportation from the conference to the party; shuttles were scheduled to depart before conference presentations had even finished for the day and we heard that the next round of shuttles would be two hours later. Suddenly, like a guardian angel, Raggedy Ann appeared, literally jumping up and down when she saw me, and I enlisted her help with the bus situation. Within two minutes she'd pulled some strings and gotten the shuttles to delay their departures a half hour so we could finish up conference business. What a doll! A Raggedy Ann doll, of course! It's great to have friends in high places.

The evening's party was hosted by the mayor, and held below Shimabara Castle, a glimmering white fortress high on a hill and surrounded by a moat. Locals had cooked hundreds of platters of food for us, all of which was excellent. There were crafts on display, and I really enjoyed the bonsai exhibit, talking to an 80-year-old man about his incredibly beautiful little trees that were almost as old as he was. My favorite was a tiny maple tree, maybe nine inches tall, with brilliantly gold and orange fall foliage. Other trees had colorful fruits and berries on them. I'd have loved to have been able to bring one home. I only saw a couple of my colleagues that evening, but the locals embraced me, feeding me noodles and homemade soup while we watched performances of drumming, Buddhist chanting, and dancing. And then, a tiny woman grabbed my hand and with a frightening display of strength dragged me along with her, exclaiming, "You must help us to make the *mochi*"!

"What is *Mochi*?" you may be asking. I too was unsure, but after consulting various online resources I learned that Mochi is a Japanese rice cake made of "glutinous rice" pounded into a paste and molded into balls. Although eaten year-round, mochi is traditionally served around Japanese New Year. It's similar to a Chinese rice cake called *nian gao;* however, mochi is molded right after it is pounded, whereas nian gao is baked first to solidify and sanitize it. In other words, I'd been asked to help pound out some raw, unsanitized rice cakes. Yum!

Arriving in front of the stage where the Buddhist monks had just been chanting, I was given a gigantic wooden sledgehammer and instructed to pound a mushy, thick rice mixture as hard as I could in rhythm with a man who was beating a drum. It was a little like making homemade ice cream in the old days when you had to crank the handle for hours to get the ice cream to harden. After a few minutes my arm felt as if it'd fall off, but my hosts relieved me of that task and led me to a kitchen-like area behind the stage. An older woman was kneading a huge, white, ugly mass of pounded rice and throwing flour over it.

Without there being time or any place to wash my hands, I was told to cover my hands with flour and start molding round balls of this stuff in an assembly-line like process. It felt eerily reminiscent of that episode of *I Love Lucy in which* Lucy and Ethel tried to keep up the pace working on an assembly line at a chocolate factory! Someone grabbed my camera from my shoulder and took my picture, as flour flew every-where, and I struggled to make my little balls even vaguely resemble those being made by the experts.

And then, the cruelest blow was struck! A young man working across the table from me grinned and exclaimed, "You must taste the mochi!" Although I like candy; I really didn't want to try one of these things that we were making. I'm more of a dark chocolate truffle kinda guy. No one seemed to have washed their hands prior to joining this mochi assembly line, the consistency of the little balls of dough was disgusting, and the darned things were covered in raw flour! However, I didn't want to offend my hosts as they were all so kind.

Mochi-making mania!

Again, from the Internet I learned that because mochi is very sticky, it can be tricky to eat. After each New Year, the Japanese media report the number of people who died from choking on it. Because it's so sticky, it is difficult to dislodge via the Heimlich maneuver. To summarize some cheery facts from *Wikipedia:* "Suffocation deaths are caused by mochi every year, especially among the elderly. In 2015, the Tokyo Fire Department, which responds to choking cases, reported that over 100 people were hospitalized for choking on mochi in Tokyo alone. Japanese authorities issue yearly warnings, advising that mochi be cut into small pieces before consumption." According to a 2015 article in the online magazine *Quartz,* Japanese fire departments suggest using vacuum cleaners to help people choking on mochi, inspiring one medical device manufacturer to offer a suction nozzle attachment for over-enthusiastic mochi eaters." No, I'm not making this up!

I'm glad I hadn't consulted the Internet before I'd gotten myself into this predicament. As soon as I popped one of these mochi balls into my mouth, I recalled another episode of *I Love Lucy* when Lucy took her first taste of the alcohol-based health tonic, "Vitameatavegemin" while filming a TV ad and had to recite the pitch line, "It's so tasty too! Just like candy!" I made a Lucy-esque face, then valiantly tried to smile without gagging. This was NOT just like candy! With great difficulty, I managed to lodge the mochi into the pouch of my cheek until I could excuse myself, then ran to the nearest dark alley, found a trashcan, and spat it out. If this is how they celebrate New Year here, I'll be sure that all future December 31[sts] are spent in Italy, France or the good old U.S.A. sipping champagne and dining on some tasteful appetizers!

After the grueling process of mochi making and the trauma

of mochi tasting, I sought solace at a tea house near the castle where locals were introducing us to the traditional tea ceremony. Raggedy Ann showed up and insisted on getting a picture of us together, which started a trend as four or five elderly women then joined suit and wanted their pictures taken with me too. I don't know if it was the novelty of my hair or what, but I was amazed that these people would want their photo taken with a perfect stranger! Of course, the Japanese seem addicted to taking photos, and I saw many of them at the conference taking photos of each and every one of a presenters' boring PowerPoint slides. In comparison to that, I suppose I seemed like a veritable super-model!

It was a long, festive evening, but eventually I returned to the hotel and the onsen, soaking in the hot water while gazing at an almost-full moon and a brilliantly red Mars rising in the east. I realized that it was now Thanksgiving morning back home and I felt a momentary pang of loneliness, wishing I were back in New England with friends and family. I'd have given anything for a big plate of turkey, stuffing, and cranberry sauce to get the lingering taste of *mochi* out of my mouth! Nevertheless, I fell asleep that night feeling very thankful for the opportunity to visit this amazing place and to meet so many of its charming people.

The next day the conference's closing ceremonies were held in a cavernous hotel ballroom. There were countless tables heaped with nothing but sushi and sashimi of every size, shape, and color, garnished with lemons, ginger and wasabi. As 500 greedy conventioneers launched into the food with gusto, a children's choir sang in angelic voices, beer and *sake* flowed like water from a volcanic hot spring, and the party went on for two hours. I don't think I've eaten as much sushi throughout my entire life as I did that night. While chatting with a Japanese colleague, I motioned to the endless tables and asked, "Do you think there are any fish left in the sea?" After a few seconds of silence in which he seemed to be translating what I'd said, he roared with laughter.

The conference over, I was on my own again, heading south by train to Kagoshima City. The terrain became more dramatic and hillier, and decidedly more tropical, with foliage changing from pine trees to red-leafed maples to bamboo. Kagoshima is another city in peril; with over 600,000 residents it sits across a beautiful bay within ten miles of Sakurajima, the most active volcano in Japan. The city is often called the "Naples of Japan" because of its similarity to its Italian counterpart that sits beneath Mt. Vesuvius. Since its last devastating eruption in 1914, Sakurajima has continued to produce minor eruptions, resulting in ash blowing across the bay and falling like rain over Kagoshima City. Over on the volcanic island itself, there are numerous towns that are the targets of flying volcanic rocks and debris that are sometimes ejected from the crater. All along the main road on the island, small concrete shelters resembling large dog houses are strategically placed so that people can run for cover if rocks start flying. Residents have them in their back yards, too, as sometimes the flying rocks damage roofs. I used to show a video about this area in the Natural Disasters course I taught, so it was exciting for me to see this place in person.

The bus ride along the bay shore was truly lovely, with adorable bobbing fishing boats and nets strewn across the water as the volcano steamed in the background. I stopped to tour the Sakurajima Volcano Observatory. Shoes had to be removed at the door and replaced by slippers they provided; believe me, it was no fun having size 10.5 wide feet mashed into a size 6 narrow sandal, but the museum was fascinating. It was filled with high-tech displays like a 3-D movie in which the viewer becomes part of a lahar or volcanic mud flow as it rages down the volcano's slopes. My favorite part was when the lahar and I took out a couple of grazing deer, smashed a few houses into kindling, and wiped out a bridge as we made our way from the summit to the sea!

My hotel back in Kagoshima City was magnificent, situated on the waterfront and decked out with thousands of Christmas lights. I had a deluxe, western style room with a full view of Sakurajima across the bay. By 8PM I was starving and set out to find a place for dinner. There were dozens of places to choose from, but the longer I searched, the more I knew I was in trouble. Not one place had an English menu or English-speaking staff. Many places had photo menus, but it was difficult to discern whether the item in the photo was chicken, fish, pork, vegetables, or a ball of *mochi* and no prices were listed. And before long several restaurants were already preparing to close.

I screwed up my courage, went into a bustling restaurant and got a table. My waitress stopped and made a motion that indicated she wanted to know what I wanted to drink. I wanted water, but I had no idea what the word for that was and she didn't understand the English word. I vainly searched nearby tables to see if anyone else had water so I could point to it, but no one did. I tried to mimic getting water out of a faucet and she looked at me as if I were crazy. In desperation I raised a finger to indicate that I needed a minute and frantically searched my guidebook; water wasn't even listed in the vocabulary section. I stared blankly at the photo menu; I tried to look up certain foods in my guidebook but couldn't pronounce them. Totally out of character for me, I had a near panic attack, grabbed my backpack and made a run for the door. In all of my travels, even the most exotic ones, there was always someone who could speak a little English, I knew enough of the language to get by, or there were other tourists around that I could consult with. This was not the case here. I'd spent the whole day in Kagoshima, and I hadn't seen even one Caucasian face and hadn't heard anyone speaking English. It was a surprisingly isolating experience. The people I encountered were friendly and wanted to try and help me, but the language barrier made it impossible; this was a first for me.

I continued to walk the streets, stomach growling, wondering if I should just give up and head to a McDonald's I'd passed. Just then I spotted an Italian flag in front of a small bar down the street. A photo menu was posted outside with Japanese characters under each photo, but there were also Italian captions! When I'd started studying Italian a few years prior I'd never have guessed that it would come to my rescue in Kagoshima City, Japan! *Fettuccine, linguine, insalata, tiramisu*: words I knew and music to my ears! The staff all spoke Italian, and while the food didn't rival that of my favorite haunts in Rome or Venice, I was just grateful to have familiar food and to be able to speak to someone. *Viva Italia!*

The next day I explored the city, walking everywhere, marveling at streets lined by koi ponds as long as a city block, filled with colorful fish and bordered by beautiful flower gardens. I climbed an unbelievably long, steep staircase to a park from which I could see all of Kagoshima, with Sakurajima puffing across the bay. As I admired the view and tried to catch my breath, I was approached by an older man who'd been sitting with friends. In very halting English he asked me where I was from and wanted to tell me a bit about his city and the volcano. I was touched by his kindness, but I also wanted to know where'd he'd been last night when I really needed his help with the menu situation!

View of Sakurajima from Kagoshima City.

In the afternoon I took the ferry over to Sakurajima and traveled by bus to a place called Furasato Onsen, a sacred Shinto shrine at the foot of the volcano with an outdoor hot spring right on the sea, surrounded by lava rock. This onsen isn't segregated by gender, so they provide a *yakuta*, a rough-textured white cotton robe to be worn in the pools. It was a truly magical spot and I got there in the late afternoon, so the light was already fading and soft. As I relaxed in the hot pools, I heard the surf. A gnarled tree stands over the pool and shelters a Shinto altar and I watched people entering the pools making praying gestures or giving two hand claps in a row as they faced the altar, seemingly giving thanks for this place. I soaked as long as I could before needing to get out of the hot water to cool down. I also met two young women from Virginia who teach English here and they confirmed that in this part of Japan, it's very hard to get by without knowing any Japanese, so I felt reassured after my prior night's experience.

Soaking at Furasato Onsen.

After returning to the city, it was time to search for dinner again and I was really apprehensive but determined to overcome my fears. I looked up a place in my guidebook that supposedly offered fixed-price, multi-course menus, so I figured I could at least point to one of those and be assured of several different dishes. Ironically, as I entered the place, the hostess approached me and began to explain the menu in slow, but understandable English. Then a waiter whose English was even better explained the finer points of the menu and I chose one of the multi-course meals. There were ten courses, and each one was as beautiful to look at as it was delicious. My favorite was sashimi made from a fish with white, black, and silver stripes. It was wrapped around vegetables and placed on a robin-egg blue plate; the strips of fish looked like a foil Christmas bow on a package. It didn't look real. Following that were local specialties of fried fish cakes, pork ribs with black sugar glaze, grilled chicken, various vegetables, rice, miso soup, and a sweet potato ice cream, which I'd been hoping to sample, as I knew it was a local specialty. It was all such a treat and one of the best meals I had on the whole trip.

I enjoyed chatting with the waiter. When he learned that I was born in Massachusetts, he shared that he'd been to Boston, was a big history buff, and excitedly talked about visiting Bunker Hill and the Boston Tea Party site. As I was leaving, he saw me to the door and said, "I think in your country you say, 'Home is where the heart is.' If this is true, then my home is in Boston!" It was very sweet, and I'm so glad that my final night in Japan was filled with great food, warm hospitality, and the gift of communication.

Back in my room I retired to my balcony, relishing the warm night, the sound of the ferry horns, the full moon rising over the bay, and the dark silhouette of Sakurajima, steam still rising from its summit and visible in the moonlight. What an amazing place this is!

I loved what I saw of Japan. The natural scenery is stunning, and I admired the order and calm of Japanese society. I've never stayed in quieter hotels anywhere: no loud voices, banging on walls, or slamming doors. I loved the cleanliness of everything and the lack of litter. I enjoyed the cuisine, especially when I knew what I was eating and when what I was eating wasn't *mochi*. Most of all, I loved the people I encountered. The Japanese were some of the friendliest and most polite people I've met anywhere in the world, and despite the significant language barriers, their warmth and hospitality were constantly in evidence.

I hope to return to Japan someday, but I'll either need to stick closer to areas where English is more widely spoken or learn a bit of the language next time. During the conference I felt safe because we were being watched over carefully, but on my own, it was surprisingly stressful to accomplish even the most basic things. Waiting for my flight home at the airport, I asked someone how to say "water" and learned that the word is *mizu*, a word I won't soon forget. Armed with that knowledge, at least I know I won't go thirsty on my next visit.

6. Now I Understand the Motivation for the Exodus
EGYPT and JORDAN

My journey across Giza with "Michael Jackson"

I'd read that the name Cairo is Arabic for "Victorious One," but after only an hour in the Egyptian capital I wondered if something had gotten lost in translation; to me Cairo must certainly be synonymous with the word "chaos." First, there was my arrival at the airport. My hotel forgot to send a driver for me, leaving me surrounded by over a hundred desperate men trying to convince me to let them take me to my destination. Once the hotel driver finally found me at the airport, he took me on an adrenaline-filled ride through the city. I witnessed countless women dressed either in colorful headscarves or in solid black burqas, babies in their arms or huge parcels balanced on their heads, simply walking out into the streets despite three lanes of traffic bearing down upon them. They were trying to hail one of Cairo's primary forms of public transportation: Microbuses, dilapidated mini vans that look like they're held together by duct tape and a prayer. Seemingly on a whim, microbuses stop without warning, often in the middle or fast lane of major thoroughfares to pick up people who rush through the traffic to hop aboard. This causes drivers of every car or bus within a two-mile radius to blast their horns. Once "aboard," microbus passengers often stand on the bumper and hang on if there's no room inside as the van weaves through the nightmarish traffic. When I ventured out for dinner on my first night, I tried crossing a street. Drivers switching lanes and traveling at breakneck speeds, coupled with the fact that about twenty percent of Cairo's drivers actually believe that using headlights wastes gas meant that I stood a one in five chance of being flattened by a car I'd never even seen coming.

This was my introduction to Cairo. It was January 2010, and I was meeting a group from my university for a ten-day, study abroad tour of Egypt. I'd arrived a day early, and after seeing what lay outside the walls of my hotel, I decided to relax by the pool in serene safety until my comrades arrived. We assembled over a buffet breakfast at the hotel the following morning and I became an instant fan of hibiscus juice, which looked and tasted somewhat like cranberry; it's purportedly good for high blood pressure, so I drank with gusto! We then met our guides, Mohammad, a spectacled man in his fifties and his assistant, Hassan, much younger with a beaming smile and a more western appearance and manner. They herded us onto a tour bus, and we began our first day of sightseeing.

Our first stop was Saqqara, an ancient gray stone pyramid older than the famous pyramids at Giza. Muhammad called it a "wedding cake" pyramid, and I did like that image, despite having never seen a gray wedding cake. We saw the enormous statue of Ramses, the Egyptian king said to have fathered 114 children. I chuckled at the irony that a brand of condoms is named after him. As we left the site, we were assailed by the most aggressive vendors I'd ever encountered anywhere in my world travels. "Hey mister, where are you from?" "What are you looking for?" "I have what you need!" I hate to be impolite, but it was impossible to make them stop so I tried to ignore them and push my way through. Had they left me alone, I'd have loved to have looked at things they were selling, but with the insane pressure, I felt cornered and panicked and couldn't get away from them quickly enough.

From Saqqara we went to see the great pyramids of Giza. We were told that for an extra $20, we could crawl inside some of the tunnels at the base of one of the pyramids, but all I wanted to do was walk around and take pictures in the fading afternoon light. I'd dreamed of seeing the pyramids all my life, and I wanted to revel in the fact that I was here and to soak up the amazing ambiance of the place. I soaked up the ambiance for maybe ten seconds before hordes of vendors came at me from every direction, across the desert sands and from nearby parking lots, with only one objective in mind: to sell me something, anything. I wasn't able to talk with my friends or take a picture. It was unbelievable. With some difficulty I broke away and headed toward the back side of the great pyramid, but then I made the fatal error of taking a picture of a man riding a camel off in the distance. He saw me take the photo and virtually galloped over to me. As a Social Psychology professor who'd taught students about research on persuasion for years, I really should have known what was coming, but this man quickly pulled me into his web.

"Take a picture of me with my camel, my friend!" he said, with a broad, friendly smile. He dismounted and invited me to stand beside the camel, grabbed my camera and took my picture. It all happened so fast. "Put your foot in the stirrup like you're mounting the camel! It will be a great picture to show your friends!" You can likely guess where this was going. I soon found myself sitting atop a kneeling camel, and when it suddenly stood up, I had to hang on for dear life, dangling precariously eight or nine feet above the ground. This man still had my camera and called his son over to walk the camel out into the desert. I looked back and saw that my group was already returning to our bus and I started to panic. I pleaded with the man to stop the camel and let me off, but my pleas fell on seemingly deaf ears. I spotted my friend Dan, called out to him for help, and he rushed over and asked the man to let me down. After a few minutes of arguing, the man, acting wounded and hurt, got hold of the reins and made the camel kneel, allowing me to dismount. I was in such a hurry to do so that I banged my right shin bone pretty badly on the wooden horn of the saddle; a nasty bruise and lump formed almost immediately.

Meanwhile, the camel's owner still had my camera and was demanding payment for the "use of his camel." He wanted 100 Egyptian pounds (about $25) and when I offered him twenty pounds, he nearly spat at me with anger. I offered him thirty pounds, and he became even angrier, demanding 100 pounds. Finally, I tossed a twenty-pound bill at him and threatened to get the police if he didn't return my camera. He threw it on the ground in front of me, ripped another ten-pound bill from my hand and stormed off. Thankfully my camera wasn't damaged, but I was shaking by the time I got back to our bus. When Hassan heard the story, he disappeared and returned minutes later with my thirty pounds, even though I told him I really didn't deserve to get it back after being such a fool and getting entangled in such a mess to begin with!

In an ironic twist, the next activity on our tour was a pre-arranged sunset camel ride. Under any other circumstances, I'd have been excited about this, but I was extremely nervous about getting back on that horse, so to speak! I tried to be a brave cowboy atop my second camel in an hour and our group began crossing the desert, being led by children in a long caravan. When I asked the young boy leading my camel what the animal's name was, he replied, "Michael Jackson," which I found both amusing and disconcerting. Thankfully Michael did not moon-walk his way across the desert and the view of the pyramids from atop him was iconic. I later learned that my friends LeeAnn and Dan, who'd been riding together on one camel, had been in an accident when their camel suddenly knelt to let them off and LeeAnn got slammed into the wooden horn of the saddle with full force. She was bruised, but OK. As we returned to our tour bus, I laughed myself silly when I saw a T-shirt for sale that said, "Leave me alone! I came to see the Pyramids!" Unfortunately, it was about twenty sizes too small for me, but it certainly summarized my experiences after my first full day in Egypt.

After the pyramids and a dreadfully salty buffet dinner at a local hotel, we were off to the Giza Sound and Light Show, a laser and music "extravaganza" - their words, not mine - taking place in the shadow of the Sphinx. The show was laughably silly as "the Sphinx" discussed his past over a booming loudspeaker. He described the sorrow he felt when Napoleon's troops used him as target practice, making him ugly by destroying his nose, a legend that I believe has since been refuted. I was sitting with one of my students, Clayton, and we entertained ourselves by making sarcastic jokes about hoping to buy a DVD of the show or a CD of the music soundtrack or wanting to see the companion show down at Aswan or Luxor later on in our trip. We thought we were pretty amusing, but evidently some of the members of our group actually liked the show and HAD wanted to buy the DVD, so we shrunk down into our seats and kept our mouths shut on the bus ride back to the hotel.

The next day we saw three famous mosques in Cairo, which were indeed beautiful, but by the third one, we were "mosqued-out." At each exit, a crowd of vendors lay in wait, forcing us to run back to the bus, which was difficult for me with my badly injured leg. Lunch that day was at the Hard Rock Café, and I was both put off at the thought of eating at a chain restaurant and excited by the prospect of being able to order off a menu after all the buffets we'd been eating. For some odd reason I craved a tuna melt and fries, but alas, it was not to be. We had to eat from a buffet of the same old stuff: rice, pasta, meatballs, overly salted carrots and broccoli, hummus, and pita bread. Each meal was exactly the same and we joked about how wonderful Lunch Buffet #3 was or how we'd never forget Dinner Buffet #2.

After lunch we visited the Egyptian Museum, but by now we were all hot, tired and cranky. The museum wasn't air-conditioned, and we weren't allowed to roam and look at things we were interested in, so we had to follow the guide for two and a half hours, standing and listening to long descriptions of certain pieces. The only thing that kept me going was to hear that we'd be returning to our hotel by 5:00, leaving an hour for a swim in the beautiful pool which closed at 6:00. Ultimately, we arrived at the hotel by 5:45 and I raced as fast as my injured leg could carry me to get my bathing suit on and get in the water. We were told that the hotel would keep the pool open an extra half hour for us, but I was asked to leave at precisely 5:59. Sigh. Then it was off to another dinner buffet.

Mosque of Ibn Tulun; Great Pyramid of Khufu and the Sphinx.

After three long days in Cairo, we had a 5AM wake-up call and were off to the airport for a flight to Aswan in southern Egypt. Our first stop was the great Aswan Dam, erected in the 1970s to control flooding on the Nile River. For years I'd lectured about the detrimental effects that this dam has had on the Nile Delta in my Natural Disasters course, so it was interesting to see it in person, but let's face it, a dam is ultimately just a dam. Next, we took a short boat ride to see the Temple of Isis, originally built on an island in the Nile, but moved piece by piece and reassembled like a gigantic jigsaw puzzle to protect it when the dam was built, flooding the area upriver. We also rode a *felucca*, a traditional Egyptian sailboat, to visit some ruins, a botanical garden, and a museum on Elephantine Island. Museum guides stood amongst the ruins and followed me around, pointing to a flower or a bird. "Mister, look! It is a lovely flower! See the bird over there!" They then wanted money for imparting this knowledge to me. Again, I tried to avoid all eye contact and refused any unsolicited narratives.

After yet another buffet lunch, we checked in at the boat dock for our Nile River cruise, which would be taking us down river toward Luxor the following day. I went to the pool on the top deck, only to discover that the water was ice cold and the jacuzzi was barely lukewarm, but I dangled my sore feet and legs in the cold water. I'd noticed that my feet and calves were swelling up badly, most likely from a combination of the heat, high salt intake, being on my feet ten hours a day, and my injury. It was unnerving, and I tried to prop my feet up whenever I could. Our cruise ship had a five star "luxury" rating, but I'd give it two stars at best. For security, every time we boarded, we had to pass through a metal detector, but we all chuckled nervously over the fact that the thing beeped every time we walked through, yet no one ever stopped us.

After another boring buffet, we walked to a nearby bazaar for a shopping expedition, accompanied by the armed security guard who'd tailed us all day. At the bazaar he seemed very uptight and on edge and wouldn't let us out of his sight. If we fell behind to take a picture or look in a shop window, he'd firmly nudge us along. Perhaps this was just as well, as the onslaught of vendors at the Aswan Bazaar was truly awful. Many vendors called me *Ali Baba*, referring to the character from the folk tale *Ali Baba and the Forty Thieves*, but I later learned that this is a common nickname given to any Caucasian with a beard. The high-pressure sales pitches were exhausting. "Come in here, my friend. Good prices! What you want? I help you spend your money! What do you look for? Ali Baba, where you are from? America? America good! We have your big size – come, try!" These vendors are adept at watching your eyes; if you so much as glance at something, even without stopping, they immediately notice and start bargaining. The only solution was to look down and keep walking, but even then, some vendors followed me, accusing me of being rude for ignoring them.

Our cruise ship set sail the next day, giving us glimpses of the countryside along the Nile as we headed north toward Luxor. This was the Africa I'd always imagined, with men in long white robes tending cattle or sheep along the riverbank, waving as the boat passed. It was one of the most pleasant couple of hours I'd spent in Egypt up to that point. After dark there was a big party onboard, but most of our group opted out when they learned that our wake-up call for a twelve-hour day of touring would be at 5AM. The rest of us attended and watched a spoon dance event in which ten women danced in a circle around a pile of nine spoons quickly grabbing one when the music stopped - a bizarre version of musical chairs. Then it was the men's turn. Four guys dangled a foil-wrapped potato from a rope tied to their waist and had to use their potato to hit another potato across the floor. The object was to see who could push his potato across the finish line first - a weird take on croquet! Eduardo, a handsome young Spaniard won the race, no doubt due to his very deliberate hip motions!

Our wake-up call came far too soon and what I'll refer to as "Temple Tour Hell" began. By 7AM we were waiting in line outside the colossal Temple of Edfu. It seemed that most other tour groups had the same idea and when the gates opened, there was such a stampede to get in I actually had to shield some of the smaller members of our group with my larger bulk. Then we were whisked off to the Valley of the Kings where we toured three tombs. I only did two of them and skipped the third; it was getting hot, my feet were tired, and there were horrendous crowds and endless stairs. It was getting to be too much. Our next stop was a tomb for a goddess whose name I can't recall, but it was a beautiful place, carved directly into the face of a mountain.

By mid-afternoon we finally stopped for lunch, but alas, it was another buffet and immediately afterward, we were herded to the temple of Karnak, another amazing site spoiled for me by the fact that we were marched through on a fast tour with no time to simply sit, stare and contemplate the place. By the time we got to the famous Temple of Luxor at sunset, half the group had mutinied, choosing to sit in a shady area, too exhausted to move or care about anything anymore. It really was a shame, because the temples were all magnificent, but it was just too much for one day. Of course, each temple exit led directly into a bazaar where we endured more sales pitches; it was like going through a fraternity hazing in order to re-board the bus.

A graceful felucca on the Nile.

We got back to the ship just in time for our evening buffet but found that the housekeeping staff had prepared "surprises" for us. They'd arranged bedspreads, towels, and articles of our own clothing like hats, t shirts or sunglasses to make it look like there was a person in our room, which was scary as hell as we entered our darkened cabins. There were several screams as people discovered their "surprise" and later, a few students reported money was missing from their rooms. This was definitely not a five-star cruise! As if we weren't having enough fun, several people became sick with food poisoning at this point in the trip. Luckily, my stomach was fine, but after twelve hours of temples, desert heat, and salty buffets, my feet looked like purple balloons. I sprawled on the floor of the upper deck with my legs elevated on a chair, trying to get the swelling down. Rarely have I wanted to leave a place as much as I wanted to leave Egypt at that moment. I thought, "Now I understand the motivation for the Exodus." Feeling like a modern-day Moses, I mused, "Let my people go!"

We were told to expect a 4AM wake-up call the next day to catch our flight back to Cairo. I awoke at 5:05AM and with horror realized I'd either slept through my wake-up call or had never received one. I freaked out and was showered, dressed and out the door of my cabin in five minutes, but my group had already gone. Why no one had come looking for me was a mystery, but I ran down the dock dragging my bag behind me and saw that the group's luggage was still being loaded onto a bus. I'd had no breakfast and was totally disheveled. By the time we reached the airport things had gotten worse; more members of our group were dropping like flies from "King Tut's Revenge" and some were so ill that Mohammad arranged for a doctor to meet us at Cairo airport. When we arrived, many were given shots to counteract food poisoning.

There was also a mix-up with our luggage; many bags bore the wrong name tags and some folks lost their bags and never got them back. I was beginning to wonder if those who'd opted to crawl around the tunnels of the Giza Pyramid had invoked a Mummy's Curse. We got back to Cairo at 10AM and several people went to their rooms to sleep. I got myself to the pool and spent my time trying to relax and soak my swollen leg.

Those of us who were well enough went to a very ornate restaurant for another lunch buffet, but this was probably the best meal we had in Egypt, the highlight of which was the most fluffy, fresh pita bread and the best hummus I've ever tasted, washed down with hibiscus tea. After lunch we entered the El Khalili Bazaar in downtown Cairo and were allowed to wander for two hours. I paired up with Clayton, my partner in crime at the Giza Sound and Light Show and we helped one another bargain to get the souvenirs we wanted for a good price. The behavior of the vendors here was much more manageable; they tried their usual tricks but weren't as aggressive as we'd encountered elsewhere. Some actually had a good sense of humor, and it was almost fun bargaining with them. I ended up finding a set of ceramic miniatures of the Giza pyramids for a collection I have from all over the world: the Coliseum, the Eiffel Tower, the Parthenon, the Sydney Opera House, etc. However, there was one street within the bazaar that Clayton dubbed "Aswan Street" because in this area, the merchants were as nasty as they'd been in Aswan. Again, I was called Ali Baba, but more often it was "Rambo." Rambo? I never knew that I bore such a striking resemblance to Sylvester Stallone. One vendor approached me, patted my belly, and asked, "You have baby? You pregnant? Maybe two babies? Three babies?" I thought I'd heard it all, but this was the height of rudeness, and I couldn't fathom why he'd think this sales tactic would make me want to buy anything from him.

After the bazaar, we visited the sixty-seven story Cairo Tower, which provided an amazing night view of the city. From our high perch we looked down at the seemingly endless traffic jams and heard the accompanying horn honking. We ate Dinner Buffet #6 at an outdoor restaurant below the tower, and in an attempt to eat something healthy, I piled my plate high with carrots and broccoli, but after a couple bites I realized they were so salty I could barely eat them.

On the final day of our trip, my legs were in bad shape, so I skipped that morning's tour to see the hotel's house doctor. He gave me three medications to combat swelling, infection, and inflammation, and said that while walking was good for me, I shouldn't stand in one place for long periods of time and should avoid salty food at all costs. I almost couldn't stop laughing! It turned out to be a good day. I spent time in the pool with some other folks who'd also skipped the tour because they'd been sick. We went to lunch at the hotel's rooftop cafe where I ordered a club sandwich and fries. It wasn't the tuna melt I'd craved, but it was close, and it wasn't a buffet. From the restaurant we could see the nearby pyramids, looming in the smoggy haze that covered everything that day. It was the calmest day of the entire trip, and the hotel was an oasis amidst the chaos that was my Egypt experience.

That evening, we took a Nile River Dinner Cruise through downtown Cairo, featuring – you guessed it – a buffet - followed by live entertainment. The buffet was better than some, worse than others. The singer was pretty sappy, playing elevator music versions of songs by everyone from the Beatles to Ricky Martin. Then there was belly-dancing, but I wasn't going to risk my non-pregnant belly getting dragged out on the dance floor, so I ran as fast as my swollen legs would carry me to the upper deck. Several others from my group were up there too and we tried to enjoy the night air and city views, though we were unnerved by the fact that our ship was being shadowed by three police boats with their lights off, which felt a little spooky. At one point one of the students came up to tell us that the belly-dancing was over and now a whirling dervish was performing. She said she'd tried to video tape the performance, but given her still-queasy stomach, the rocking boat, and the swirling motions of the dervish she'd become too nauseous to continue filming, which I found, perhaps inappropriately, hilarious.

As we debarked from the ship, my group said goodbye and boarded a bus bound for the airport to take a red-eye flight back home. I was now on my own and heading to Jordan the next day, fervently hoping that it wouldn't be as stressful as Egypt had been. I spent that night alone at the hotel, then headed for the airport in the morning. As my plane took off, I looked at the deserts of the Sinai far below and this modern-day Moses said a silent prayer of thanks for having been safely delivered out of Egypt.

In Amman I'd arranged to meet a Bedouin guide who'd take me to the famous archeological site of Petra and then to his camp near the Saudi border. However, I immediately ran into a problem at the airport trying to enter the country. Visitors to the formally titled Kingdom of Jordan need an entrance visa costing ten *dinars*, the equivalent of about $15. However, I didn't have any dinars yet, there were no ATM machines available until you exited the Customs area, and I couldn't exit Customs without a visa! I tried to explain my predicament to the man at the visa booth, but he just shrugged and said nothing. As I was about to seriously panic, out of nowhere, a blond woman who'd been on my flight walked over and handed me a bill worth ten Jordanian dinars! Before I could say anything, she said, "I've been in exactly the same situation you're in now. Take this with my blessing." This kind gesture left me almost speechless, but I managed to find my voice in time to thank her profusely and was then able to purchase my visa. The door to the Kingdom was now open to me.

Outside Customs I found my guide, Obeid waiting for me, dressed in full Bedouin headgear. He showed me the cash machines and the toilets, and I debated which I needed more. After getting my Jordanian cash, I scanned the airport looking for the angel who'd given me the money for my visa, but she'd vanished as quickly as she'd appeared. My attention returned to Obeid, a young-looking man in his late forties, with piercing black eyes and a wide smile. He tossed my luggage into the trunk of his car, and we exited the airport. He proudly showed me the award plaque he'd just received that morning from the Queen of Jordan herself to honor his success in the tourism business. With this royal endorsement, I was confident that I was in good hands.

It was a three-hour drive to Petra, the ruins of an ancient city where I'd be spending my first overnight. Obeid was a spirited conversationalist and we talked about many things during the trip. I learned that he'd just lost his mother three weeks ago due to diabetes and circulatory problems, which was unsettling for me to hear given that I'd spent the last ten days with swollen ankles and painful legs. I was grateful when the topic changed to politics, even though as we all know, this is a topic that should be avoided at all costs in polite conversation. I did more listening than talking, but throughout my stay in Jordan I heard many strong, negative opinions about Egypt, Saudi Arabia, Yemen, and Iran, yet the people I spoke with seemed rather indifferent when Israel or the United States were mentioned. Of course, this could be because they knew I was an American, but still, I found it interesting. I shared my experiences in Egypt, and Obeid complained that many Egyptians had recently entered Jordan to find work in the tourist industry. He said this was a problem because, "They treat our tourists like they do in Egypt! They're aggressive and often try to find ways to take advantage. This is not what the Koran tells us to do and it's not how we treat our guests in Jordan!" I was certainly relieved to hear that.

As we neared Petra the terrain changed from a flat, unimpressive desert to more dramatic, mountainous scenery. Soon Obeid was negotiating our passage through the security barriers of the Crowne Plaza Petra Hotel and a striking Jordanian bellman with black hair and ice blue eyes got me checked in and showed me to a beautiful room overlooking the otherworldly hills surrounding the ruins of Petra. After ensuring that I was happy with my room, Obeid said goodbye, promising to return at noon the next day.

I'd signed up for an 8PM candlelight walking tour of Petra. I headed to the hotel restaurant and was informed that the dinner buffet would begin shortly; I almost ran screaming into the dark Jordanian night at the thought of yet another hotel buffet, but the hostess said I could order from the menu and sit in the bar area if I preferred. I ordered the daily special; my first meal in Jordan was the tuna melt I'd been strangely craving for a week, accompanied by fries and a huge salad, all delicious. God bless Jordan!

Walking through the Siq; first glimpse of the Treasury.

After dinner I joined dozens of people gathered at the nearby Petra Visitor's Center. Petra had been inhabited by a group called the Nabateans at least 2,500 years ago, and like so many other parts of the ancient world, eventually found itself under Roman control. Entrance to the site is through a mile long, winding, narrow canyon called the *Siq* that eventually opens up into a city that was literally carved out of the walls of the wider canyon beyond. I remembered that *Indiana Jones and the Last Crusade* was partly filmed in Petra and in fact there was an Indiana Jones Coffee Shop near the entrance. Despite having seen the movie and photos of Petra, nothing could have prepared me for seeing it in person.

We were led by a Bedouin guide who insisted on absolute silence as we walked for twenty minutes to the Treasury, the first major building beyond the Siq. The entire path was lit only by candles placed inside canvas bags, similar to the *luminaria* seen at Christmastime in the American southwest. During these candlelight tours 1500 candles are used to light the way! I can't imagine how tedious it must be to set it all up, but it was so impressive! I walked at the front of the line behind the guide, as I didn't want to be in the middle of a whole pack of people who were disobeying orders and chatting loudly. I had to carefully watch my footing because I was so drawn to the amazingly bright, starry sky above us and the way that the candles and the starlight illuminated the surrounding white sandstone hills. I felt a million miles away from civilization and as if I'd been transported back in time a couple of thousand years.

Once we reached the Treasury, long mats were placed on the ground for us to sit on and we were served a sweet tea. Bedouins played long musical pieces for us, one on a flute and one on a stringed instrument called a *rebab*, and that was followed by a bit of storytelling. When the festivities ended, we were told to take our time walking back through the Siq at our own pace. That was good news, as I was feeling a bit winded as I hiked back out of the canyon on a gradual but constant uphill grade. In addition, my leg still hadn't fully healed from "the camel incident" so I walked slowly, soaking up the atmosphere and pausing to scan the night sky.

I rose early the next morning to walk back to Petra and see it by daylight. It was a cool, sunny morning and to my surprise I had the trail pretty much all to myself. I could hear the hooting of owls that are believed to have been in the area since the city was founded; in fact, the owl is the symbol of the city. The ruins were even more magnificent by day, but by 9:00 AM the sun was already baking, and tourist groups were pouring through the *Siq* like a noisy flash flood, so I made my way back to the hotel. I avoided the breakfast buffet and had a simple omelet, packed, and checked out, only to find an unfamiliar young man waiting for me in the lobby.

In somewhat halting English he said, "I am Subhi. I here for Obeid. His cousin die, so I take you to Wadi Rum." At that moment Obeid called me to confirm the change of plan, so off I went with Subhi for the ninety-minute ride to Wadi Rum, an area near the Saudi border where Obeid's camp is located. Subhi didn't speak much English, but he was a chatterbox, nonetheless. When I said I'd just come from Egypt, he went on a tirade about how annoying Egyptians can be, then launched into an attack on the Philistines (Palestinians). He said they now outnumber Jordanians in their own country and characterized them as not willing to work hard and of only wanting to destroy things. Anyone who believes that the people of the Middle East share a monolithic view of the world's geopolitics is sadly misinformed.

Morning in Petra.

He showed me a picture of his baby daughter and if I'm not mistaken, I think he said her name was Muhammad, which I didn't think was a typical girl's name. He complained that he'd recently gotten a ticket for fifteen dinars from the police for driving while on his cell phone. "They take milk from baby Muhammad's mouth!" he moaned. However, he apparently hadn't learned his lesson, checking his cell phone about once every two minutes as he drove. There were police parked along the road every ten miles or so; sometimes they pulled us over to check ID, and sometimes they just waved us through the check-points. They were always armed with both radar guns and machine guns.

Sunset at Wadi Rum.

The scenery became absolutely stunning as we neared Wadi Rum, with jagged mountains and brick red sand - a cross between Utah and Mars. Obeid greeted us at the entrance to the valley and brought me to his camp which was tucked into a sand-filled valley. There were two long, dark, Bedouin style communal tents and a bit further away, three individual tents. I was given a choice of which I preferred, so I opted for my own tent and dropped my luggage off. Obeid invited me to join him in one of the communal tents for lunch where I met his teenaged son and we all dined on some canned tuna and a bit of chopped salad and pita bread - not exactly a tuna melt, but it hit the spot.

Over lunch I met two other guests, Emma and Richard, a British couple on their honeymoon. They were fun, though Emma never seemed to stop speaking and Richard could barely get more than two words out before being interrupted. They were planning to stay for four days, and Emma gushed about how Jordan was their favorite place ever. They'd just come from Syria. and were now arguing about whether to try to go to Israel next; Richard felt it might be too dangerous, which struck me as odd, since Syria seemed like a much riskier destination than Israel.

Obeid's son then loaded me onto a couch-like seat in the bed of an old pickup truck – a Jordanian version of Tahiti's *Le Truck* - for a tour of places where the film *Lawrence of Arabia* was filmed, where Lawrence himself had supposedly set up camp, a natural arch, and a Bedouin camp where people tried to convince me to go on a camel ride, which I politely but firmly declined. At sunset we drove to a remote promontory, and he invited me to go watch the sunset, so I hiked out a bit and sat on a huge rock, watching the changing colors. It was wonderfully quiet, except when the wind died down and I could hear him screaming into his cell phone off in the distance. Even in this remote outpost, the modern world intruded.

Like lunch, dinner was also held in the big tent. A campfire was built in a pit in the middle of the floor, and it was smoky, but there were openings near the top of the tent so the smoke could exit. We sat on the floor, leaning against large pillows. Dinner was cooked outside in a huge metal pot that was covered and buried in the sand, not unlike a New England clambake or the Māori *hangi* meal I'd had in New Zealand. It consisted of rice, a tasty mixture of onions, tomatoes and zucchini, pita bread, and chicken. We also had a refreshing sweet tea and slices of lemon cake. Both Obeid and his son seemed concerned that I wasn't married, and their issue seemed to center on the fact that I'd have no family to take care of me when I got older. I wondered how they'd have reacted if they'd known I was gay. Meanwhile, I couldn't help but chuckle as Obeid, this Bedouin in his tent in the middle of nowhere, spent much of the evening playing on his Blackberry device: Lawrence of Arabia with a cell phone.

Since the Bedouins usually sleep by 9:00, once our hosts retired, Emma and Robert invited me to come sit outside their tent and have some wine. As soon as the wine was poured, Emma surprised me, asking if I could tell how desperate she was to get to back to civilization. I laughed because she gave the impression of being totally into this whole experience, but she confessed that she was actually hating it! She said they hadn't taken a shower in two days because she was so freaked out by the communal bathing facilities. Evidently this was not the honeymoon of their dreams. They'd reserved four nights here, but Emma had been hinting to Obeid that Robert wasn't feeling well and perhaps they needed to move to a hotel down in Aqaba on the Red Sea. Unfortunately for Emma, Obeid was either not picking up on her hints or was ignoring them.

Obeid's Camp at Wadi Rum, Jordan.

I will say that while this was an exciting way to spend a night or two, it was a little rugged and I was looking forward to the comfy hotel room that I knew awaited me in Tel Aviv. The only amenities in my tent were a gas lamp and a bedroll with pillows. The bathroom and shower were housed in a tiny concrete building 143 steps down a sand dune from my tent; yes, I counted! Still, staying in a Bedouin camp in the middle of this remote desert was an unforgettable experience. I loved it!

In the morning I gathered up my toiletries and trudged down the dune to the bathroom facilities. I was grateful to score the last three sheets of toilet paper, and then hopped into a lukewarm shower. Over the sound of the shower, I heard Emma screaming from the toilets that there was no toilet paper. Poor Emma.

Breakfast was pita bread, salad, and the scariest looking scrambled eggs I'd ever seen, so I grabbed a hard-boiled one instead! Emma, arriving late for breakfast, nervously confessed that she never did get any toilet paper, and I didn't want to imagine how she'd dealt with that situation. Despite her hints to Obeid about wanting to relocate to a hotel, he reminded her that he'd arranged a six-hour horseback ride across the desert for them that day. Emma threw me the kind of panicked look that hostages display when they know no help is coming for them, and I admit, I had to stifle a giggle as I headed back to my tent to pack my stuff. As Obeid and I drove away from Wadi Run, I saw his son at the stable getting Emma and Richard ready for their marathon horseback trip. It would be a long day for them, I feared.

On the drive back to the Amman airport we passed through a dozen little towns, each consisting of a smattering of stores selling some combination of bottled water, Coke and Fanta, or tires! That was it. No postcards, no bumper stickers and no fancy t shirts proclaiming, "I hiked the *Siq*" could be found. We stopped at a little roadside stand to get a Turkish coffee. I learned that the first three sips of a Turkish coffee are OK, but if you drink it down to the bottom, you'll find a thick sludge of Nescafe instant coffee and sugar waiting at the bottom that will make you gag if you accidentally swallow it. Jordan's answer to *mochi*. You have been warned.

At the airport, Obeid went inside to be sure we were at the right terminal. While he was gone, a porter grabbed my luggage and despite my protests, started to walk away without a word. Obeid came back just in time to stop the guy and asked if I'd given this man permission to take my bag. When I said that I hadn't, he said, "I could tell from how he spoke that he was Egyptian. He does things the Egyptian way, like I told you before! It's always the same!"

With a laugh and a big thanks, I bid my Bedouin host farewell and headed off through security to check in for my flight to The Promised Land, Israel. As I settled into my seat, anticipating the comforts waiting for me in Tel Aviv, I pictured Emma and Robert, likely in the fourth hour of their horseback ride under the cruel desert sun and chuckled softly.

7. From Guns & Moses to Jesus Christ Superstar
ISRAEL

Bobbing like a cork in Israel's Dead Sea.

After a lifetime of hearing the names of so many Biblical locales central to both Christianity and Judaism, as well as endless political discussions concerning Israel's very existence and its contentious relationships with Palestine and the Arab world, I was filled with anticipation to see this country for myself. After my visits to Egypt and Jordan, Israel was my next stop. As the plane began its descent into Tel Aviv, I looked out the window and was struck by the fact that Israel is such a narrow strip of land, surrounded on three sides by relatively unfriendly neighbors, with its back up against the Mediterranean – a very precarious position.

I arrived at 5PM on a Friday, the start of the Jewish *Shabbat* or sabbath. From sundown Friday to sundown Saturday, public transit, stores, and many restaurants close down. The airport was a ghost town, and the intense security screenings I'd anticipated when entering the country didn't happen at all. Since trains and buses into the city weren't operating, I was forced to take a cab. My driver played beautiful, soothing music as we drove into Tel Aviv and told me that we were listening to a radio broadcast of Greek music that airs once a week. He was born in Greece, but his family was Jewish and had moved to Israel sixty years ago when he was only three years old. We were traveling on modern freeways, the lights of Tel Aviv's skyline twinkled in the distance, and beautiful trees and flowers lined the highway. It was a stark and jarring contrast to my prior evening's stay at the Bedouin camp in Jordan.

My hotel was small and cozy, located only a block from the Mediterranean, which was visible from the window of my second-floor room. I laid down to rest my eyes but fell soundly asleep for almost two hours, only to be wakened by the phone. I had two acquaintances in Tel Aviv: a former student, Tanya, now doing graduate study at a university here, and Ben, an Israeli online pen pal with whom I'd been corresponding for several months. It was Ben who'd called, so we met for dinner, and I was fascinated to hear about life in Israel from a native's perspective.

Ben was in his mid-thirties and worked as an accountant. His father was a sixth generation Israeli, and his mother was Jewish but born in Libya. Ben grew up in a small village in southern Israel bordering the volatile, Palestinian-controlled Gaza Strip separating Egypt from Israel. He recounted frequent instances of his town being shelled in attacks emanating from Gaza and said that his mother, who still lived in that town had been traumatized by a recent explosion from a shell that struck a mall close to her apartment. Like many I spoke with in Egypt and Jordan who feared the prospect of Iran developing nuclear capabilities, Ben shared his concern that Israel will one day be attacked with a nuclear weapon. It was as if news headlines came to life as I listened to his stories. Of course, our conversation was not all doom and gloom; Ben was warm and funny, and I really enjoyed meeting him.

Tanya called the next morning, and we had brunch at a place called Orna and Ella, a popular restaurant that was featured in an excellent Israeli film I'd seen called, *The Bubble*. Tel Aviv is referred to as "the bubble" because it is a cosmopolitan, secular, liberal city that is seemingly far removed from - or in denial about - the turmoil, conflicts and stresses faced by the rest of Israel and its feuding neighbors. In the film, a restaurant is blown up by a suicide bomber; Orna and Ella was the location for those exterior shots and the restaurant's owners even appeared in the film. Thankfully, no such fate has befallen the restaurant in real life, and Tanya told me I simply could not miss their famous Shabbat brunch.

After weeks of mostly forgettable meals in Egypt and Jordan, the food in Israel was a welcome change. I was introduced to the standard Israeli breakfast, which typically consists of a basket of warm bread and rolls, accompanied by a huge spread of butter, jam, sun-dried tomatoes, olive tapenade, chocolate, sour cream with chives and more. This is washed down with freshly squeezed, pulp-filled orange juice and strong coffee, and then you order an entree of your choice. I chose a dish consisting of corn bread topped by poached eggs, so when the yolks were broken, they seeped into the cornbread, and the result was wonderful! There were also legendary pumpkin pancakes accompanied by orange syrup that are only served at Saturday brunch, so I had to sample those too. In the Bible Israel is often referred to as "the land of milk and honey," but I was quickly discovering that it had a lot more to offer than those simple pleasures.

During the next couple of days, I explored Tel Aviv on foot, visiting the city's vast markets, which were bursting with stalls selling fruit, candies, pastries, spices, and various clothing and gifts. I strolled the beachfront along the Mediterranean, soaking up some winter sun, but I was both impressed and intimidated by the athleticism of the citizens. They don't seem to understand the concept of relaxation; everyone was jogging, performing sit-ups or push-ups on the sand, throwing frisbees, playing paddleball, or sweating through rigorous games of beach volley-ball. I was exhausted just watching them. I met Ben for coffee one after-noon and then took a long walk through the old port area of Jaffa where I got some nice sunset pictures and had some pleasant chats with friendly locals.

Israeli Breakfast: way beyond milk and honey...

The quality of the food here and throughout Israel was top notch and beautifully prepared. I'd planned to meet Tanya and her friends for dinner at a Japanese place called Moon, but due to some crossed wires, I got stood up and went by myself. I was a little skeptical about ordering sushi in Israel, but I had memorable shrimp and vegetable tempura, salmon sashimi, and a sweet potato roll. Another day I met Tanya at a Tel Aviv breakfast institution called Benedict, and had one of their specialties: salmon Benedict, accompanied by the full Israeli breakfast spread. I've never been a morning person, though I've always loved going out for breakfast and here in Israel, it made crawling out of bed worth the effort. On my last night in Tel Aviv, I met Tanya and her friends back at Orna and Ella, and dinner here was even better than brunch. We all shared a huge appetizer of sweet potato pancakes with a cucumber and dill sauce. I ordered a bruschetta served on sweet brioche bread and topped with Roquefort cheese and fresh figs which I ended up getting for free. Our waiter took our massive order without writing anything down, and I commented that he must have an amazing memory. Well, my bruschetta got lost in the shuffle and he ended up bringing it much later into the meal. Good-naturedly he said, "This is

on the house because it's so late, but it IS your fault. When you compli-
mented me on my memory, you jinxed me and made me forget!" My
main course was pasta with fresh lamb and tomatoes, and for dessert
there was chocolate hazelnut torte served with cream and raspberries.
When I spoke to Ben later in the evening and told him where I'd dined,
he joked, "You DO know we have other restaurants in Tel Aviv, right?"

The next morning, I picked up a rental car to start my exploration of
the rest of the country. The woman at the Hertz office asked if I was
enjoying Tel Aviv and when the topic of food came up, she asked if I'd
been to either Orna & Ella or Benedict and was surprised and impressed
when I said I'd been to both. "Wow! You've gone to the very best local
places!" And then she added, "Now, if you like sushi..." and I finished
her sentence with, "I went to Moon, too!" We had a good laugh over
that before she handed me the keys and off I went, heading out of the
city toward the Dead Sea.

Flashing back to 1971. one day my mother came home from work
with a copy of the musical *Jesus Christ Superstar*. She'd borrowed it from
a co-worker as she couldn't afford to buy the double album set at that
time. I was twelve years old, and I remember my mother playing the
songs, reading the libretto with me, and explaining the context of each
scene. In 1973 we saw the film version, which was shot at various locations in Israel and my mom bought the movie soundtrack. While
Sunday school classes and boring Protestant sermons never really
sparked my curiosity about the story of Jesus, that musical did. To this
day I can sing almost every line of every song by heart. It wasn't long
after this when my mom was diagnosed with cancer and as her condition
worsened, I'd often play one particular song from *Jesus Christ Superstar,*
"Could We Start Again Please?" It's from a scene in which Mary Magda-
lene and Peter lament Jesus' arrest, longing for things to be as they'd
been before. I played that song over and over as a plea both to God and
to my mother to let us go back to the days before she got sick. That song
and the entire musical have had special significance for me ever since. For
much of my adult life I engaged in a rather unorthodox Easter tradition
of taking a long drive through California's Mojave Desert while playing
the entire two-CD soundtrack from start to finish.

Thirty-five years later, here I was driving a rental car across the Israeli desert, blasting the *Jesus Christ Superstar* CD set I'd brought with me. At one point, "Could We Start Again Please?" began to play, and I started sobbing so intensely that I had to pull off the road to compose myself; I was that scared fifteen-year-old boy all over again. And I swear to you, at that very moment, through my tears I noticed the most beautiful white bird, probably a crane or egret, sitting by the side of the road just staring at me. It stood out because it was so brilliantly white against the red desert rocks and because it was the first living thing I'd seen for hours. After a minute or so, it took flight and disappeared, but I couldn't help thinking that my mom had been right there with me at that moment.

Salt formations near Sodom.

As I pressed on toward the Dead Sea the air was warm and fresh despite some drizzle. The scenery became more dramatic, and I gasped as I rounded a bend and got my first glimpse of this bluish-green, otherworldly salt lake, nearly 1,400 feet below sea level. It's surrounded by salt formations with the reddish-brown mountains of Jordan looming in the distance on the opposite side. When I reached the shoreline, I followed a road sign directing me toward Sodom, the famous city that along with Gomorrah was supposedly destroyed according to the Biblical story from the book of Genesis. There is absolutely nothing here now but rocky badlands of sulfur, some salt mines and an interesting rock formation called "Lot's Wife" that resembles the woman who was, according to the story, turned into a pillar of salt for disobeying God's order to flee from Sodom without looking back to witness its destruction. Whatever one's beliefs, this is a lonely, eerie place.

I spent that evening in the town of Ein Bokek, ten miles north of Sodom. I stayed at one of the dozen spa hotels located here. The hotel pool was comfortably heated with water from the Dead Sea which contains so many minerals and salts that it's virtually impossible to sink or even submerge yourself in the water; all you can do is bob like a cork on the surface. The water leaves your skin feeling silky and smooth, unless you have any small cuts, which sting quite a bit from all the salt. I happily floated from the indoor pool through a sort of plastic "doggie door" into the outdoor pool, relishing the contrast between the cool desert night air and the warm water. It was still raining a bit and there was a lot of thunder and lightning all around, which provided a dramatic backdrop.

Back in my room I watched TV for the first time in almost three weeks and caught an episode of what I believe was actually an American reality TV show called *Shalom in the Home* in which a rabbi visits with and tries to solve issues faced by a different family each week. It seemed so appropriate to be watching this in Israel. I flipped channels, hoping there might be some epic Biblical film like *Ben Hur* or maybe even *Jesus Christ Superstar*, but alas, that was not to be!

The next morning, I headed inland toward the ruins of the ancient city of Masada, which was a thriving outpost built by King Herod around the year 35 BC. Rome eventually conquered most of the area, but Masada was one of the last rebel holdouts, a heavily fortified city built high atop a steep plateau. According to an account by the Jewish-Roman historian Flavius Josephus, the Romans tried to starve the residents into submission. They built a giant ramp to reach the city, then attempted to break through its walls using battering rams and fire.

Sensing that the end was near and that the Romans would soon over-power them, the approximately 950 people in Masada supposedly elected ten soldiers to slay all of them, then one soldier was chosen to slay the other nine before killing himself. When the Romans finally entered the city, they were shocked that these rebels chose death over life under Roman occupation.

I'd read that on one side of Masada there was a cable car that could be ridden to the top but on the other side there was only a long, steep trail. I'd planned to take the cable car, but ended up on the side with only the trail and mine was the only car in the parking lot. Inspired by the athletic population of Tel Aviv, I hiked the trail that runs alongside the Roman ramp, still visible after 2,000 years. It was certainly worth the effort; the city ruins are impressive and the views of the Dead Sea looming far below on the eastern side and the Judean desert to the north and west were stunning. It is one of those rare places where you can still almost feel the energy and emotion of what happened so long ago. It was truly a highlight of the trip.

The Dead Sea and The Roman Ramp leading to Masada.

Leaving Masada, I drove back down to the Dead Sea, passing a group of Bedouin kids riding mules and herding at least a dozen camels up a steep slope, which made for a great photo opportunity. I then proceeded north along the shoreline, stopping at Ein Gedi, where there was a rocky beach from which I could easily enter the sea. Despite it being January, it was quite mild that day and I couldn't miss an oppor-tunity to float in the sea itself. The water temperature felt warmer than the air and I felt like a child as I bobbed on the water. I called out to a woman who was taking pictures of her family nearby, asking her to take my camera from my backpack on the beach and snap a few shots of me floating around out there and they really captured the carefree feeling I had that day.

Soon after leaving Ein Gedi, I approached a military checkpoint dividing the Palestinian-controlled West Bank from the rest of Israel. The soldiers barely gave me a second look as they waved me through. This highway is a narrow safe zone. As you head north, the West Bank is to your left; rental cars are not allowed to enter this area and the U.S. State Department strongly suggested that Americans avoid it. To the right was the border with Jordan and there were miles of barbed wire fencing on both sides of the road that appeared to be electrified, with cameras and radar stations lining the highway at regular intervals. After passing through another military check point, I reached Israel's Highway 1, another small strip of roadway cutting across the West Bank toward Jerusalem, which lies just twenty miles from the Dead Sea.

Shortly after sunset, I reached the city. It was raining, traffic was nightmarish, and other drivers were impatient and aggressive. As I found throughout Israel, many signs are not in English and in the dark and with a fair amount of road construction, I had a terrible time matching up my location with the map I had. I saw a policeman and tried to stop to ask him for help, but he insistently waved me on. Farther down the road I saw a place to pull over, rolled down my window and flagged down an older man wearing a yarmulke. I asked if he could tell me how to get to the famous King David Hotel, not because I was staying there, but my hotel, the Three Arches, was across the street from this landmark. He looked genuinely perplexed as to how to describe what I needed to do, but finally said, "Well, at the bottom of this hill turn right at the stoplight. Then, somehow, you'll need to make an immediate left and at the next main street, take a right. You should see a gas station there and the hotel is just past that. Sorry I can't be more specific, but it's hard to explain." I thanked him and said, "I'll get there!" He leaned in the window and quite earnestly said, "With God's help, I know that you will!" It was an interesting introduction to Jerusalem.

I followed his directions and despite the challenge of trying to weave across several lanes of traffic to make my turns, I found my hotel. The

Three Arches is an art deco style building from the 1930s designed by the same man who designed the Empire State Building. The lobby was elegantly decorated, but the room was rather spartan, resembling a monk's cell.

It was cold and wet outside, and I was too tired to venture to the old walled city, so I found a small restaurant close by, the Tmol Shilshom Bookstore Café that I'd read about in a guidebook. It was a cozy place with comfortable chairs, and grey stone walls lined with bookshelves and hundreds of books, all in Hebrew of course. The staff was young and friendly, and I had a great meal starting with a sampler of three soups: French onion, lentil-pumpkin, and sweet potato, served in drinking glasses with wonderful homemade bread. I had ravioli stuffed with pears and gorgonzola cheese that would make an Italian chef envious, and for dessert my waiter recommended apple pie. I laughed, saying that apple pie didn't sound very authentically Israeli to me, but I was presented with a beautiful tart surrounded by sliced apples arranged in an artistic pattern accompanied by ice cream and dollops of whipped cream.

Comfort food in Jerusalem.

Early the next morning it was still cold and rainy, and I really had to bundle up. I set out on foot toward the Old City, entering through the Jaffa Gate and discovered a labyrinth of covered streets and corridors making up the city's bazaars. I soon began to suffer traumatic flashbacks to Egypt as I was assailed by vendors wanting to sell me everything from "Guns & Moses" souvenir T-shirts to jewelry and perfume to hideous candies that looked as if the main ingredient was artificial food coloring.

There were shops selling exotic spices; one even had a sale on frankincense and myrrh! I'd liked to have wandered the market to take it all in, but the vendors took all the fun out of it. I was followed, teased, and harassed for almost a block by one aggressive salesman, before crossing into the turf of a new, equally unpleasant vendor. I hadn't been bullied this much since junior high school! I wondered how much Jerusalem had really changed over the past 2000 years, and I smiled at the thought of Jesus making an appearance to overturn the tables of these nasty merchants.

A unique Jerusalem souvenir.

Another disappointment about my time in Jerusalem was that I never got to visit the Dome of the Rock on the Temple Mount, a very holy site for both Jews and Muslims. The Muslims pretty much control this sector of the city and severely limit the hours when non-Muslims may visit the site. In addition, everyone I asked, from police to merchants to people leading tours, gave me different answers regarding when I could visit. Every time I tried to go, the site was closed to non-Muslims. I did visit the Western or "Wailing Wall", probably the most sacred pilgrimage site in the world for Jews. After passing through metal detectors and security checks, I donned a yarmulke provided at the entrance and quietly approached the wall where I joined dozens of others in saying prayers for all of my loved ones. I then exited the city walls and headed east toward the Mount of Olives and the Garden of Gethsemane.

Of all the religious sites I visited, I'd have to say Gethsemane was perhaps the most moving to me. The site has a basilica built atop it, but the Garden itself is still here. I walked a path amongst gnarled olive trees, looking back to take in the vista of walled Jerusalem on the hill above me. It gave me chills, thinking that this must have been the same view Jesus would have had on the night of his arrest. In the basilica I knelt at the altar and read a passage taken from the Book of Matthew that was posted on the railing in front of me describing Jesus' visit to the Garden. I was overcome with emotion, sobbing intensely from the sheer power of where I was. I was a little perturbed that none of the priests standing nearby asked if I was OK, but perhaps they see such reactions often.

Jerusalem from Gethsemane.

From there I hiked up the Mount of Olives to an ancient Jewish cemetery where the stone sarcophagi of at least 2,000 people cover the western side of the mountain facing Jerusalem. The sun had finally come out and the view was spectacular. I planned to descend from the mountain to make another attempt to visit the Temple Mount but wanted to take a different route. Unfortunately, this road wound around the mountain and led me into the Palestinian-controlled area of East Jerusalem. I noted that the neighborhood changed abruptly; dumpsters of trash were full to overflowing and dozens of stray cats mulled over the scraps. Bottles, cans, broken glass, and paper littered every street. More disturbing, in another Jewish cemetery I passed, the sarcophagi were covered in trash; everything from bleach containers, soda cans, beer bottles, paper, and plastic had been tossed over the fence. It seemed so disrespectful, and it made me angry.

Taxi cabs stopped for me twice and their drivers offered to take me anywhere I needed to go. I declined, but the neighborhood deteriorated even further, and I started to notice people eyeing me in a most unfriendly way. Perhaps the cab drivers knew that I was in the wrong place and were trying to come to my aid. I remembered a story I'd heard many years before which I think was told by a rabbi:

A man with great faith in God was drowning in the sea. Someone came along in a small rowboat and asked if he needed help, but the drowning man replied, "No, I'm fine! God will save me!" A second boat came along, and the same exchange happened, then a third boat and again, the drowning man refused help. He finally drowned and when he found himself before God, he asked, "Why did you let this happen to me? Lord, I was faithful! I waited for you to save me, but you let me drown! How could you do that?" God replied, "Well, I sent you three rescue boats."

Chuckling nervously to myself, I vowed to accept a ride from the next cab that stopped for me. Of course, I never saw another one, but thankfully, I safely made it back to the city walls without a problem.

I then decided to walk the Via Dolorosa, the route taken by Jesus as he carried his cross through the city to the place where he was crucified. Along the way are the stations of the cross where plaques explain what happened at each place. I began at the Lion's Gate and as I stood there contemplating what had happened here, a taxi screeched up next to me and the driver, whom I believe was Arab, asked where I wanted to go. It's hard to tell the difference between Hebrew and Arabic for me, except that in Hebrew the greeting is *shalom* and in Arabic it's *salaam*. I hadn't hailed a cab, but the driver tried to sell me a city tour. After quietly saying "no thanks" three times, he finally demanded, "Well why are you just standing here? What do you want?" Frustrated, I said, "I want to be left alone to pray and think about what happened to Jesus here." At that point, to his credit, he at least apologized, but then sped off with squealing tires.

Inside the gates I walked the Via Dolorosa, which is all uphill, and stopped at the place where Jesus first fell under the weight of the cross. I was reading a plaque posted on this spot when suddenly, a loud voice cried out behind me, "*As-salamu alaykum*, my friend! Come look in my shop. What you want to buy? I have scarves for your girlfriend! Tell me what you want! I give you good prices! I have big T-shirts, your size!" There was no peace to be had here, so I moved on.

A little farther along, I heard lovely singing coming from a small chapel, walked through the open doors, and sat in the back to listen to nuns singing hymns. It was beautiful – for about four minutes. Suddenly, all hell broke loose. It was time for the Muslim call to prayer; I'd truly enjoyed listening to these haunting chants that echoed across Cairo and in Jordan, but here they just seemed offensive and intrusive because they were being broadcast over huge, crackling loudspeakers on virtually every block of the city. It was like having someone with a bull-horn shouting at you from five feet away. Though we were in the same room, I literally could not hear the nuns' singing any longer, and the call to prayer went on for about fifteen minutes, drowning out everything. I couldn't help but consider the unfairness of being forbidden to peek inside the gates of what Muslims consider their holy site, yet I was assailed by the call to prayer while I was actually inside a Christian church.

Finally, I reached the Church of the Holy Sepulcher, built over the spot where Jesus was supposedly crucified and entombed. A group of kids was playing soccer in the alley beside the church and the ball thudded against the church wall every twenty seconds. Seriously? Inside the church there was pandemonium. It's divided into a dozen different chapel areas: Greek Orthodox, Lutheran, Catholic, Russian Orthodox, Methodist. I had no idea what I was even looking at as nothing was labeled. I eventually found what appeared to be the Holy Sepulcher, but there was a long line of people waiting to go inside it, people were talking loudly on their cell phones, and a man was approaching people in the line trying to solicit business for his tour company! "*Saalam*, my friend. I can take you on a tour to Bethlehem. I can show you the Mount of Olives! How much you want to pay?" I couldn't take it anymore. I just left.

As I exited the Old City, I sighed with relief to be out of the craziness. I wondered whether Jerusalem has always been like this; was it this chaotic in Jesus' time? How long can it last in its present form, given the tension, the religious and racial prejudices, the violent disagreements over who even owns it? I left feeling sad, frustrated, angry and confused. It was an emotionally tiring day, so I returned to the friendly Tmol Shilshom Café for dinner, and met three Jewish women from Buffalo, New York and one of their daughters who's lived in Jerusalem for two years. They asked me to join them for dinner and were eager to hear my impressions of Jerusalem. I hesitated a bit, but one of them reassured me, "Don't worry, you don't need to be politically correct. I don't like Jerusalem at all!"

So, I shared some of the day's experiences, like the intrusive call to prayer and the desecrated Jewish cemeteries and it turned into an interesting discussion. The daughter sympathized with my complaints, but also shared stories about Jewish settlers in the West Bank playing religious music on loudspeakers twenty-four hours a day to drown out the Muslim call to prayer. She said that in one area the Israelis are engaged in urban renewal and are bulldozing through Muslim cemeteries. I know there are always at least two sides to every story, and that this is probably one of the most complicated parts of the world and I wondered whether it's even possible to understand the full truth about what's happening here. But on that evening, I simply enjoyed the solace of good company and sought comfort in a bowl of sweet potato soup, some Swiss chard pancakes, and a decadent slice of cheesecake.

The sun was shining brightly the next day as I left the city and headed north into the Jordan River Valley, passing more military checkpoints and barbed wire all along the Jordanian border. The desert blooms within this valley due to irrigation from the river; there were date palms, bananas, oranges, pomegranates, and any vegetable you can name. Soon I reached Yardenit, the site where Jesus was supposed to have been baptized by John, and where pilgrims from all over the world come to be baptized. A large group of people from Kenya was there during my visit, and I watched them don long white robes and step into the rather murky river. One big, muscled man was the "dunker", taking his fellow pilgrims one by one in his arms and submerging them in the river for a second or two. It was fun to watch the varied reactions: some people shrieked from apparent rapture, others laughed and hugged their comrades. It was a beautiful place to spend an hour.

Soon after, I reached the Sea of Galilee, also well below sea level, but unlike the Dead Sea, it is a freshwater lake surrounded by beautiful green hills. I stopped at the Mount of Beatitudes where Jesus is believed to have delivered his Sermon on the Mount and I toured the church built on its slopes which offered a panoramic view of the entire area. In the nearby town of Tabgha, I stopped at the Church of the Multiplication, located on the site where Jesus reportedly performed the miracle of feeding the multitudes with the five loaves and two fishes. I walked the shores of the Sea of Galilee in the area where Jesus first encountered Peter and Andrew, and finally visited the ruins of ancient Capernaum, where Jesus spent several years of his adult life. Throughout the day I felt a sense of disbelief that I was actually seeing places I'd heard so much about but had never been able to picture. It was a religious experience for someone who'd never felt particularly religious before.

On the eastern side of Galilee, I gazed up at the lush, green Golan Heights, an area formerly owned by Syria that had been used to stage attacks on Israeli villages below. The area was taken by Israel during the Six-Day War in 1967 and has remained occupied ever since. It looks peaceful and calm, but guidebooks warn that straying off established roads or trails puts one in danger of being injured by old land mines placed there during the war. Again, the modern world intruded into this otherwise idyllic setting.

The shores of the Sea of Galilee; The Jordan River at Yardenit.

At Home in the World

At the end of what had been an amazing stay in Israel I drove to the airport, but trouble arose when I needed to refill the tank of my rental car. I exited the highway just before the airport to find a gas station and drove thirty minutes without seeing a single one. At the Dead Sea I'd seen stations every ten miles; here in suburban Tel Aviv, there was nothing. Finally, I gave up and decided just to head to the airport and face the music at Hertz for not refueling the car. They weren't happy, but I didn't have time to argue, so I quickly explained what happened and ran for the terminal as my flight was leaving in under two hours.

As I entered the airport, I was approached by security personnel who asked a lot of questions. I'd been warned to expect this, but arriving in Tel Aviv had been so effortless, I'd assumed leaving would be easier. They asked me where I'd been, why I was there, whether I knew anyone in Israel, whether I'd accepted any packages, and then a stern female security officer asked the big question: "Why are you arriving for your flight so late? You should have been here three hours in advance!"

I tried to explain my gasoline woes, but the woman looked at me as if to say, "We know you are a terrorist; your gas excuse is the oldest trick in the book!" Ultimately, she took pity on me and let me pass, sending me on to run my bags through an x-ray machine. Just when I thought I was home free, I was instructed to take my bags to a nearby table and wait for an inspector. I watched in horror as security personnel were opening people's bags all around me, taking every single item out and scanning them with a wand. All I could think was, "Oh Lord, don't let them drag all my dirty underwear out onto this table!" But I didn't panic and after waiting a few minutes, a man came over, put some tags on the bags without opening them and said I could go! I guess I have an honest face. By the skin of my teeth, I made my flight to Rome and soon watched from the window of the plane as the coast of Israel faded from view.

Of all my travels, that visit to Israel was one of the most memorable experiences I'd ever had. Since then, I've returned to Israel three more times, and in 2015 I arranged to get baptized in the Jordan River at Yardenit by Tom, a Christian pastor from Tennessee who lives in Israel part-time. There was no one else there that day, and both of us donned long white robes and waded out into the river. As Tom started the ceremony, something I hadn't expected was the presence of so many fish in the river, some almost a foot long. They congregated around us and began nibbling at the hairs on my legs. I felt like a kid giggling inappropriately in church as Tom prayed with me while the fish tickled me incessantly. Finally, it was time; Todd dunked me for a few seconds, and I popped up again into the warm sun. We talked quietly for a while, then he left, telling me to take my time and to meet him back at the reception area. I stood waist deep in the Jordan River, fish still tickling me, gorgeous flowers and trees swaying in the breeze, watching the water slowly making its way downstream. The whole scene was perfect, and I felt so content, it was hard to pull myself away. By the time I showered, dressed, and went to the reception area, Tom was gone without a trace - my phantom baptizer.

Israel isn't a place to go for a relaxing, restful vacation. It is challenging, requiring you to think about your own values and beliefs and how they differ from those of other people. It brings you face to face with your own religious or spiritual beliefs, whatever those might be. It makes you ponder the past and the future. How much of what occurred in the past was true? Was it all predetermined? Will what's been prophesied actually come to pass? Israel gives the impression that the answers to such questions are all there waiting for you but doesn't guarantee that you'll necessarily find them.

8. "Is First Time in Hamam?"
TURKEY

The prehistoric-looking town of Goreme in Cappadocia, Turkey

After having explored nearly every corner of Europe, in 2014 I set my sights on Turkey as my next summer travel adventure. I began my visit by flying into Kayseri, a rather rough and tumble little desert city in the middle of Turkey's Cappadocia region. Things got off to a rocky start when I was left empty-handed at baggage claim, but thankfully, other passengers were in the same boat and we learned that if our flight had originated in another country, our luggage would be arriving at the International Terminal, despite the fact that we'd changed planes in Istanbul and had arrived at the domestic terminal here. We were led outside onto the tarmac in the blazing sun and ushered to the other terminal where we were reunited with our luggage. I then needed to collect my rental car, but from baggage claim at the International Terminal there was no way to get to the rental car offices without re-entering the terminal and passing through security again. My flight from Istanbul hadn't taken this long!

Luckily the rental car process was easy, and I was soon leaving the airport with the air conditioning cranked up full blast and some traditional Turkish music on the radio. My first impression of Turkey was that the drivers were a lot more civilized than in many other places I've driven, including my native Boston. People stuck to the speed limit, didn't honk, and didn't tailgate. Additionally, the scenery was impressive, with a 12,000-foot, snow-capped volcanic peak looming to the south stealing the show. My destination was Goreme, the most unique and heavily-touristed town in the region of Cappadocia, which reminded me a lot of parts of Utah except the rock here is gray instead of reddish orange. But what gives the area an exotic, prehistoric look reminiscent of an episode of the old *Flintstones* cartoons are enormous stone formations, several stories high, shaped like a gnome's hat into which people carve out homes, shops, and hotels. I've never seen anything quite like it.

Goreme was not large, but I had some trouble finding my hotel, so I rolled down the window and asked a man in a suit and tie where the Kelebek Hotel was. He started to describe how to get there, then said, "Let me get in, I'll show you!" He just hopped into the passenger seat and directed me: right, left, left, up, down, right. We had to stop twice so he could ask for directions, but we finally arrived. Before he left, he told me that his son sells carpets and invited me to come by the shop to see them while I was in town. I soon learned that this is typically the motive behind many seeming acts of kindness in Turkey, but I was still really grateful for his help!

At Home in the World

It's difficult to describe the Kelebek Hotel in words, but I'll try. It is perched on a hill high above the town and is a sprawling complex of terraces lined with couches and pillows, covered areas of grass with lounge chairs, a small but lovely pool, stairs adorned by flowerpots everywhere, and two big "gnome's hat" rock formations, one of which housed my own little cave room. It was almost sunset when I checked in, and after an amazingly tasty dinner of stuffed grape leaves and lamb kebabs at an outdoor table in the hotel's restaurant, I settled in on a couch on one of the terraces, looking out over the amazing landscape, watching as the city lights were gradually illuminated, and enjoyed the cool evening breezes. As it got darker, dogs barked and howled in the distance, children could be heard giggling, and the clinking of cutlery and dinner dishes could be heard from a dozen other terraces. The Muslim call to prayer was conducted twice from a nearby mosque, echoing beautifully across the entire town. The stars twinkled brightly overhead, there were two fireworks displays (people celebrating weddings, I was told), and the hotel staff served me delicious apple tea as I sat out there taking in this whole scene. I really didn't want to go to sleep!

The next morning, after a huge buffet breakfast of fresh fruits, breads, cheeses, olives, tomatoes, jam, and honey, I tried to decide what to do for the day. I discovered that I'd apparently lost the battery charger for my camera; without that, my photo-taking days were severely numbered. The hotel staff recommended that I drive to a mall in nearby Neveshir for the best chance of getting a replacement. Neveshir was a pretty big place but relying on the map-reading skills I'd been honing since the age of six, I found the mall quite easily, a very modern, beautiful three-story building that looked out of place amidst a backdrop of rather run-down buildings and a mosque on every corner. Mosques are to Turkey what Dunkin' Donuts franchises are to New England; you'll find one on almost every block!

There was an electronics store in the mall, and I was optimistic, but no one could speak any English at all. As I'd learned all too well in Japan, it's frustrating to be unable to communicate. I had no knowledge of Turkish beyond a handful of words I'd managed to pick up: *merhaba* (hello), *kebab* (as in steak or chicken), *kelebek* (butterfly, and the name of my hotel) and *cikis* (exit - which I learned aboard my Turkish Air flight). So how in the hell could I say, "Do you have a battery charger for my Panasonic Lumix camera?" Well, I couldn't. I played a valiant game of charades and I do think the guys at the store finally figured out what I needed but shook their heads and said "no". Dejected, I left the mall and made a stop at a bakery and got into another game of charades when I wanted one large cookie and the man thought I wanted a one-kilogram box of cookies.

I then headed off to explore the Ihlara Valley, a scenic area along a river about an hour from Goreme. I drove back roads and meandered through tiny villages where I'd wager no redhead had ever gone before. I came upon a particularly scenic area of the valley right along the river where people had set up little orange juice and drink stands. Some had built covered wooden platforms extending into the river with tables and chairs set up for dining. I parked my car and started to walk along the river. I didn't get far before a man called to me from one of the refreshment stands, "Where are you from?" One of my fears about visiting Turkey was that it might be like Egypt, where people had so aggressively tried to sell me things. Turkey was different; here they do want to sell you things, but they kill you with kindness: "Where are you from?" "I have a cousin in San Francisco!" "My brother lives in Boston!" "I love American people! How do you like Turkey so far?" I hate being rude or ignoring people, so I often found myself enmeshed in long conversations with strangers here.

Typically, it seemed that the ultimate goal of these pleasantries was to sell me a Turkish rug, but the guy here in the Ihlara Valley had a smaller goal: he just wanted to sell me something to eat or drink. I was thirsty and the offer of freshly squeezed orange juice sounded good. He said the oranges had arrived yesterday from Cyprus and were squeezed that morning. I'd planned to take my juice to go, but my host took out a chair and motioned for me to sit and enjoy my drink. His English was limited and my Turkish, unless I wanted to talk about butterflies or exit row signs, was of no help. Nevertheless, we just sat together, staring at the river, listening to the sound of some far-off thunder. Old men wandered down the road, smiled, said something to my host, nodded to me and moved along. It was like a weird Turkish version of a 1950s TV sitcom, with characters like Andy, Barney and Floyd sittin' on the front porch in Mayberry, tipping their hats to passers-by. It was charming. Eventually I indicated to my host that I had to go. I asked the price of the juice and was surprised when it came to about $5 - an expensive juice, but worth it just for the experience.

The next day I decided to go hiking at Love Valley, which gets it rather corny name from the fact that it is filled with giant, phallic-shaped rock formations. And so, I took a walk amongst the giant penises, so to speak. It was extremely hot, the sun was brutal, and in the valley itself there was no wind at all. As I climbed higher, at least there was a slight breeze and I tried to stay out of the sun and in the shadow of the penises as much as possible. I also visited a place called Sunset Point and hiked portions of Red Valley and Rose Valley, both reddish-pink and requiring some very strenuous climbs. At one point I had to use a chain ladder to get down from a high point on the trail. It was a workout. When I finally got back to the parking area, I immediately headed for a fruit stand with about 10,000 oranges displayed out front and ordered another fresh squeezed juice. I don't know if these oranges came from Cyprus or not, but the guy squeezed them for me on the spot, it was delicious beyond belief, and it cost about half of what I paid in "Mayberry, Turkey."

Hiking through Love Valley; afternoon shadows in Rose Valley.

Returning to the hotel, I made a beeline for the pool, which was frigidly cold, but felt great after all the hiking. At the pool I met a U.S. Marine Corps chaplain named Dan and his family. He was stationed in

Bahrain, an island nation in the Persian Gulf, and the family was taking a vacation. I listened with interest as he talked about the soldiers he counsels and their reactions to the deteriorating conditions in Iraq. He described the heavy burden of trying to comfort them and said his days are filled with non-stop appointments with disillusioned soldiers. "All the wasted lives, the missing limbs, the destroyed villages and now the country is being allowed to fall back into chaos again," he said.

As I got ready to leave the pool area, Dan asked if I'd join him and his family for dinner, and so we all ate together on the big terrace that evening. It was nice to have some company for the evening in this far-away place. His children were so well-behaved... but I suppose that's a result of having a father in the marines! Before we said goodnight, Dan asked if I'd mind if he prayed for me; he prayed for my health, my safe travels, and for resolution of some of the struggles I'd shared with him about issues I faced back home. He went on for two or three minutes, and I wanted to say, "Dan, enough! God has too much on his plate already!" He gave me his e-mail and told me that I ever wanted to come to Bahrain, I'd have a place to stay.

My flight to Istanbul wasn't until mid-afternoon the next day, so I'd signed up for an early morning excursion called Kelebek's Organic Valley Breakfast. About twelve of us, guests of the hotel, were loaded into a huge wine barrel that had been converted into a cart that was pulled through the streets of Goreme by a tractor. We were taken to a rural area, hiked down a steep flight of stairs carved into the rock and found ourselves in a shaded valley encampment where local women had prepared a breakfast feast of eggs, bread, cheeses, vegetables, stuffed walnuts, olives, jams and honey, tea, and homemade wine.

This property belonged to the owner of the Kelebek Hotel and had been his family's farm for several generations. The farm had fruit orchards, grape vines, and olive trees and the harvests are stored in caves over the winter. There were also pigeon houses, and the birds produce the fertilizer used for the crops. It was a little Garden of Eden, hidden deep in this desert canyon. Breakfast was great fun, despite the presence of many bees who didn't seem to appreciate the fact that honeycomb was one of the things being served on the table. It was a torturous walk back up out of the valley in the now blazing sun; I took a cold shower when I got back to the hotel and alas, it was then time to check out and say goodbye to Cappadocia.

A couple of hours later I found myself in a totally different world, riding a modern Metro train from the airport into Istanbul, traveling several stops, then transferring to an above-ground tram line that took me within half a block of my hotel. To use the transit system here, you must first purchase *jetons*, little red disks made of plastic resembling a small checker piece; insert one into a turnstile and you're on your way! I got to the hotel in less than an hour and along the way, I gazed out the window and got my first glimpses of Istanbul.

As in Cappadocia, it seemed that there was a Mosque on every corner, with a kebab stand and a carpet store beside each mosque. I studied the people around me and out on the streets; some looked very trendy and western in their dress and appearance, while in contrast, many women wore black burqas that covered them from head to toe with only a slit for the eyes. Often these women were wearing giant sunglasses so that not even their eyes were visible. The city felt simultaneously familiar and exotic, and I suppose it's always been this way, since Istanbul has been a major east/west cultural crossroads for centuries. It's a huge city of fourteen million people, and geographically, it is vast, straddling both sides of the Bosphorus Strait which connects the Black Sea to the Mediterranean. Therefore, Istanbul literally has a foot in both Europe and Asia.

It was hot and much more humid here than in the deserts of Cappadocia; sweat poured off me even though I was just sitting on the poorly air-conditioned Metro train. I shook my head in amazement at men dressed in three-piece business suits who seemed perfectly comfortable and wondered how they could manage to look so put together while I was melting. I arrived at my hotel, the Nomade, and at check-in the desk clerk told me I'd been upgraded to a bigger room for two nights at no extra charge if I was willing to move to a smaller, single room on my third night. That sounded great to me, and I got a beautiful room with a double bed, hardwood floors, bright windows overlooking a small lane filled with restaurants and cafes, and best of all, a high-powered air-conditioner that quickly brought the room temperature down to something akin to a meat locker. After showering and sitting beside the air conditioner for a few minutes, I felt totally refreshed and ready to hunt for dinner.

I'd read about a restaurant called Aloran, so heading in that direction I walked through a crowded park that separates two famous landmarks. On one side was the famous Blue Mosque, an amazing structure with multiple domes and six tall minarets. On the other side was the Hagia Sophia, a Byzantine church that was later converted into a mosque. As I made my way through the park, I was approached and stopped several times by handsome young men who approached me with big smiles. "Where are you from? Ah, San Francisco! My cousin lives there now! It's a great city! I love America! How long will you stay in Istanbul? How do you like it so far?"

Inevitably these jovial conversations led to, "You must come and see my rugs. I have a small store and I give discounts to people from San Francisco!" This offer was changed to a discount to anyone from Boston when I told some of them that I was originally from there. They were all so polite and friendly it was hard to just ignore them, but after being stopped several times and realizing I'd wasted half an hour in chit-chat, it was beginning to get old. I soon began to avoid eye contact and walk with my head down, but as in Egypt, some salesmen followed me, demanding to know why I was being rude by ignoring their attempts at conversation.

I found the street where the restaurant was located and was scanning the businesses up and down the block when another friendly young man approached me and asked if I was looking for something specific. I said I was looking for a restaurant named *Aloran*, and he laughed and pointed; I was standing directly in front of the place but had my back to it! Of course, after sharing a laugh, this good Samaritan politely informed me that his rug shop was next door to the restaurant, and he hoped I'd visit after dinner because he had a cousin in Boston...

I sat outside and enjoyed a truly delicious meal: lentil soup, amazing puffy loaves of pita-like bread that resembled gigantic, foot-high mushrooms, olives, salads, and lamb cooked with apricots. By the time I finished dinner and navigated stealthily past another army of carpet salesmen, it was 11PM, so I retired to the cool oasis of my hotel room and dozed off to the sounds of late-night Istanbul below my window.

Blue Mosque (and the popcorn sign).

Breakfast was served on the hotel's sixth floor outdoor terrace, featuring a beautiful view of the Blue Mosque, marred only by a huge box labeled "POPCORN" that sat atop the roof of the building next door. It was impossible to take a decent photo of the mosque without having the popcorn "caption" underneath. It was another hot day, so I decided my first tourist stop would be the ancient cisterns built during the last days of the Roman Empire when its eastern headquarters was Constantinople, Istanbul's former moniker. The cisterns are underground caverns filled with water transported into the city via an aqueduct. Hundreds of columns support the roof, the place is lit by candle-like lanterns, and you can listen to the sounds of dripping water while watching the wriggling fish that inhabit this underground lake. It was cooler down here than in the streets above, but the humidity was intense, and the sounds of sweat pouring from my face melded with those of the water droplets from the ceiling.

Exploring the cisterns.

By the time I'd finished my tour of the cistern, I had less than an hour until prayer time ended, and the Blue Mosque would be open to visitors. I walked there but as I got close, I was stopped by a young man who politely informed me that the mosque was closed now, which I knew. "It will open at 2:00" he offered. I knew that, too. "Where are you from? I have a carpet store in the bazaar nearby. You can come and have tea until the mosque opens!" Politely but firmly declining his offer, I went into the open courtyard in front of the mosque and as I wandered around taking some pictures, this same man approached me again and said, "The mosque is closed, I told you! Come see my rugs!" I almost pleaded with him to just leave me in peace, and then joined the line that was forming to enter the mosque. Removing my shoes and throwing them into my backpack, I began to walk around the carpeted mosque, wondering where they'd bought their rugs.

The mosque is a breathtaking space, with towering domes and cool blue tiles lining the walls, creating intricate patterns. There was a roped-off area in the middle where the afternoon prayers were still finishing up.

I'd noted that the Muslim call to prayer here in Istanbul seemed a lot more melodious and well-broadcasted than it had been in parts of Cappadocia, where a man sounding like he had "morning voice" chanted over a very crackly P.A. system.

Inside the Blue Mosque.

Late that afternoon I met up with an online pen pal I'd been corresponding with for a few weeks prior to my trip. His name was Adam, and he actually drove ninety minutes into Istanbul from his place in the suburbs just for the chance to meet me in person. What I didn't know about Adam, and something he'd never shared with me online, was that he was deaf and could not read lips, though even if he could, it wouldn't have helped; his English vocabulary was only slightly more extensive than my Turkish one! But where there's a will, there's a way and thanks to the miracles of modern technology, we sat in front of his laptop and WROTE to one another, as we had been doing in our online interactions. We used Google Translator to type things from Turkish into English and vice versa, and it actually went pretty well! While we were "talking" there was a huge demonstration going on in the streets, which he didn't notice because he hadn't heard it. When I pointed it out, he wrote a lengthy explanation saying that due to troubles in Iraq, several staff from the Turkish Embassy in Baghdad had been kidnapped by terrorists and these demonstrators were protesting the incident. Adam shook his head silently, and then typed, "There are too many troubles in this world today. I can't make sense of it." I nodded in agreement. If only Google Translator could help us figure everything out, I mused.

After spending a couple of hours visiting with Adam, I then rendezvoused with Lynn, a colleague from my university who'd just arrived with her husband for a visit to Istanbul. We met at a restaurant called the Anatolia Café; they'd already eaten dinner, but they had drinks and kept me company as I dined on a wonderful meal of lentil soup with lemon, fried calamari, chicken in garlic sauce, and baklava. Baklava is a dessert I've never been a huge fan of, but online reviews of this place unanimously mentioned the baklava. They served it warm from the oven and it was truly out of this world, converting me to a baklava believer! It was refreshing to spend much of the day having real conversations, first with Adam and now with Lynn and her husband, as opposed to the stilted banter I'd been exchanging with every rug salesman in Istanbul.

After dinner I took a long walk and made a stop for ice cream at one of the many stands that are found throughout the city. Turkish ice cream vendors wear cute little hats with a tassel, and they are amateur magicians. As they prepare your cone, they use a long utensil not only to fill the cone with ice cream, but also to place the half-created cone into your shirt pocket or touch it to your nose, quickly removing it when you try to reach for it. They may play with you like this for two or three minutes before finally handing over your ice cream. The show was a bit more entertaining than the ice cream itself, which had a strange, chewy consistency. However, I liked the ice cream much better than the other "treat" here: Turkish Delight, a candy that is for sale everywhere and is served with your coffee at restaurants or as a dessert if you don't order one. It comes in various flavors, has a starchy, chewy consistency like a gummy bear that's gone stale, and is dipped in powdered sugar. I hadn't experienced anything quite so unappealing since I was presented with *mochi* a few years earlier across the world in Japan and just tasting the Turkish Delight triggered "mochi flashbacks." So as not to appear rude to my hosts, I was constantly trying to hide these decidedly un-delightful Turkish treats under my napkin or by shoving them into my pants pockets to dispose of later.

I visited Istanbul's Grand Bazaar, an enclosed marketplace that covers a total of fifty-eight city blocks. I'd feared there would be an intense onslaught by the vendors, but I was pretty much left alone to browse at my leisure while enjoying a delicious glass of fresh-squeezed pomegranate juice from one of the shops. Perhaps word was out around the city that the big, redheaded guy from San Francisco (or Boston) was not buying any carpets. I did manage to find a battery charger adaptor, so thankfully I was back in the photo-taking business again.

The lights of Istanbul: lamps at the Grand Bazaar; the Blue Mosque.

At the top of my Istanbul bucket list was to experience a traditional session at a *hamam* or public bath. Before coming to Turkey, I'd read dozens of online reviews of various hamams, but they were very confusing and contradictory. Reviews stating, "Here you can find the genuine, traditional hamam experience!" and "They rush you through the process, it's very touristy, and it wasn't worth the money" referred to the same place. After seemingly hours of research, I finally settled upon the *Kılıç Ali Paşa Hamam*, which had gotten excellent and consistent ratings online. I was glad I'd read so much about the experience before-hand, as I found it to be a rather complicated process and at least I had a vague idea of what to expect.

I arrived fifteen minutes before my appointment and was directed to a table in a beautiful, marble-covered room in a 700-year-old building. I had to fill out paperwork about any medical conditions I had and was rewarded for this with a glass of juice and a cup of sherbet. At 5PM sharp, a young man escorted me to a locker room where I was to remove all my clothes. He gave me a pair of insanely undersized sandals and a loin-cloth-like towel to wear and told me to meet him downstairs once I was ready.

The "lobby" of the Hamam.

With my feet sticking out of the back of my sandals by several inches, I hobbled down the stairs, trying not to fall, and was guided into the main bathing area. My host motioned for me to sit, pointing toward an area with two huge tubs, shaped like open scallop shells, each with a faucet spigot at the top. He left, so I took a seat inside one of the scallop shell tubs and waited for further instructions. When he came back a few moments later he had a somewhat quizzical look on his face. "Sir, if you please, you must to sit on the steps to the side of the tub, not inside." As

I sat inside this giant scallop shell, legs dangling over the side I must have been as red as a pomegranate with embarrassment. I felt a strange kinship to that zany redhead, Lucy Ricardo, as she found herself in yet another crazy situation on *I Love Lucy*.

"Is first time in hamam?" my gentle host asked. I laughed out loud and said, "Yes, it is. But how did you guess?" as I awkwardly climbed out of the shell and sat on the steps as directed. My host then filled giant bowls of warm water from the faucets and proceeded to dump them on my head as a sort of "pre-rinse". He then led me to a huge, round marble slab in the middle of the room, upon which several men were lying on their backs. This hamam is associated with a mosque, so women use the baths from 8:00AM till 4:00PM, and men from 4:00 till midnight. This room was similar to a sauna or steam room, but was not as hot and uncomfortable as some I have been in. In fact, I've been on non-air-conditioned buses in Rome that were hotter than this! The marble slab was heated from within, and I was asked to lie directly atop the slab, on my back with my head cradled by a silver bowl that looked like a pet's water dish. There I simmered like meat on a hotplate for about thirty minutes, feeling the warmth emanating from the marble slab into my legs and back, sweating out all the toxins, breathing deeply, and staring up at a dome lighted by white stars and geometric patterns. I almost dozed off a couple of times; it was so magical and utterly relaxing.

I was then gently roused by a new man wearing only a towel who introduced himself as Ahmed, and as I continued to lie on the marble slab, he poured four big bowls of warm water over me to rinse me off, then guided me back to one of the steps beside the scallop tubs. For the next twenty minutes Ahmed used a luffa mitt on my entire body, scrubbing the skin vigorously. Every so often he'd show me all the dirt and dead skin that was coming off on the luffa, a part of the experience I could easily have done without! Occasionally he'd toss another bowl of warm water over me and then kept scrubbing. After this, he used what seemed like giant pillowcases filled with soap bubbles and warm water, squeezing the bubbles over me from the neck down, repeating this about ten times and then scrubbing me some more.

Next there was a facial scrub, a brief massage of my arms, neck, and back, then a shampoo, and last, a final rinse starting with bowls of very hot water to progressively colder ones, both to cool me down and evidently to close my pores. Once I was thoroughly rinsed, Ahmed took my hand and guided me into another room, and I did not refuse the help: I felt as mushy as an overripe banana by this point! He dried me off completely, then wrapped me in a series of plush towels: one around the waist, one over my back and shoulders, and one wrapped tightly around my hair. I was then led out into the foyer area, where I was met by another attendant and taken to the periphery of the room, which was lined with big, elevated couches and pillows. I sprawled out on one of the couches in this much cooler room where I was served herbal tea and told I could remain as long as I wanted. I think I fell asleep for a while, and in my entire life I'd never felt so relaxed. The wear and tear I'd accumulated after a few weeks of travel just floated away. Finally, with great difficulty, I dragged my limp body back to the lockers, got dressed and went out into the steamy air of Istanbul. The whole experience lasted two hours and cost me far less than what a good massage would be back home. It was definitely one of the highlights of my time in Turkey.

Since I was now in a new part of the city far from my hotel, I explored the area around Taksim Square and what is purported to be one of the longest pedestrian streets in all of Europe. I was blown away by the sheer number of people on the street on this Friday night. It felt like a huge festival or concert had just ended; thousands of people strolled, ate, and window-shopped. I'm not a big fan of crowds and didn't particularly like pushing my way through it all. At the end of the street was Taksim Square and when I saw it, I was happy I hadn't stayed in this part of town. It was a tacky, Times Square-ish place with a McDonalds and Burger King, and throngs of young people standing around smoking. Not exactly my scene, so I took a tram back to the old town again, had a few more conversations with polite and persistent rug salesmen, and called it an early night.

Unfortunately, that morning I'd had to move from my beautiful room into the smaller single for my final night. It was half the size of my big room and had only one tiny window looking out on a concrete wall. Worst of all, the air conditioner not only didn't keep the room cool, but made hideous noises all night, alternating from the sizzling sound of a giant insect coming into contact with a bug-zapper on a hot summer night to the whirring blades of a police helicopter flying low in pursuit of a fleeing criminal! It was not a restful night, but I tried to comfort myself with thoughts of plush towels, cascades of warm water, slabs of heated marble, and elaborate scallop shell sinks.

The unforgettable landscape of Cappadocia.

My time in Turkey was all too brief, but I can say that Cappadocia was one of the most exotic and beautiful places I've ever traveled to. As for Istanbul, I know I barely scratched the surface of what is a dynamic and complicated city. I'd like to return some day when time, money, and world events permit. When I do, I'll at least know not to climb into the scallop shell tubs in a hamam. And who knows? I may just buy a rug!

9. The Sun Doesn't Always Shine in Tuscany

ITALY

Italy's stunning Tuscan countryside.

When I first "discovered" Italy in 1998, it was pretty much love at first sight. Since then, I've made countless trips and cumulatively, I've spent almost two years of my life there. I've traveled the country extensively and Italian friends joke that I've seen more of their country than they have. Venice is probably my favorite city in the world. The country's scenery is varied and stunning and I challenge anyone who has driven across the Italian Alps, meandered through the hill towns of Tuscany, or explored the Amalfi Coast to say they haven't at least developed a crush on Italy, if not having fallen head over heels in love with her.

As I mentioned previously, Italy played a pivotal role in my career. With the help of my Italian colleague Tullio, I conducted the very first research studies on how residents living close to the volcanoes, Etna and Vesuvius, perceive their risk from eruptions and how much confidence they have in the evacuation plans for their towns. I also attended professional conferences and led several student trips to Italy as part of my university's study abroad program. But it hasn't been all work and no play; I've spent plenty of leisure time there, undoubtedly helping to bolster the Italian economy with my generous contributions to their restaurant industry! I've been fortunate enough to cultivate cherished friendships, study the language, and experience the culture. I had considerable trouble writing this chapter because I have so much to say and so many tales to tell about Italy. Therefore, rather than describing just one or two trips, I decided to share a series of "snapshots" about Italy and its people and I hope they will convey why Italy has such a special place in my heart.

When in Rome: Italian Social and Cultural Norms

In the Social Psychology classes I taught for over thirty years I discussed the importance of social norms, rules that govern much of our behavior. Some norms are formally integrated into our legal system: stopping at red lights, not stealing, filing taxes on time, etc. Other norms are more subtle, learned by watching the behavior of others as we grow and develop: maintaining certain physical distances from other people, shaking hands when meeting someone, or waiting in lines. Adhering to norms keeps us out of trouble and earns approval from others; deviating from norms can lead to being punished or socially ridiculed. If you doubt how powerful such norms can be, try an experiment: violate an innocent social norm like having a conversation with someone without making any eye contact, or turning to face people behind you in a crowded elevator. The level of discomfort you and those around you will feel may surprise you! While many social norms are universal, others tend to be culturally specific.

One aspect of travel that I find fascinating is being exposed to the different social norms of places I'm visiting. I've encountered many interesting cultural norms, like refraining from nose-blowing in public in Japan or removing one's shoes before entering a home or certain public buildings in Japan, as well as in Hawaii and some Muslim countries. In the Middle East never use the "thumbs up" sign and in Brazil avoid the OK gesture; both of these have very different connotations than they do in the U.S. It's customary to greet acquaintances with a quick kiss on each cheek in many European countries, but there are exceptions; in some places they do three kisses, one on each cheek and then back to the first. In some countries the kissing starts on the right cheek, while in others it starts on the left. Because of these differences in cultural norms, I recommend doing some research about the place you're visiting to avoid insulting someone, being laughed at, or creating embarrassing mishaps like banging heads with the person you're trying to politely kiss on the cheek.

Because I've spent more time in Italy than in any other foreign country, I've become intimately acquainted with and thoroughly entertained by the many customs that Italians follow, particularly around dining and food. One of the first rules to be aware of is that if you're invited to dinner at someone's home, don't arrive on time. Yes, you read that correctly; strive to be fashionably late. My friend Fabio in Rome invited me to dinner and told me to come over at 7:30PM. I dutifully rang the buzzer at 7:30 sharp, waited a while for him to answer the intercom and buzz me in, and when he did, he sounded flustered. I climbed the stairs to his sixth-floor apartment - there is no elevator – and when I reached his door, he'd left it open and was dashing toward his bedroom with a towel wrapped around his waist.

"Sorry, I wasn't expecting you yet. I forgot, you're American!"

According to Italian norms, 7:30 really means 8:00 or so. Lesson learned.

Here in the U.S., many Italian restaurants offer diners a basket of bread and a bowl of herb-infused olive oil to dip the bread into. After several visits to Italy, I realized I'd never seen this custom practiced there, so I asked my Italian friends whether this was actually an Italian custom. The answer that I most vividly recall was, "*No! È barbarico!*" (It's barbaric!). I wondered if perhaps this was a practice in just one or two of the country's diverse regions, but everyone I asked assured me, "No Italian would ever do this!" Bread may be served before a meal, usually for a price, and Italians don't put butter on it; its primary purpose is to sop up the remainder of a very good pasta sauce.

In fact, when you're dining out in Italy, you'll find that bread plates aren't even included in the table setting. Once at a family dinner in Italy's Veneto region, I noticed my friend Cristoforo's mother seemed obviously perturbed. When I asked what was wrong, he said that I was being rude by balancing a piece of bread on the edge of my dinner plate. I learned that I should place my bread directly on the tablecloth. Restaurants across Italy use a fresh tablecloth for each new guest; by not placing my bread on the table, I was implying that perhaps the tablecloth wasn't clean enough.

When I brought my study abroad students to Italy, I drilled these norms into them. Nevertheless, on one trip at our first group dinner, my student Clayton asked our waiter for olive oil and an extra plate. Other students gasped, chiding Clayton for ignoring my lecture. Indignantly, he pointed out that the waiter hadn't protested and when he returned to our table, Clayton asked him if Italians dip their bread in olive oil. The waiter rolled his eyes and said, "No! I brought you the oil because I know Americans like it, but we think it's disgusting!" A friend of mine who owns a restaurant in Rome has expressed his exasperation with American and British tourists in this regard. "We serve very fine oil to our guests, but they use half a bottle of oil for bread! It's like they're drinking it!" I assured him that I was doing my part to get the message out.

Another amusing example of this culture clash happened while I was dining at a trendy pasta and wine bar in Florence. Shortly after ordering my meal, a young American couple entered and sat near me. The waitress brought them a basket of bread and headed back toward the kitchen, but the young man called out, "Um, could we get some olive oil, please?" She turned and stared intently at him without saying a word. He pointed at the basket and stammered, nervously, "You know... for our bread." The waitress eyed him suspiciously, uttered a very definitive "No!" and continued toward the kitchen. When I finally stopped laughing, I turned to my neighbors and said, "Let me explain what just happened here."

Another thing to know is that some of your favorite "Italian" dishes may not be Italian at all or may not be what you expect. Spaghetti and meatballs and fettuccine alfredo are not Italian. Chicken is never used in pasta dishes or on pizza and there's no such thing as pepperoni pizza: the Italian word *peperoni* refers to green peppers, not meat. Pizza in Italy is usually thin crust and isn't loaded with cheese like "Chicago Style" pizza. Other than oil and vinegar, there's no choice of salad dressings. And Italians don't typically eat eggs or bacon for breakfast; pastry and coffee is the norm.

So, you like cappuccino? I do too. Italian coffee is delightfully strong, and I prefer to take it with steamed milk rather than as a shot glass of espresso. But beware: you should only order a cappuccino before noon; to do otherwise will make you the object of ridicule and scorn. At the very least, your server or bystanders nearby will look at you strangely; at worst, the person behind the counter will simply refuse to make a cappuccino in the afternoon or evening. I'll admit that this is an Italian food norm I've rebelled against, as I really don't like espresso, but conformity is a powerful thing. After a nice dinner with friends in Rome, the waitress came by and asked, "*Caffe*?" I simply raised my eyebrows in an impish manner as if I might dare to make the forbidden request for a cappuccino; my friend Fabio threw me a look that would scare a pit-bull and whispered, "I will kill you!" There was no cappuccino for me that night.

At my favorite restaurant in Rome, because I know the staff well, I've sheepishly asked my servers, Barbara or Zeljan, whether I might possibly break this rule, prefacing my request with, "I know it's wrong, but..." Barbara shrugged indifferently, but with a demeanor that communicated that she thought I was a major loser, replied, "If you pay for it you can have whatever you want." Zeljan didn't make a big deal about my request, but when he delivered the cappuccino, he leaned in and whispered, "I won't tell anyone what you have done. I will keep your secret!" I've asked my friends the reason for this rigid code regarding cappuccino. They say something vague about it being bad for digestion to have milk after noon, but they cannot explain to me why things like cheese and gelato can be eaten at any time of the day or night. Until I understand the rationale for this rule, I'll probably continue to ignore it – but only when I think it's safe to do so!

Now, picture yourself in Venice, a beautiful platter of linguine with clam sauce placed before you. Your dinner companion is receiving a flurry of freshly grated, fragrant Parmesan cheese on his or her spaghetti with a hearty meat sauce, causing you to think about how nice it would be to add some to your dish too. However, the waiter doesn't ask if you'd like some and as he starts to leave, you consider asking him to come back to top your dish with some cheese as well. I beg of you, don't go there! Don't do it! You see, cheese and seafood are not supposed to be eaten together. Period.

Cappuccino never after noon; Mr. Shrimp says "No cheese!

During an early visit to Italy, I didn't know this rule. I ordered linguine with clams at lunch with my friends Alex and Patrizio and asked them to pass the Parmesan that was on our table. Patrizio's face became a mask of pure, unadulterated horror. He seemed momentarily speechless, so Alex quickly explained the "no cheese on seafood" rule to me. I pressed him, saying that I love fresh cheese on my pasta. He started to hand me the cheese and I thought Patrizio might leap across the table and throttle me. In a dramatic scene that could have been out of a movie, he literally stomped his foot and pleaded, "Alex! Please! Tell him! It's just not right!" You'd have thought he was trying to keep me from jumping off a bridge, such was the level of his passion. Calmly, Alex who was a bit more worldly and well-traveled than Patrizio and therefore, more forgiving of my violation of the norm, said, "It's his dinner. He can put cheese on his pasta if he wants..." I sighed with relief and started to spoon the Parmesan over my pasta as Alex finished his sentence: "...even if it is wrong." Patrizio shook his head sorrowfully. Message received. These days I follow the rules and don't even consider adding cheese to my seafood pasta; it's an easier road to take.

Another rule I'd read about before I'd ever set foot in the country was that salad is eaten after the main course, but on one of my early visits to Venice, I was in a very empty restaurant, and I was hungry. My waiter, an older gentleman who seemed to have nothing else to do but stare and scrutinize my every move, delivered my salad before my pasta had arrived. I knew the rule, but hunger and boredom led me to grab my fork and take a few tentative bites of salad. The waiter noticed my transgression and without saying a word, came over and moved my salad to the other side of my table, almost out of reach. He then returned to his stool and continued to watch me until my pasta finally arrived. I hadn't learned enough Italian at that time to explain or defend my actions, so I timidly finished my pasta and only then did I dare reach for my salad.

One of the most common complaints I see in online travel forums or hear from fellow tourists is that a waiter or waitress was rude, keeping them waiting too long without bringing the bill. What these folks fail to understand is that their server was being polite, not rude. In Italy it's customary for patrons to ask for the check when they're ready to leave, using the phrase, "*Il conto, per favore.*" A server wouldn't want to make you feel pressured to leave by bringing you the bill before you've requested it. And never ask for a "doggy bag" or a to-go container in a restaurant; it's just not done in Italy.

The moral of these stories is that whether you're planning a trip to Italy or to any other country, do some research on the cultural norms, etiquette, or traditions of the places you intend to visit. You'll feel more at ease when you're there, avoid embarrassing incidents, and the locals will be impressed by the fact that you're familiar with and respect some of their customs and traditions.

Mangia, Mangia! Memorable Meals in Italy

One of the joys of travel is meeting strangers who become new friends. At a café in Rome, I met Scott, an American professor who was living there while working on a book. After some conversation it was apparent that we were kindred spirits. He'd planned to go to a restaurant called Sora Margherita the next day and asked me to join him. That evening I became a bit uneasy when I found many negative online reviews of this restaurant. Most of the bad comments weren't about the food, but focused on the service, in particular, a surly waitress who "abused" customers by forcing them to finish uneaten food on their plates. I was intrigued.

The next day I met Scott at the restaurant, and we'd barely been seated when I noticed a waitress eyeing us suspiciously and thought "Uh-oh" as she swaggered over to our table. In Italian she asked us what we wanted, but we hadn't even seen a menu yet. Before we could answer, she told us to trust her, and she'd bring us what she thought we should eat. She had a look about her that told us not to argue and for some reason she seemed to like us, so we agreed to go with the flow and allow her to choose our dishes.

I was glad I'd been forewarned by the online reviews, because otherwise I'd have been even more taken by surprise than I was when our waitress returned with a dish of marinated vegetables, spooned up a healthy portion, and shoved it into my mouth before I could react or protest, a strange, triumphant look on her face as she posed for Scott, who had whipped out his camera to capture the moment. I was laughing, but also trying not to choke to death on my food as she proceeded to break off some bread and shove a piece into my mouth as well. She attempted to force-feed Scott, but the look he gave her was enough for her to back off and focus her attention solely on me.

During our meal we learned that her name was Tiziana; she really was good humored, but with enough of an edge to know that I wouldn't want to get on her bad side. I imagine that many of the online reviewers complaining about her rudeness hadn't taken her behavior with as much of a sense of fun as I did. Aside from these antics, the food was quite good; my favorite was a warm ricotta cake with black cherries for dessert. All in all, it was an entertaining afternoon. By the time we left I'd made a new friend in Tiziana, who gave me a gentle kiss on the cheek that seemed to suggest that she does have a tender side, despite all evidence to the contrary!

Don't piss Tiziana off!

One of the first friends I made in Italy was Cristoforo, a serious young man with a sarcastic sense of humor who grew up in the Veneto region. I've been invited to many memorable dinners at his parents' home. I refer to his mother as *Mamma*, despite the fact that she's only a couple years older than me as she embodies all of the stereotypical characteristics of an Italian Mamma. According to Cristoforo, she's happiest when preparing and serving food. When I'm invited to dinner, I avoid eating for the entire day to prepare for what I refer to as a "*Mangia-*thon." Mamma brings out platters of succulent fruits, cheeses, and bread, a vat of her intoxicating spaghetti with mixed seafood, and various main courses: grilled fish, shrimp, chicken, or even horse meat with lemon, a very Venetian dish. There are vegetable dishes and salads, and always dessert, coffee, and after dinner liqueurs. After everyone at dinner has surrendered, refusing offers of more food, Mamma seems deflated and sad. Once, when I changed my mind and decided that I had room for some cookies with my coffee, she dashed into the kitchen to fetch them. Cristoforo rolled his eyes and said, "You have just given my mother a reason to live for another few minutes!"

My favorite restaurant in Rome is Trattoria Monti where I had a magnificent dinner one summer. Months later, finding myself back in Rome, I returned to Monti and to my astonishment, the waiters recognized me. "Ah yes, the *professore* from San Francisco!" I couldn't believe they'd remembered me and jokingly wondered whether they'd had any other customers since my last visit. That was twenty years ago, and I never visit Rome without visiting Monti.

On study abroad trips, I wanted my students to have an authentic dining experience. Because Monti is a small restaurant, I'd take groups of six to eight students at a time to three separate dinners or lunches, happily benefitting by getting to dine there three times! One memorable lunch found us seated near the kitchen, watching the chef, Mamma Camerucci working her magic. Her sons, Enrico and Daniele, are the headwaiters and that day, Enrico brought his baby daughter Sophia to the restaurant. She was absolutely adorable, with eyes the size of saucers; Uncle Daniele joked that she looked like a lemur. Every so often, grandma came out from the kitchen to hold Sophia and bounce her on her lap.

Meanwhile, the students adored their food, sharing stuffed olives, red onion flan, fried zucchini flowers, and exquisite homemade pasta dishes. When Chef Camerucci visited our table, they showered her with love and thanks, though one rather odd female student made her uneasy, repeating, "*Ti amo, Mamma! Ti amo!*" Italians typically only say "*Ti amo*" to a lover. Using me to translate, "Mamma" told the student she needed to find herself a man. Another student, Andrew, was having such a wonderful experience he actually got teary-eyed, and Mamma wiped his eyes with her apron. He asked her to choose a dessert for him, but she surprised all of us by bringing out a collection of amazing treats to share: ricotta pudding, peach torte, apple cake, wild strawberries in gelatin with peach sauce... a dessert orgy! Weeks later when I reviewed students' evaluations of our trip, ratings for the Coliseum and the Vatican paled in comparison to those for our afternoon at Trattoria Monti.

Enrico, Mamma and Daniele.

After the students had flown home, I dined at Monti one last time before leaving Rome. I went all out, ordering more dishes than usual, just wanting one more taste of everything. At the end of a stunning meal, Enrico and Daniele came to my table and said that my dinner was free... a gift for being such a faithful customer and bringing so many people to their restaurant. I was so touched I could have used Mamma's apron to wipe the tears from my eyes. Daniele said, "You're like a brother to us now!" Given their dark, handsome good looks I guess that makes me the red sheep of the family!

Lost in Translation

Brent and Boner, Priello.

On one of my first excursions through Tuscany, I discovered a B&B called Priello, a mile or so up a rough gravel road on a mountaintop overlooking the hamlet of Caprese Michelangelo, birthplace of the famous artist. My gregarious host was Brent, an American who fell in love with Italy, purchased and painstakingly restored a 1,000-year-old stone farmhouse and turned it into a B&B and working farm. Brent could write his own book about his struggles to get established in Italy and create the masterpiece that was Priello, and I enjoyed listening to his tales of woe because his delivery was hilarious. Once, in reference to the film *Under the Tuscan Sun,* the story of an impetuous American writer who finds true love and personal fulfillment while she restores a decrepit Italian villa, Brent deadpanned, "I'm going to tell my story and I'm going to call it, *The Sun Doesn't Always Shine in Tuscany!*"

During one visit, I expressed frustration about wanting to speak Italian more fluently, and Brent told me a story about his first year at Priello. An old woman named Signora Innocente lived at the bottom of the steep road leading to his property. After a hard day's work, on a whim, he decided to walk down to Signora Innocente's and bring her a basket of fresh eggs from his chickens. When she opened the door, he became tongue-tied and couldn't think of what to say in Italian, so he just awkwardly shoved the eggs at her. She motioned to invite him in, but since he was sweaty and dirty from working all day, he attempted to say, "No, I need to take a shower now!" In Italian this would be, "*No, devo farmi una doccia adesso!*" However, Brent had mistakenly and unknowingly responded with, "*No, devi farmi un dolce adesso!*" (No, you must make me a dessert now!")

Brent went home and about two hours later, Signora Innocente came trudging up his steep driveway looking frazzled, hair flecked with bits of flour, and presented him with a huge cake! He was so touched, and thought, "Wow, I've made a new friend here!" But days later Brent learned that Signora Innocente was going around town talking about the crazy American who'd come to her house, forced eggs upon her and demanded that she make him a cake! His tale made me feel a little better about my own struggles with the language.

Amici nel Cuore

My friends Claudia and Marco live in a small village in the Veneto region near Padova. Claudia is among the sweetest and most charming people I've ever known, and we've been friends for almost twenty years. At parties or group dinners, she often checks with me to make sure I'm following the fast-paced Italian conversations and fills me in on details I've missed. Despite having an impressive command of English, she often struggles with colloquialisms or slang. One evening when she was making dinner for me, she said I could help by "dressing the table." I chuckled and told her that in English we say, "set the table." She furrowed a brow and displayed the same frustration I feel when I find I've used an Italian expression incorrectly, but her frown dissolved into a hearty laugh when I asked, "Wouldn't it sound strangely sexual to talk about UN-dressing the table after dinner?"

Another time, Claudia was taking an English course and asked for help on some homework. Her teacher had introduced the expression, "I'll see you when I see you!" - making it sound like a jolly way of saying "See you soon!" I explained that unless you were expecting someone who was running hopelessly late and wanted to reassure him not to hurry, this phrase could sound almost dismissive or rude, as if to say, "I really don't care when or if I'll see you!" Later, when I was getting ready to head back to my hotel, Claudia offered directions, saying I needed to go north and then *"Dritto, sempre dritto!"* (Always straight). I quipped, "If I do that, then I'll be in Austria by midnight!" She laughed and came back with, "Well, in this case, I will see you when I see you!"

Claudia is married to Marco, a somewhat shy man with dark hair and ice blue eyes. He understands English quite well, and valiantly tries to speak it, but it's a struggle for him. I often urge him to speak slowly in Italian to me and chances are good that I'll understand, but he painstakingly searches for just the right English words. On one occasion he was trying to share an Italian proverb with me, and after thirty minutes of Claudia and me suggesting words and trying to guess what he wanted to say, he proudly proclaimed, "When a man is burned once, he then fears the fire." Simultaneously, all three of us dissolved into laughter as we couldn't believe he'd spent so much time trying to convey such an anti-climactic message. Later that night, Marco sent me a text: "Matt, I will be sure to think of more proverbs for your next visit!"

Marco and Claudia.

I was deeply honored when they invited me to their wedding and was thrilled to be able to be in Italy for the ceremony. Before I arrived, Claudia said, "I must warn you that in Italy, when there is a wedding, you can expect that all we will do is eat for about three days!" Had I not already agreed to come, that would have clinched it for me. It was a fairy-tale wedding held at a tiny rural church on a beautiful afternoon in April. The happy couple traveled from the church to the reception in a horse and buggy while the attendees followed on foot. It's a memory I'll always cherish. Claudia and Marco once explained that I'm a very special type of friend that Italians call, *un amico nel cuore* – a friend of the heart.

I couldn't think of a more beautiful way to express my feelings for them as well.

Another member of my Italian family is Emanuele, whose nickname is *Ciube* because of his hirsute appearance. *Ciube* is Italian for "Chewie" or Chewbacca, Han Solo's furry sidekick in the *Star Wars* films. Ciube always greets me with an affectionate arm around my shoulder, looking deeply into my eyes and earnestly asking how I've been since we last saw one another. He's given me a nickname: *Matto*, which means "crazy" in Italian.

Emanuele and "Matto"

Ciube plays in a band called The Beards and they've released several CDs of traditional music from the Veneto, as well as tribute albums to Bob Dylan and Johnny Cash. It's amazing to hear the band, a group of men who speak with very thick Italian accents, singing *Ring of Fire* and sounding like they were raised just outside of Nashville. A few years ago, they did a short concert tour in the U.S. and Ciube's prized souvenirs from the trip were ten speeding violations he'd accumulated, one from each state they'd visited! "Matt, I can no longer drive in your country; you have too many driving rules!" he declared. And he calls ME, Matto?

My friend Fabio, born and raised in Rome, is a free spirit who shares my love of travel, the sea, and good food. He's taken me on excursions to coastal towns like Nettuno and Anzio, the volcanic mountains and crater lakes of the Alban Hills, and to Castel di Tora, a beautiful hill town near the border between Lazio and Umbria. He's also shown me some of Rome's lesser-known ruins, monuments, and viewpoints and provided me with a classic Roman experience: riding on the back of his motorbike, winding our way through traffic in the Eternal City on a warm summer night.

One day we explored the neighborhood where Fabio lived as a child, and he showed me a field littered with ancient Roman tombs where he'd played as a boy. Thinking back to my own childhood, I asked, "In America we played cowboys and Indians when we were kids. What did you play?" Looking at me with an expression that told me the answer should have been obvious, he replied simply, "Gladiatori" (Gladiators). I laughed hysterically; what else would a little Roman boy play as he crept around ancient ruins and tombs virtually in his own backyard?

My friend Fabio from Rome.

I got another peek into Fabio's childhood when he expressed a strong hatred for Halloween, explaining that as a child, his mother always came up with obscure costumes for him to wear. One year he was Pulcinella, a character popularized in 17th century Italian comedy theater and puppetry. Another year she wrapped him in robes and a crown and dubbed him "The Prince of Russia." As he recalled these memories, I tried not to laugh, but it was almost impossible. His face took on the look of a pouty young boy and in a far-off voice he sighed, "I just wanted to be a robot or Superman!"

I often learn new Italian words or phrases from my Italian friends. One day Fabio and I were driving in Rome and heard thunderous bass off in the distance; I thought it was a concert or a neighborhood street fair, but Fabio shook his head. *"Truzzo!"* Truzzo, he explained, is a term for what Americans might call a *Guido*... a stereotypical Italian man with an inflated ego, adorned with lots of jewelry, and driving a flashy car. Sure enough, the booming sounds got closer, and a canary-yellow Lamborghini pulled up beside us. The young driver's shirt was open to the navel, displaying numerous gold chains, and he was wearing multiple bracelets and rings. He kept peeling rubber and weaving in and out of the traffic. *"Che truzzo!"* moaned Fabio. "You see what I mean? No one drives a Lamborghini down Via Tuscolana unless they are a truzzo! If you have a Lamborghini, you drive it on the Amalfi coast, not in this neighborhood!" Heed Fabio's words: don't be a truzzo!

Italian Pop Culture: TV and Music

Having taught a course in Media Psychology for many years and being a fan of many genres of music, various aspects of Italy's popular culture have interested me. Following a busy day of distributing surveys at Vesuvius, my colleague Tullio and I relaxed by watching TV in the lobby of our hotel. I was introduced to a program called *Ciao, Darwin* in which two opposing groups debate some social issue and the audience votes on who won the argument. Of course, this was not a reasoned, cerebral discussion; it was trashy reality TV. That night's episode featured two groups of women, the Virgins, and the sexually experienced Experts, who screamed at one another about whose lifestyle was better. Periodically the camera cut to a scantily clad woman reclining on a sofa, casually spinning a globe. I was confused and asked, "Who is she?" Tullio, seemingly transfixed by the screen replied, "She is Madre Natura."

"OK... but, what does Mother Nature have to do with any of this?" I wondered. "Nothing. We just like her," he replied.

On another occasion while channel-surfing in a hotel room one night I came across a middle-aged woman apparently sitting at her own kitchen table, a giant telephone beside her. I gleaned that she was a psychic and she was urging viewers to call in for a reading. As a phone number flashed across the screen, she whispered, "*Chiamami. Chiamami adesso!*" (Call me now!) After a while she casually got up, made herself a cup of tea, straightened a few things around the kitchen, then returned to the table, staring intently into the camera. "Chiamami!"

Transfixed, I watched this for over thirty minutes; her phone never rang, and I almost called her just to break the tension. I love television.

When Cher released her *Believe* album in the late 1990s, it included the song *Dov'e L'Amore* in which she sings a few lines of Italian. The song was a hit in Italy, but my friend Cristoforo gave it a brutally honest assessment: "We applaud Cher for her attempt to sing in Italian, but her accent makes her sound very much like an Albanian prostitute." Somehow, I think Cher would be amused by that comparison.

Eros Ramazzotti in concert.

Since my first road trip in Italy, I've listened to Radio Italia, a station that plays only Italian pop music. I discovered a number of musical artists that caught my ear right from the start, but in particular, two singers became favorites: Eros Ramazzotti and Laura Pausini. With careers spanning over thirty years, they are arguably among the most famous entertainers in Italy, but also have large followings outside Italy too, as they release their albums in both Italian and Spanish language versions. I've seen both of them in concert and own all of their music, but most of my younger Italian friends aren't fans. I once asked Cristoforo if he'd purchase a ticket for me to an upcoming concert by Eros when I wasn't able to do so online. He agreed, but with the stipulation, "When I buy the ticket, I will tell them that it is not for me, because I don't want anyone to think that I would ever go to an Eros Ramazzotti concert!"

Eros has a distinctive, somewhat nasal voice that people seem either to love or hate, but I think he's an amazing singer/songwriter. I recall talking about music with our Italian guide on a study abroad trip; when I mentioned Eros, she exclaimed, "*Ah, la voce brutta!*" (The ugly voice!) Grimacing, she continued, "No! You mustn't like him! He's too sentimental and he sings always about love! I hate this!" Then she added, "But please don't tell me that you also like Laura Pausini!" Busted. Strike two! She shook her head in disgust. "Both of them depress me! They are always in love! Then they fall out of love, but they still want to be in love, then they find another love, but they know it can never work. I hate this!" Well, I couldn't argue with someone who hates love, but I can safely say, I love Eros Ramazzotti.

Naples: "They Won't Kill You; They'll Just Rob You"

Three hours south of Rome lies a totally different world, far removed from the rest of Italy. It's called Napoli, Europe's most densely populated metropolitan area. It also has the dubious honor of being the city with the highest crime rate. Napoli lies in the shadow of one of the world's most dangerous volcanoes: Vesuvius. Nearby, the ancient ruins of Pompeii and Herculaneum, cities destroyed in the famous eruption of 79AD, have been rebuilt and renamed: Pompei and Ercolano, just two of the dozens of communities that lie at the base of the volcano. The area is rather shabby and chaotic, not terribly affluent, and has traffic that must be seen to be believed, yet while conducting my research in this area, I fell in love with these cities and the earthy, friendly people I met here.

During our month-long stay in the area for the research project, my colleague Tullio and I found a gelato shop in one of the towns on the slopes of Vesuvius. We stopped by each afternoon for a refreshing ice cream break before continuing our work and got to know the owner, Sandro. He didn't speak English, so I tried to converse in Italian, which was challenging; people here speak a Neapolitan dialect characterized by lots of B and SH sounds not commonly heard in standard Italian. Many words in the dialect sounded to me like, "Bushta, bushta!" I made Tullio laugh several times as my imitation of the general sound of the dialect was evidently spot on.

On a visit to the area years later, Sandro invited me to dinner at his home, and despite my misgivings about how we'd communicate for an entire evening, I gratefully accepted. When I arrived, Sandro immediately warned his daughter and four sons, *"Parlate Italiano, non Napoletano!"* (Speak Italian, not Neapolitan!), and as he did so he gave one of the older boys a playful smack on the back of the head. Every so often one of the boys forgot the rules and received a smack on the head from either Sandro or one of the other children, accompanied by emphatic shouts of what sounded like "Bushta, bushta!" I sipped my wine and tried not to laugh, but the scene was like something out of a comedy skit.

Naples and Vesuvius.

There was so much head-smacking and so many shouts of "Bushta, bushta!" at the table that evening it was hard to focus, but I did manage to speak with Sandro's wife a bit. She seemed nervous about living so close to Vesuvius, and at one point asked, in Italian of course, "When will Vesuvio erupt again?" Of course, no one knows, but I playfully responded with, "*Forse tra cento anni... o forse domani!*" (Maybe in 100 years or maybe tomorrow!) Her eyes widened and I instantly realized that I'd made a big mistake joking about this issue with her. Throughout the rest of the evening, amidst more shouts of "Bushta, bushta!" and the never-ending smacking of heads, she'd lock eyes with me and ask, "*Domani? Veramente?*" (Tomorrow? Really?) At that point I wanted to smack myself on the head for freaking this poor woman out! Contrary to the stereotype that people here are in denial about their risk, my research and my conversations with locals indicated that they're well aware of the danger. Of course, for most of them, this is the only home they've ever known, and since Vesuvius has been dormant since 1944, an eruption isn't something they worry about on a daily basis; life's everyday problems take precedence most of the time.

After dinner, Sandro's oldest son, Roberto, who speaks English fluently, drove me back to Naples. As we descended from the slopes of Vesuvius, many small fireworks displays were going off across the entire region. I asked what the occasion was, and Roberto said, "It's like this each night. Either someone is having a birthday, someone is getting married, or someone just got out of prison." I checked his face and saw that he was completely serious. Then he added, "It's usually the third reason."

I've stayed in Naples itself several times and I recall walking through a busy zone pedestrian one evening with Tullio and a friend of his who lived in Naples. "That looks like an interesting area to explore." I said, pointing to neighborhoods perched on the hills above us. Tullio laughed and said, "That is one of the most dangerous areas in Napoli. You could be killed ten minutes after you climbed the stairways to get up there!" But Tullio's friend scoffed and said, "No! They won't kill you! They'll just rob you!" Now that is a slogan the city of Naples might not want to include in tourist brochures.

While attending a conference in the city, I needed to get to a meeting and decided to hop on the Metro train, momentarily forgetting I was in Napoli where chaos reigns and nothing works as it should. The train station was completely deserted, and there was only one automated ticket machine. I selected English to conduct the transaction and tried to purchase my ticket. A loud, metallic, heavily accented female voice shouted at me: "You are advised to be at all times aware of the presence of PEEK-A-POCKETS!" This warning reverberated throughout the empty station, and I ruefully thought, "Great, now every pickpocket within a three-block radius knows exactly where I am!" I climbed multiple flights of stairs in stifling heat and humidity to get to the train platform because every escalator was blocked by signs reading, *Fuori*

Servizio (out of service) and the signs looked as if they'd been there since the 79AD eruption of Vesuvius! I then waited almost forty minutes for a train to arrive; it honestly would have been simpler and faster to have walked.

On another evening I entered a Metro station to find the only two ticket machines adorned with the dreaded *Fuori Servizio* signs; how could I buy a ticket? An older woman faced the same dilemma, so we approached the ticket office. There was a transit worker inside, but she was busy smoking and chatting on her phone. I waited politely to be acknowledged, but the Italian woman had no such reservations, pounding on the window and forcing the employee to interrupt her phone call. She rudely informed us that the office was closed, and she had no tickets to sell.

My new friend motioned for me to follow her down a long hallway where we found a decrepit ticket machine that looked like it hadn't been used in years. She indicated that we could get a ticket here, so I took out my loose change and she carefully selected coins, counting them aloud to reach the required fare. She put the coins into the machine, which promptly spat them all out. She replaced them in my hand and selected others, again counting out loud as if to assure me that she wasn't trying to cheat me. This time the machine accepted all but one coin. She rubbed it several times with a napkin, scraped it against the side of the machine, then redeposited it and *voila* (or as they say in Italy, *ecco*); a ticket slowly printed, and she handed it to me with a triumphant smile.

Allora...

Allora is one of my favorite Italian expressions, and is a word frequently used to begin a sentence or before sharing a thought or observation. Its closest English equivalent might be, "And so..." or "Well then..." Allora... what else can I tell you about Italy? What comes to mind when I think about her?

Gelato and homemade pasta, two of Italy's greatest gifts.

Italy is horn-honking, boisterous, manic celebrations that clog Roman streets when the regional soccer team wins. It's also the silent alleys of Venice at night when all you hear is the gentle lapping of water in the canals and the echo of your own footsteps on brick. It's the smell of oranges and lemons in the Cinque Terre and on the Amalfi Coast, the intense flavors of blueberry, melon, or dark chocolate gelato, and the amazing comfort that results from a bowl of homemade pasta.

Italy is breathtaking vistas of red poppies and deep green poplar trees that adorn the Tuscan countryside. Italy is ancient hill towns made of stone or colorful fishing villages perched precariously above the Mediterranean. And most of all, it's the warm, generous people who have welcomed me, treated me like family, and made me feel that I have a second home. Allora... this is Italy.

Sunset over Venice and her quiet streets by night.

10. Where English Seems Like a Foreign Language

GREAT BRITAIN

The Dark Hedges: Northern Ireland

Scotland: I'm Not Sure Stanislaw is a Member of My Clan

My first trip abroad was in the summer of 1986 when I visited England, Scotland, Paris, and Amsterdam. I was in graduate school then, traveling on a shoestring budget, but it opened the door to international travel for me. During the trip I met up with my friend Carol and we drove through northern England and Scotland. Though it was a brief stay, I associated Scotland with rolling green hills, rainbows, more sheep than you could count, and hospitable people with a wry sense of humor.

One British custom that Carol and I adopted wholeheartedly was breaking for afternoon tea and scones and one day we found ourselves in a mad rush to get to a place for tea before the shop closed at 5PM. We saw an older man walking along the road and though I rarely stop to ask for directions, I pulled over to ask him the quickest way to get to the tea shop. He pondered the question a moment and in a heavy Scottish brogue, rolling his r's to the point where it sounded almost like parody, he said, "Ah, but you've passed the rrroad you needed to take! Oh my, what can we do?" He thought long and hard as the time crept ever closer to 5PM. "You need to take this rrroad a wee bit further into town, but at the firrrst stop sign you'll want to go rrright. Don't go left! Go rrright! After a bit you'll see a wee, white church. At the church make a left. Don't go rrright! Follow that strrraight to the town squarrre. At the squarrre, go rrright. Don't go left! And in a mile or so you'll see the place on your rrright."

As the man spoke, it took everything we had to keep from laughing, because his directions and his accent were hilarious, but he was so earnest and sincere in trying to help us that the last thing we wanted was to hurt his feelings. I looked at Carol tentatively, asking if she'd remember all this; her voice said yes, but her eyes looked frantically into mine saying, "No! No!".

We thanked the man, but before I could pull away, he called out, "Wait!" Leaning into my window, he said, "Orrr... you might go back the way you came and when you see the wee stone church, go left. Don't go rrright! Then a mile, no, maybe two miles further along there's a road on the rrright, but don't go rrright. Just keep strrraight on..." I honestly felt like we were trapped in a comedy skit. I assured the man that we'd try the first route he'd suggested and thanked him profusely for his "help". We laughed until we cried, but we did reach our destination in time to slather some clotted cream and raspberry jam over our warm scones.

In 2008, twenty-two years later I returned to Scotland as part of a longer Europe trip. I was flying from Venice to London and London to Glasgow, but a gigantic monkey wrench was thrown into my plans when my flight to London was delayed six hours, causing me to miss my connecting flight to Glasgow. Like a row of dominoes my schedule toppled piece by piece. I had to pay a hefty penalty for missing my Glasgow flight and book a new one for 9:30PM. I called the rental car company in Glasgow to inform them of the late arrival and then called the owner of the B&B where I was staying north of Glasgow. She said she'd leave the door to my cottage unlocked, so I'd be OK no matter when I arrived. In other words, she'd see me when she saw me!

First visit to Scotland... castles and cream teas.

I got to Glasgow at 11PM, grabbed my bag and ran straight to the rental car office, then departed the airport bound for my B&B, exhausted, but thankful to be in Scotland and to know I had a bed waiting for me, even though it was a two-hour drive away - or so I thought. Forty minutes out of Glasgow, the A82 motorway was closed to traffic. A workman sat in a truck, blocking the way, so I wearily got out and asked how I could get to Glencoe given the road closure. He responded in the famous Glaswegian accent, known even among the British as among the most difficult to decipher. It was so heavy that I understood only three concepts: turn rrright (My mind inserted, "Don't go left!"), then turn left at some point ("Don't go rrright!"), and then follow signs toward Tyndrum. This detour added an hour to my trip, but I eventually found Tyndrum, and got back on A82 only to encounter many flashing lights and a long line of stopped cars with their engines turned off. A redheaded policeman who could have been a cousin of mine came to my window telling me to turn off my engine. A mobile crane had gone off the road ahead and workers were attempting to get it removed. I think he said they hoped to reopen the road soon, but he had a Glaswegian accent too! Ninety minutes later the road finally reopened, and I reached the B&B at 3:30AM. I stumbled from the car, found the unlocked door to my cottage, and collapsed onto the bed, falling into a dead sleep instantly. The total travel time since leaving my Venice hotel: twenty-one hours!

I woke a few hours later and I honestly had no idea where I was. I'd been traveling across Europe for almost three weeks, and after the nightmarish travel delays and my extreme fatigue I felt like a character in a bad soap opera, waking from a coma with a case of amnesia. I lay in bed trying to remember where I was. Ah yes, I'd arrived in the wee hours of the morning, found an unlocked door to a cottage in the woods; a note with my name on it was pinned to the door. As I tried to piece together my memories, I heard people talking softly outside my door, but couldn't understand them. Was it Italian I heard? Was I still in Venice? No, it definitely wasn't Italian. Wait, was it the Venetian dialect? No, that wasn't it either. As my brain fog cleared, I remembered I was in Scotland! Was I hearing English being spoken in that almost unintelligible Glasgow accent? But I couldn't understand even one word. Was it Gaelic?

I got up and headed toward the bathroom to splash some water on my face and had a flashback to a famous scene from TV's *Dallas*. One morning Pam Ewing woke to the sound of running water in the bathroom and found her dead husband Bobby, alive and well, casually showering and leaving her shaken and speechless. The explanation: Pam had awakened from a bad dream and none of the events of the show's prior season had ever happened. Gosh, I miss *Dallas*! Anyway, Bobby Ewing was not in my shower, so at least I knew I wasn't in Texas. I threw on some clothes and ventured out to the common area of the cottage where I met a man who introduced himself as Stanislaw.

Stanislaw? That didn't sound like a member of some Scottish clan. I'd heard of Scottish names like Hamish, Gwyn, or Gareth, but this was a new one. The mystery was finally solved when Stanislaw, the B&B's

on-site host, explained that he was from Poland. Soon his wife Luisa appeared, also Polish, but fluent in Italian, so I began to get my linguistic bearings again. They cooked me a huge breakfast and we had a good chat. Stanislaw shared a humorous story about his early days in Scotland as he was learning English. He was speaking to one of the guests at the B&B who found his Polish-accented English unfathomable. The exasperated guest said, "I'd heard about the Glaswegian accent, but this is ridiculous!"

After breakfast I continued north toward the Isle of Skye. Since I'd arrived in the dark, it was nice to see the countryside by the light of day. I found myself in an emerald green, heavily forested landscape punctuated by placid blue lakes (*lochs*) that reflected beautiful, barren green mountains. I kept entertained on the drive listening to bagpipe music on Radio Gaelic; the DJs on that station might as well have been speaking Polish, as Gaelic sounded just as foreign to me.

I found my B&B, set high on a bluff overlooking the sea, some nearby islands, and far-off mountains. I was greeted by my hosts, John and Pam, settled into a comfortable room, then headed out to explore. Driving south toward Elgol the scenery was nothing short of spectacular. I found a parking lot at a trailhead and decided to hike to the top of one of the nearby small mountains to watch the sunset. I wasn't sure how long my hike might take, so I fortified myself with a bag of Scottish shortbread cookies and a basket of fresh raspberries I'd picked up along the way.

It was a fairly strenuous uphill trek, but I did pretty well. Guideposts said it was two and a half miles to my destination and within an hour I was approaching the top of the ridge. The sky to the west was cloudy, but the sun peeked through, causing rays of light to strike random patches of the mountains, lighting them up in countless shades of green. At the top I was treated to one of the most beautiful views I've ever seen. To the south, dramatic cliffs overlooked the sea, and I could see far-off islands. West, across a narrow bay were rugged shoulders of mountains, looking almost black because they were backlit by the sun. To the north the magnificent, stark Cuillen Mountains loomed in the distance, while closer to me was a deep blue loch and more green hills dotted with white sheep. Many of the hills had waterfalls pouring down their slopes, and even from a mile away I could hear the sound of the rushing water. I sat there for almost an hour, not seeing another soul, taking in this amazing panorama. I chuckled, thinking that if Heaven doesn't look like this, it will be a disappointment.

A glimpse of Heaven? The Isle of Skye.

Unfortunately, like a flashback to my adventures in Tahiti, the other guests at the B&B were French and spoke no English. I've studied French for more years than any other language, but after three years of focusing on Italian, I barely remembered anything in French past *merci* and *bonjour*. I sat with the French group at breakfast, and it was a bit uncomfortable given the language barrier that separated us. I noticed that they didn't even speak much amongst themselves, so I dined in awkward silence until one of our hosts would burst into the room to offer us more coffee or toast. They tried speaking French to their guests, but with horrible accents. Granted, I couldn't remember my French tenses or vocabulary, but I do know how to pronounce *Bonjour!* John mangled even that, making it sound like BON-jer!

I dined on a beautiful platter of smoked salmon and scrambled eggs, with hearty bread and great coffee, but the French folks had ordered the Scottish breakfast: eggs, ham, sausage, soggy cooked tomatoes, and blood pudding. They kept looking over at me, eyeing my eggs and salmon with obvious envy. I suspected that the hosts hadn't clearly communicated to them that salmon and eggs was a breakfast choice. I smiled and mustered at least one French phrase: "*Le saumon est tres bon!*" (The salmon is very good!) They glared at me; they had pushed their sausages and ham to the side of their plates and one woman pointed to her meat, saying, "*pour les chiens*" (for the dogs). I made sure to order the salmon again the next morning!

I spent a leisurely day driving and exploring the Isle of Skye, covering almost every mile of the roads there. Nothing quite rivaled the beauty of my hike the night before, but it is a beautiful place with strange, brooding mountains, and lots of dark, volcanic rock covered in greenery and sheep. One highlight of the day was a hike to Coral Beach, a series of beautiful white sandy coves and aqua water that looked like a Caribbean island except for the presence of cattle and sheep on the beach. The weather was overcast, but as I climbed a bluff overlooking the beach, the sun lit the scene beautifully. Along the trail I overheard some hikers speaking a familiar language. Glaswegian? Polish? No, Italian! They seemed shocked when I said, *Buongiorno!* and began a conversation. "But, why do you know Italian? It's not common for anyone to speak it outside Italy!" True, but of course they couldn't begin to fathom just how much I love their country.

I had a delicious dinner in a seaside hamlet called Stein: a slab of fresh halibut, potatoes, veggies, and sun-dried tomato soup. When I returned to the B&B, John and Pam invited me to join them for a glass of Scotch whisky. I'm not much of a drinker, but I must say this stuff was very smooth and tasty. John claimed it was the best in Scotland. They were welcoming hosts, though both seemed a bit nervous, perhaps in response to their brooding French guests. Still, they were welcoming and helpful, fed me smoked salmon and good whisky, so I had no complaints.

I reluctantly left Skye and stopped for a contemplative hike at the ruins of Kilchurn Castle, built in the 1400s near Glencoe. I had the entire place to myself, allowing my mind to wander and wonder who'd lived there in the past and what might have happened within its walls. For lunch I stopped at an organic food restaurant near Tyndrum, where I had possibly the best fish and chips of my life. One of the young guys working behind the counter looked over and spoke to me, but I didn't understand one word. I asked him to repeat himself. To my ear it sounded like, "Ah who ya busta fret in a whore day?" Hmmm. This wasn't Italian, nor the Neapolitan dialect, though it sounded a little like "Bushta! Bushta!" Not Gaelic, nor Polish...it was that strange form of English only spoken near Glasgow! I was embarrassed because I hadn't a clue what he'd said to me. Finally, a co-worker with a far less pronounced accent saved me. "He's asking you if you're here on holiday." Ahhh! First contact established! I smiled, said yes, and told him where I was from. After that I have absolutely no idea what else he said for the next three, uncomfortable minutes as I waited for my order, but he certainly was friendly and jovial.

I thought I'd leave you to ponder this thought-provoking Scottish proverb that perhaps you can apply in your own life: "Woo din ya gut da radushta!" Didn't understand that? Well, neither did I, but now you've had just a little taste of Glasgow!

Northern Ireland: Land of the Giants

One of my dearest friends is Maggi, a 92-year-old woman I met in college in 1976. Maggi was born in Belfast, Northern Island, but married an American and moved to Massachusetts in the 1950s. She was a rather famous storyteller in her younger days, performing traditional folk tales as well as sentimental, thought-provoking reminiscences about her Belfast childhood. At the age of forty-four, Maggi decided to earn a bachelor's degree in German; I was an eighteen-year-old Psychology major fresh out of high school. We met in our Freshman English class and became close friends, despite our different ages and backgrounds.

Because of our friendship, I probably know more Irish dialect than most Americans, and have adopted many terms because no other word quite captures the sentiment they convey. Foolish, stupid, or annoying people are *gormless, bloody nits, eejits,* or *right gits.* If you're disgusted with something you want to *boke* (gag or vomit), a gossipy conversation is a good *craic,* and of course adjectives like *bloody, bleeding,* and *flaming* are generously sprinkled into any description. Though I'd visited England, Scotland, and Ireland before, I'd never seen Northern Ireland, but in 2011 as part of a longer trip in Europe, I decided to explore Maggi's homeland.

I flew into Dublin in the Republic of Ireland and drove north from there, assuming that when I crossed into Northern Ireland, or Ulster as it is also called, there'd be a border crossing of some kind, since Ulster, like Scotland and Wales is part of the United Kingdom. But I only realized I'd crossed the border when I noticed that houses in the little towns I was passing were flying the British Union Jack flag. I exited the highway in the border town of Armagh to get cash, since Euros are used in Ireland, but British Pounds are needed in Northern Ireland.

The first items on my to-do list were visits to the Breaghmore Stone Circles and Legananny Dolmen, ancient sites reminiscent of Stonehenge, but not nearly as big. The Dolmen was easy to find and was a popular attraction, but not so the Stone Circles. Though they appeared on my map, there was no visible road leading to them, so I surmised that maybe I'd have to hike to them. I started driving in that general direction on narrow one- lane roads, often being startled by a fast-approaching truck coming at me from the opposite direction and requiring me to rapidly throw the car into reverse and back up to allow it to pass.

I stopped at a small store to ask for directions and was amused by the responses. Although I knew I was within five minutes of these bleeding, flaming stone circles, people acted as if I were asking them for directions to Mars and some said they'd never even heard of the place. Eventually I found someone who said I was on the correct road, so I pressed on and finally saw a sign: "Breaghmore Circles, 2.5"! I drove two and a half kilometers, but saw only farms, cows, and sheep. When I'd gone three kilometers, I figured I'd passed them, so I turned around and slowly backtracked. Nothing!

Really frustrated now, as directions have always been my forte, I flagged down a passing truck and asked the guy if he knew where the stone circles were. I couldn't tell if he was trying to help me or tease me; he seemed to take some pleasure from my predicament, but he did try to steer me in the right direction. Despite decades of practice listening to Maggi's Ulster accent I understood one of every three words he said, though he was a wee bit easier to understand than some of the folks I'd encountered back in Scotland. He indicated that the stone circles were further along the road in the direction I'd been going. As I headed that way it suddenly dawned on me that because I was now in the United

Kingdom, they use miles here, not kilometers. My car was from Ireland; therefore, its odometer measured in kilometers. I'd only gone two and a half kilometers but needed to go two and a half miles! Sure enough, I finally found the circles, and while they were not exactly Stonehenge, they were worth the effort I'd invested to get there, and I had them all to myself. Perhaps no other tourists had been able to find them!

My storytelling friend, Maggi.

From there I headed for the northern coast, and along the way listened to one of Maggi's storytelling CDs I'd brought with me. It was almost like having her riding in the passenger seat beside me. I listened with great interest to the traditional folk tale about Finn McCool, an Irish giant who was always squabbling with a Scottish giant across the sea. My destination that day was Giant's Causeway, a major tourist attraction and World Heritage Preservation site. The Causeway is a geological formation created sixty million years ago when volcanic flows met cool sea water, causing the lava to harden quickly and form peculiar hexagonal columns. However, if you prefer to believe the folk tale, the Causeway is a remnant of a giant bridge built by Finn McCool in order to reach Scotland and attack the Scottish giant. Unfortunately for Finn, the Scottish Giant was tougher than he'd bargained for, so Finn quickly retreated back to Ireland. His wife dressed him like a baby to fool the angry Scottish giant, who, seeing how big this baby was, decided he didn't want to fight its dad. He returned to Scotland and peace ensued.

I stayed at a B&B located close to the Causeway, and met my charming and funny redheaded hostess, Maureen who urged me to hike to the Causeway before it got dark. Because I was staying at this B&B I didn't have to pay to park in the huge lots down the road. Instead, I had access to a private path leading to the top of the cliffs, and down a stairway to the formation. From the cliff's edge, the Causeway below looked unimpressive, but there were magnificent views of the coast. I loved the fact that there were virtually no tourists here this late in the day, so all I could hear as I walked the cliff path were the sounds of seabirds, pounding surf, and my own footsteps. Occasionally the sun broke through the clouds and lit up a hillside and I nearly had to squint and shield my eyes from the intense green color, so common in places with rich volcanic soil like Scotland, Iceland, and Hawaii.

Once I reached the Causeway, I saw what all the fuss was about. This formation looks like a cobblestone bridge jutting out onto the ocean. Looking down at it, the tops of the hexagonal columns form a honeycomb pattern; from the side, the columns vary in height and look like a tightly packed city skyline. You can use the columns just like a stairway to walk up and down the formation. It was otherworldly. I was again grateful for the solitude, because the following morning as I left the B&B, dozens of tour buses were bearing down on the parking lot; I'm sure it would have been a very different experience with hundreds of tourists swarming the place!

The Giant's Causeway

I walked back to the B&B then drove to the nearby Bushmills Inn, a charming, elegant restaurant for dinner. I ordered lamb served with *champ*, a Northern Irish version of buttery, creamy mashed potatoes, and a basket of delicious, warm Irish brown bread. I finished the meal with an Irish coffee, spiked with the Bushmills whiskey made nearby at the oldest whiskey distillery in the world. It was an almost perfect meal, marred by the presence of four men in their early sixties seated near me.

In this classy, upscale establishment, these *gormless eejits* were engaging in inappropriately loud conversation laced with lots of foul language. Unfortunately, they were fellow Americans, and one loudly complained, "I can't believe they don't take f'n American dollars here!" It took all my self-control not to scream, "If someone tried to pay you in British Pounds in New Jersey, would you accept those, you great, bloody *nit*?" However, I refrained, kept my cool and breathed a sigh of relief once they left me to drink my Irish coffee in peace.

That night it started pouring and when I returned to the B&B Maureen teased, "Aw, your hair's gone all rusty from being out in the rain!" In the morning, she prepared a home cooked breakfast called an Ulster Fry, consisting of fried eggs, sausage, Canadian bacon, tomato wedges, potato bread similar to hashbrowns, and Irish soda bread. It was delicious and fortified me for the day.

Former home of Sorely Boy.

I explored the nearby ruins of Dunluce Castle, which dates back to 1500 and sits on a dramatic cliff overlooking the sea. It was home to a rowdy Scotsman named Sorely Boy MacDonnell who was evidently a major thorn in the side of the English who were trying to seize this area. It must have been an amazing place to call home and like Sorely Boy, I'd have fought tooth and nail to hang onto it. Then I found my way to a weird attraction known as the Dark Hedge, a mile-long stretch of road that tunnels through some 300-year-old beech trees. It really looks like something out of the *Lord of the Rings,* and I spent a lot of time trying to capture its mystery and beauty in photos. From there I drove east and south along the Antrim Coast Road toward Belfast, stopping for a short walk on the beach at White Park Bay. I visited the ruins of 8th Century Dunseverick Castle, believed to have been destroyed by Viking raids, and then visited magical Ballintoy Harbor, a village so cute I wanted to pinch its little cheeks!

Once I got to my Belfast hotel, I made a quick call to Maggi to see what neighborhood she'd grown up in. She asked if I'd noticed the Strand Theater where she'd gone to movies as a child, and I laughed because it was literally next door to my hotel. The house she'd grown up in was five minutes away, so I drove there and found the little red brick duplex that had been her home. I strolled the neighborhood, taking a few pictures, until a woman suddenly came barreling out onto the street, demanding to know why I was taking photos of her house. I guess I'd make a lousy private detective. She calmed down once I'd introduced myself and told her what I was doing.

I had one of the best meals of my whole trip at a place called Beatrice Kennedy: apple-celery bisque, warm brown bread, roast duck breast over mashed sweet potatoes, and peas and asparagus so crispy I'm sure they'd come from someone's garden earlier that day. As if that weren't enough, I finished with a chocolate raspberry summer pudding, a cross between a sponge cake and a trifle. What a great find!

The highlight of my time in Belfast was a Black Taxi Tour of the city's segregated Protestant and Catholic neighborhoods. I'd heard, of course, about the violence that rocked Belfast from the 1960s through the 1990s when the militantly Catholic Irish Republican Army and equally militant Protestant groups waged war against one another. In my long friendship with Maggi, she rarely mentioned "The Troubles" as they are called here and wondered if it was too sensitive an issue to speak about, so I never pressed. But I was ashamed to realize how ignorant I'd been about the whole situation; the Black Taxi Tour was truly an eye-opener.

The short-hand version of what happened goes like this. When the English conquered Ireland, they outlawed Catholicism and leaders like Cromwell slaughtered entire villages of people. After centuries of conflict, persecution, and uprisings, England granted independence to most of Ireland in the early 20th century but kept six counties in the northeast under British rule. This became Northern Ireland or Ulster. Most of the people living here were Protestant and loyal to England, but there were Catholics living here too, and they had a rough time of things. My cabbie and guide, Rob took me down the Falls Road, where most of Belfast's Catholics live and then up Shankill Road, the Protestant area. Factories and linen mills located between the two neighborhoods had two entrances: one on the Protestant side and one on the Catholic side. Workers enter through their own doors, work together all day, and then leave through different exits.

Homes along the Peace Wall.

Because of increasing unrest during the 1960s, with groups like the Irish Republican Army calling for Ireland to be reunited, and other groups wanting the North to remain British, a wall was built between the two areas. It was called The Peace Wall and is forty-two feet high in places. Its purpose was to keep peace between the two neighborhoods. There are gates in the wall that even now, after a couple decades of relative peace, are closed each night to avoid trouble. We visited Bombay Street, a Catholic area right beside the wall where Protestant mobs burned down several rows of houses and tried to destroy a major Catholic church, and there were murals depicting this incident. I noticed that many homes adjacent to the wall had what looked like steel batting cages in the back, completely enclosing their porches and yards. These, Rob explained, protect the houses from rocks or the occasional bombs that are lobbed over the wall from the other side! I asked if this was just a reconstruction to show what it was like during The Troubles and he laughed, "No, mostly it's just kids throwing rocks today, but these are still functioning and designed to protect the occupants." I was speechless.

Rob showed me dozens of murals on both sides of the wall. Ones on the south or Catholic side display themes demanding independence from "occupiers" by "oppressed" groups in places like Palestine, Basque Country, and Iraq. Evidently an anti-George Bush mural had just recently been painted over with an anti-Barack Obama mural, criticizing U.S. policies in Afghanistan and Libya. On the north or Protestant side of the wall, murals honored people who had murdered Catholics during the troubles.

"One man's terrorist is another man's hero," Rob said quietly. He'd been doing these tours for eight years; before that he was a cab driver, which he said was among the most dangerous occupations in Belfast during The Troubles. If a cab driver was identified as Catholic, militant Protestants called for his cab, had him drive them to a Protestant area and beat or killed him. The same thing happened with militant Catholics targeting Protestant cabbies. I never had a clue how bad things had been here, and the fact that all of this animosity was between two such similar denominations of Christianity just boggled my mind.

While there is still tension these days, Rob says it is nothing like it used to be, and thankfully, tourists are returning to Northern Ireland.

The Mournes.

From Belfast I drove south into the Mourne Mountains of County Down, an area where Maggi spent a lot of her young adulthood hiking with her sister and their friends. The Mournes cover a relatively small area, but are the highest range in Northern Ireland, barren and brooding, exuding an eerie beauty. I pulled off the road near a farmhouse to take some photos and the farmer who lived there peeked out of the barn, then came over to greet me. Like my prior interactions with the locals, I understood only about half of what he was saying to me, but it was all accompanied by a warm and friendly manner that put me at ease. When I told him about Maggi, he wiped off his hands and used my camera to take a photo of me with the Mournes in the background to show her. He insisted I walk up his steep driveway to get an even better panoramic shot from up there. He said he'd never, ever seen an American in these parts and was astounded that I even knew the

Mournes existed. At least that's what I think he said. But he was kindness itself.

Northern Ireland doesn't get the attention from tourists that its sister to the south receives, but it's a wonderful travel destination. The scenery is mind-bogglingly beautiful, the food is terrific, and the combination of a vivid and often troubled history, coupled with the warmth and friendliness of its people make it a fascinating place to visit. I actually preferred the rather staid and civilized streets of Belfast to the far more crowded and rowdy streets of Dublin in the south.

When I returned home, I shared my experiences with Maggi, who listened to my impressions with great interest. She laughed heartily about the woman who'd come out to scold me for photographing her house. "That is so typically Belfast!", she roared. Then I saw tears gather in her eyes as she studied the photos of her beloved Mourne Mountains. With a gentle sigh of resignation, she whispered, "I'll probably never see them again, but the very sight of them makes my heart full."

I uploaded a photo of the Mournes onto the desktop of Maggi's computer. Like many folks her age, she's terrified of her computer and is always getting *muddled* with regard to how to use it. But now she says that when she turns it on and sees her gorgeous Mournes, she panics just a wee bit less. And now I understand why.

England: The Battle of the Cream Teas

In 2018 I'd planned to visit London as part of a longer European trip but realized that I'd be there during the Royal Wedding, which explained the astronomical prices I was encountering for hotels. Never having been a fan of Harry and Meghan and knowing that the city would be a zoo at that time, I decided instead to explore a region I'd never seen before: the counties of Devonshire and Cornwall in far southwestern England. I didn't know much about these areas, except that they were purportedly very picturesque.

As I mentioned earlier, I'd enthusiastically embraced the custom of afternoon tea and scones during my first visit to Britain. I learned that there's a debate about whether Devon or Cornwall actually started this tradition and over which county serves a better version of a cream tea.

Furthermore, in Devonshire, the clotted cream is spread on the scone first, then topped with jam; in Cornwall, this process is reversed, with jam on the bottom and cream on the top, which seems like a totally ridiculous sticking point to me. Heavy, spreadable cream: good! Fresh berry preserves: good! As long as they're both present, who cares which one has the top bunk? At any rate, I decided that it was my duty as an impartial American descended from British heritage to help resolve the debate between these competing counties once and for all.

Along the Devonsire Coast.

Shortly after leaving the airport, the urban sprawl of London gave way to pastoral countryside, rolling hills and eventually, the stunning northern coast of Devonshire. I stopped at the charming town of Lynmouth, built along a river, with cute shops and restaurants lining the banks on one side, and parks and gardens on the other. I headed for the Lynmouth Bay Café, which I'd read was the place to go for a cream tea. I sat outside and my tea and scones were served by a jolly waitress. I'd almost forgotten how decadent Devonshire or "clotted" cream is – a hybrid between butter and heavy cream, and my scones were served with whortleberry preserves, a European cousin of blueberries. The scones were great, though you could put whortleberry preserves and clotted cream on a cracker and it'd still be good. This tea definitely gave Devon a strong start in the competition, but I had to give Cornwall its chance too.

My B&B was on a farm along a tiny country road in the town of Helston in Cornwall, and I do mean tiny. Like parts of Scotland and Ireland, this area is laced with small roads barely wide enough for a car. In most places they are bordered on both sides by six-foot walls of hedges, grasses, and wildflowers. It's beautiful until you dare sneak a glance at the flowers. Then and only then, a car is sure to speed around the next bend, coming at you like a bullet train. Often one or the other of you must back up a considerable distance to find a place to pull off and let the other pass, so it can take a while to go even a short distance, and of course there always seemed to be an impatient lunatic virtually riding in my trunk, chomping at the bit to pass me. It's a shame; the place is lovely, but it was hard to relax and enjoy it.

On my first full day in England, I visited Lizard, a ramshackle town filled with colorful houses, tourist shops and restaurants. The highlight of the day was a visit to nearby Kynance Cove, which lies beneath steep cliffs covered in bizarre rock formations. The rocks are porous and wildflowers of every color, shape, and size grow from holes or cracks in them. I hiked down to the cove on steep trails and seemingly hundreds of stairs, but it was worth it to reach the sandy beach at the bottom and hiking was far more relaxing than driving!

Kynance Cove.

I had dinner at a restaurant in Cadgwith, a tiny fishing village accessible only by hiking from a parking lot down a steep path to the seafront. It is noted for its fresh seafood and the fishermen who supply it perform sea shanties at 10PM on Fridays. Unfortunately, I couldn't get a reservation any time after 7PM, so shanties weren't in the cards for me. In hindsight, I should've skipped dinner and just come for the shanties! I ordered lobster claws for an appetizer, then fish and chips. The waitress brought my claws, asking if I knew how to open them. I laughed and said that as a New Englander, I've cracked many a lobster claw in my time. Moments later, I began to think I was on *Candid Camera*; I couldn't crack the first claw to save my life! It was as hard as a rock, the tool they provided was too small to wrap around the claw, and I wondered if this was the lobster equivalent of trick birthday candles that won't blow out. I imagined the staff back in the kitchen, "We'll show that smarty pants Yank that he doesn't know lobsters as well as he thinks he does!"

When I finally managed to break open the first claw, a veritable ocean of cold water poured out; inside were mushy, cold pieces of meat. It was absolutely awful. The second claw opened more easily, but the meat in that one was no better. While I waited for my main course, a woman who'd been sitting nearby watching my valiant struggle came to my table and whispered, "It's a good thing you didn't waste your money on the seafood chowder. It was utterly flavorless and there was barely any seafood in it! Dreadful!" And out she walked. The fish and chips arrived, and I hate to say it, but dreadful is the most apt adjective I can think of to describe it. The fish tasted fresh, but the batter was soggy and wet, as were the chips under them. Meanwhile, I overheard a couple seated near me mentioning the fish and chips. In good conscience, I had to warn them, and they looked forlorn. The husband said, "Well we were thinking about the chowder, but then we heard what that woman said to you!" We had a good laugh together, as my new friends tried to figure out what to order. Maybe everything would have tasted better if accompanied by sea shanties, but as the Scottish say, *"A hae ma doots!"* (I have my doubts!)

The next day I tried my first Cornwall tea in a small cafe along a rural road that wound through booming metropolises like Mawgan and Gweek. I was excited to see butternut squash scones on the menu; my friend Joyce has nicknamed me "Butternut" due to my love of that vegetable, so I ordered these immediately. The clotted cream and jam were spot on, and the scones tasted great, but had a crumbly consistency, disintegrating into a million pieces as I bit into them. This got very messy when the fragments were slathered in jam and cream. While I was impressed by the creative flavor, the actual result was less than stellar due to the mess factor.

I left Cornwall the next day, crossing back into Devon for a last cream tea at Royal Oak Farms in Honiton. Tea was served on the lawn, but as soon as I got a table, a family of eleven arrived and was seated near me. The waitress was overwhelmed, and I had a long wait. Close to my table a cocker spaniel named Bronte was leashed to the trunk of a tree and his owners sat a few feet behind me. They had two young children; the little girl tried to pull the tablecloth off my table twice and wandered aimlessly across the lawn, causing near accidents with waitresses bearing huge trays while her parents said nothing. The little boy, Barnaby, was also getting into all sorts of mischief and for the next thirty minutes I was forced to listen to these people, speaking in rather pretentious accents, repeating the boy's and the dog's names incessantly.

"Barnaby! I say, Barnaby, what are you doing? Are you visiting with Bronte? There's a good chap, Barnaby, because Bronte would like company. Oh, no, Barnaby, don't pull on Bronte's ears! He's not fond of that, Barnaby! No, Barnaby, don't wrap Bronte's leash around the tree. Can't you see he's choking now! Poor Bronte! Barnaby, you simply must help Bronte get untangled!" On and on this went. I contemplated cutting Bronte free with my butter knife and urging him to make a run for it.

Meanwhile, the table of eleven had grown restless, so grandma decided to play an alphabet game with the children at that table, using a voice loud enough for all of Devonshire to hear. "Now children, find something around us beginning with the letter A." The children wandered around, with grandma telling them how hot, warm, or cold they were. One of the kids thankfully found an apron rather quickly. "OK, children! Now find something that begins with the letter B!" The kids wandered everywhere as grandma continued to shout. "You're cold! You're freezing! You're in Antarctica!" After what seemed an eternity of this, I simply lost it and began laughing uncontrollably. I wanted to scream, "Hey, kids, wake up! You've got Barnaby and Bronte over here under the tree. You're on a berry farm with bowls of butter on your table! How hard can it possibly be to find a bloody B word?"

The winner: Devonshire!

Before I snapped, my cream tea arrived, and I became pleasantly distracted. This was the definitive cream tea, the one that clinched the title for County Devon as far as this judge was concerned. The scones were warm from the oven and accompanied by a huge scoop of Devonshire cream with small pots of homemade raspberry and plum preserves. I made that cream tea last as long as I could, using up all the cream and jam, eating every last scone crumb, and consuming every drop of my tea. The ballad of Barnaby and Bronte continued behind me, and the kids next to me were struggling to find a word starting with C amidst the chairs they sat in, the cups on their table, and the cream on their plates... but I was oblivious.

I left the lush Devon countryside and entered the Jurassic Coast of Dorset, so named because many fossils have been found in this area, though I think it's also because one of the famous rock formations here resembles a brontosaurus or a displaced Loch Ness Monster dipping its head into the ocean. I hiked the cliffs, sighing as I descended a trail so steep it made my shins hurt, knowing I'd have to come back up again at some point. At least I'd be working off the calories from the scones and jam. The calm and quiet of Devon and Cornwall were lost here; hundreds of tourists from all over the world screamed to one another, ventured off the path despite huge signs asking them not to trample the grass and flowers, and climbed over safety walls to take photos from precarious cliff edges that looked as crumbly as my butternut squash scone.

Dorset's Jurassic Coast

I enjoyed this little jaunt to England. Now that Prince Harry has fallen out of favor and removed himself from his Royal Family obligations, perhaps he could be replaced by another redhead who'd be happy to accept the title, "Prince of Devon" or "Duke of Devonshire." I could see myself contentedly presiding over my little corner of England, home to the best cream teas in all the land. With my newfound authority, my first acts would be to issue a royal pardon setting Bronte free from his annoying owners, to ban the name Barnaby for all eternity, and to prohibit anyone from playing the alphabet game within earshot of any other living souls.

11. Surviving the Heat, the Stairs, and the Cruise Ship Hordes

CROATIA

A beautiful panorama of Dubrovnik, Croatia

In 2016 I went on a Mediterranean cruise as part of a study abroad trip with three faculty colleagues and about twenty-five students from my university. We departed from Venice and made stops at Split and

Dubrovnik in Croatia, on to Sicily and Rome, and finally Marseille and Nice in France. We held classes for the students aboard ship and went on guided tours at various ports of call. The food was very good, it was a small ship with only 250 passengers, and it was a novel experience for me, but I learned that I never wanted to take a cruise again! I'm a very independent traveler who likes to explore a place on my own and really get a feel for it. Therefore, when our cruise director told us that after our guided tour of Dubrovnik that we'd have "ample time" to explore the city, I was excited. But subsequently, due to rough seas, ample time became about forty-five minutes; I was not happy. Nope, I'm not a cruise ship kind of guy, though I realize that for many people cruises represent an easy and safe way to explore new places.

In summer 2018, I returned to Croatia to spend some one-on-one, quality time with her. I flew from Rome to Dubrovnik and at the airport, purchased a ticket for a local shuttle bus that was to take passengers to one of three stops in the city: the bus terminal, the *Pile* Gate and the *Ploče* Gate, two entrances on opposites sides of the walled Old City. I'd booked a room in a guest house inside the walls and my hosts advised me that to avoid the most stairs in the very hilly, pedestrian-only center, I should get off at the Pile Gate and walk from there.

The drive into the city took a while; traffic on the narrow road that winds over the coastal hills was bumper to bumper, moving at a snail's pace. Finally, we saw views of the city and it looked magical: a walled city straight out of a fairytale with castles, forts, cathedrals, and a jumbled, hilly skyline of red tile roofs. A few minutes later we pulled into the bus terminal where all but ten of us hopped off. We waited as people retrieved their luggage from the storage area beneath the bus, but then the driver came back on board and told us to get off the bus; this was the last stop. We all argued that we were going to the Pile Gate or the Ploče Gate, but he scoffed at us and said buses don't go there. Some passengers were belligerent, demanding that the driver either take them to their stop or refund their money, but of course he was having none of that. I sensed that this was a battle that couldn't be won, so I quietly asked him how to get to the Pile Gate. He pointed to a bus stop far down the street and said, "Local, orange bus!" OK then. Local orange bus it was going to have to be.

The brutal heat I'd hoped I'd left behind in Rome had followed me to Dubrovnik, and before I'd dragged my roller bag half a block I was sweating and panting. I got to the bus stop and waited with what seemed to be a group of locals, but they told me I had to buy my ticket at the bus terminal, so I trudged back there to get my ticket and returned just in time to catch the "local orange bus". There were no open seats, so I stood with my bags and held on tight. The first stop was the Port, and to my amazement and horror, there must have been 100 people waiting to board our bus: cruise ship passengers heading from the port to the Old City. The doors opened and they flooded into the bus, filling every space until it was impossible to move and hard to even breathe! I thought that surely the driver would stop the crowd at some point and have them wait for the next bus, but no, they just kept coming. The heat was excruciating and the claustrophobia I didn't even know I had kicked in. Finally, the bus lurched slowly forward, up and down hills, around curves, and finally coming to a stop where this sea of humanity emptied from the bus in mere seconds. We had arrived at the Pile Gate.

I've never watched *Game of Thrones,* but I know that some pivotal scenes were filmed in Dubrovnik at the Pile Gate. Despite having almost 1300 years of history under its belt, Dubrovnik now seems to exist only for fans of this TV show. The entrance gate into the city was clogged with hundreds of tourists taking selfies and shoving their way through the crowd, making it difficult for me to navigate my roller bag though the bottleneck that the gate creates. Once I reached the wide, pedestrian-only main street, the *Stradun,* things weren't much better. It was hotter than the planet Mercury in summertime; hundreds of tourists wandered aimlessly down the streets, stopping abruptly in front of me to take a spontaneous selfie, shoving me, hitting me in the face with backpacks when they made a turn, or walking directly into me because they were staring into their phones. I couldn't believe what a zoo it was.

This experience made me question my feelings about cruise ship travel in general. I'm very familiar with the plight of Venice, where hordes of cruise ship passengers make areas around the Rialto and San Marco almost impassable during the day. At least in Venice it's possible to escape to quieter neighborhoods at these times and return in the evening when the passengers have returned to their ships. In Dubrovnik the very small Old Town is surrounded by a wall, making it feel hotter and even more cramped. Some argue that cruise ships help local economies, but I've read articles that claim that because cruise ship passengers eat meals aboard ship, they don't patronize local restaurants except for fast food snacks or ice cream. In Venice, while hotel guests or apartment renters pay a city tax for each night's lodgings, cruise ship folks pay nothing, yet thousands of them strain city services throughout the day as they swarm to buy mostly Chinese-made souvenirs that say, "I Love Venice!" One Venetian shop keeper I'd purchased something from emphasized that what I'd bought was made in Italy and complained that most tourists just want cheap, foreign-made trinkets. Two years ago, a cruise ship rammed into one of Venice's piers, injuring a number of people and re-igniting the controversy about whether these ships are a blessing or a curse to the city. I don't know what the answer is, but I can say that the crowds I dealt with in Dubrovnik were worse than anything I've experienced in Venice.

After fighting the hordes under the broiling sun on the sweltering Stradun, I turned off onto a narrow, shady passageway that led toward my guesthouse. Though the crowds had thinned, a worse fate awaited: stairs. Lots of stairs. Guidebooks say that there is a total of 4,343 stairs in Dubrovnik's Old City, and I was face to face with a flight of them that looked like it had no end. Before I'd even climbed a dozen stairs I was soaked in sweat and mentally berating myself for my foolish decision to stay anywhere that required such a climb. These were uneven stone steps of varying heights, some probably as much as ten inches high, so it was very slow going as I dragged myself and my bag up one step at a time. Another flight of fifteen steps and I truly thought I was going to die.

"So, this is where it all ends, Matt," I thought to myself. "Dead in a pool of sweat on a stone stairway in Dubrovnik. Who'd have guessed?"

Suddenly a huge group of people led by a tour guide overtook me. I tried to get out of their way, but one of the young male tour leaders grabbed one end of my bag saying, "I'll help you, don't worry!" It was a godsend, but although he was sharing my burden, he was an athletic, young man bounding up the stairs at lightning speed, and after maybe thirty steps, I couldn't keep up. I begged him to stop, not wanting to hold him back, so I thanked him profusely and told him to go without me.

I seriously considered just leaving the bag behind...

In all, I climbed about 150 stairs; it felt like 1500. I found the guest-house and let myself in with a code the hosts had provided via e-mail. Inside was a note with my room assignment and keys, and I let out an exhausted laugh as I faced another flight of stairs leading to my room. Thank God I was only one floor up, another ten stairs, but I honestly don't think I could have climbed one more. I opened the door, walked straight to the air conditioner, and cranked it up to create a habitat suitable for a polar bear. I drank about five glasses of water, shed my clothes, and took a long cold shower, then threw myself down on the bed wondering if I'd even have the strength to leave my room for the next two days! The mere idea of climbing any more stairs filled me with dread.

I eventually emerged from my polar cave late in the afternoon and ventured out into the city, knowing that every step down meant I'd be having to come back up later, but at least I wouldn't have to do it with a suitcase again. I dined at a restaurant overlooking the harbor, watching glass bottomed boats, a pirate ship, and even a yellow submarine returning to their docks. Unfortunately, I had a rather terse waiter, which was especially disappointing because other waiters and waitresses were serving tables near me and were funny and talkative. Mine just scowled and tried to take dishes away before I'd even finished my food! At least it was a tasty meal of steamed mussels and seafood risotto. After dinner, even in the dark the streets were still hot and very crowded. After my arduous arrival, I was exhausted, so I retreated to my air-conditioned room and fell into a stair-climbing induced coma. I didn't count sheep that night; I counted stone stairs!

One of the most popular tourist activities in Dubrovnik is to walk the city walls, but the more I read about it online and talked to other tourists, the less enthusiastic I became. First, you're out in the sun the entire time, as there is no shade atop the walls. Second, unless you go between 8AM and 10AM, you're surrounded by the cruise ship hordes, and third, the price for all this fun was twenty-five Euros. It didn't sound that appealing. Instead, I slept in, then took myself to a delicious lunch at a quiet restaurant called Azur, featuring an Asian – East European fusion cuisine they called "Cro-Asian."

After an exceptional lunch, I walked through the city, out the Ploče Gate and arrived at Banje Beach fifteen minutes later. It was ridiculously hot, so without hesitation I decided to rent a lounge chair and umbrella, regardless of the cost. I sat in the shade of my umbrella at the water's edge, periodically soaking in the refreshingly cool Adriatic. Croatia has few sandy beaches; most are pebbled, like Banje, but some have concrete walls with a ladder providing access into the water. The sea that day was very calm, and the water crystal clear, like being in a pool, except for small fish persistently nibbling my leg hairs. It was a perfect way to spend a scorching afternoon.

Seeing Dubrovnik now it's hard to imagine that between 1991 and 1995 it was the scene of some of the ugliest battles in what the Croats call the "Homeland War." As the Soviet Union collapsed, its former satellite nations gradually began to regain their freedom. Croatia declared its independence from the Socialist Republic of Yugoslavia, which had been pieced together after World War II from the states of Serbia, Croatia, Slovenia, Macedonia Montenegro, and Bosnia-Herzegovina. When Croatia tried to break free, it found itself at war with former Yugoslav forces and ethnic Serbs living in parts of Croatia, resulting in the deaths of about 20,000 people and serious damage to the country's infrastructure.

For several months in 1991 and 1992, Dubrovnik was the target of attacks from the sea, the air, and the surrounding mountains and there was extensive damage within the Old City. Many buildings were hit in these attacks and today as you look down on the tile roofs of the Old City, you notice two colors: lighter colored, original tiles and brighter red tiles that indicate restored, post-war roofs. A local museum displays sobering photos of ruined store fronts along the completely abandoned Stradun, and video footage taken during the battle shows explosions throughout the Old City and the harbor, including directly in front of the restaurant where I'd dined on my first night. It was all just so hard to imagine.

On my third day in Croatia, I was leaving Dubrovnik and had to get myself to a local rental car office. First, I faced the obstacle of going down all the stairs I'd climbed when I arrived, though at least gravity would be on my side for this journey. Once at the Pile Gate, my GPS said that the rental car office was half a mile away. I called the rental company and asked if there was a local bus that goes to their office, and they said there was not. When I asked whether it was an easy walk, the genial man laughed and said, "It's all uphill." As I stood outside the Pile Gate, sweat dripping off my face even at 9:30AM, cruise ship passengers swarming around me like bees pissed off because I'd just bumped into their hive, I made a quick decision and ran to the taxicab stand; it was some of the best money I've ever spent.

The car rental staff were friendly and funny, upgrading me to a brand-new Opel Corsa; it was nice, but truly all I cared about was a car with an efficient air conditioner! My first destination was Mt. Srd (I'd like to buy a vowel...), a 1300-foot mountain overlooking Dubrovnik and home to a Napoleonic fort and a swanky restaurant. A cable car used to travel to the summit from just outside the Old City, but evidently, it's been closed for a couple years due to some legal issues. It's a shame, as the only way to get there now is a very strenuous hike, an expensive taxi ride, or in a rental car. The drive to the summit took almost half an hour; the road was extremely rugged, with huge rocks and potholes, and narrow areas where cars coming in opposite directions had to carefully maneuver past each other. The scenery, when I could take my eyes off the road, was magnificent, with abundant wildflowers, picturesque farms, and spectacular views of Dubrovnik and the nearby island of Lokrum.

I finally made it to the top and dined at the aptly-named Panorama Restaurant for lunch, enjoying a grilled chicken sandwich, sweet potato fries, and a million-dollar view of the Old City far below me. Mt. Srd was the scene of much of the bombing that took place during the Homeland War, and there was damage to Napoleon's fortress, a huge TV antenna, and the now closed cable car. The mountain served as an ideal base from which to reign fire down upon the city, and a museum at the summit features photos from the war.

The Old City from Mt. Srd; a daredevil greets Lokrum Island.

After another nail-biting drive down from the summit, I headed up Highway 8, which skirts the beautiful coastline for almost the entire length of the country. There was a mountainous interior to the east and a patchwork of vineyards, fields, and deep blue bays to the west. About an hour north of Dubrovnik a ten-mile strip of Bosnia-Herzegovina cuts through Croatia, requiring stops at two border stations for passport checks.

I spent a night in the small coastal town of Drašnice at a B&B run by a Croatian woman who was also a professor of English and Italian. I loved my apartment, which had a first-class air conditioner, a parking space right out front, and was located about ten steps away from the Adriatic on a beautiful beach. I had a nice swim before going to dinner in nearby Podgora, a resort town with a lively boardwalk lined with restaurants and bars. I dined at the water's edge and enjoyed the sunset while dining on good, but seriously overpriced food. I'd been under the impression that Croatia was an economical travel destination, but it seems it's been discovered, with prices similar to France or Italy.

The next day I continued up the coast, skirting the city of Split and continuing north to my stop for that night, a B&B in Privlaka, twenty minutes past the coastal city of Zadar. Although this property was lovely, a villa with beautiful gardens, it fronted an unusual stretch of coastline that unlike most of the beaches in Croatia, was shallow and muddy. It wasn't very appealing at all; you'd have to walk in knee-deep muddy water for quite some time just to reach a place where it was possible to swim. My room was stiflingly hot, so I promptly turned on the small air conditioning unit, anticipating a burst of refreshingly cool air. Instead, the fan had less force than a hummingbird's wings, and in terms of cool air, I'd have been better off opening the small refrigerator and sitting in front of it. It was pathetic! I closed the windows and drapes and left the air conditioning on while I was out in hopes that when I returned, the room would be a bit more comfortable.

Pag Island vista.

I drove about forty minutes further north to Pag Island, a much-photographed barren landscape that resembles the surface of the moon, if the moon had any bodies of water on it. At the bridge leading to the island, there was a small refreshment stand and I hadn't had lunch, so I pulled in and ordered a cheeseburger for the equivalent of under $3. I wasn't expecting much, but the quiet woman who ran the place brought out a very large, freshly cooked burger with lettuce, tomatoes, and pickles, that was quite delicious. I explored a picturesque fortress nearby, then proceeded north, stopping at a stand along the way to sample some Pag Island cheese that the area is noted for. It's made of sheep's milk and is said to get its distinctive flavor from the high amount of salt in the grasses that the lambs feed on here. I liked it a lot, and happily alternated between bites of the cheese and some dark red cherries I'd picked up at another roadside stand.

I'd really hoped to swim at some remote beach on Pag, but I found that the famous Bošana Beach required a hike down some steep hills and there was nowhere to park the car. Another place that sounded promising was Čista Beach, a bit further north, but to my dismay, the road that was supposed to connect Bošana with Čista according to the map ended abruptly in a dead end that seemed to have been caused by landslides, neglect, or a little of both. By now it was getting close to sunset, and so I gave up my search for the perfect beach and headed south to the city of Zadar. Zadar is famous for its Sea Organ, an artistic endeavor consisting of a series of tubes carved into the seafront that produce sound as the waves move through them. People sat quietly on a staircase above the tubes listening to what sounded a bit like whale songs. Nearby was another interesting creation by the same artist called Greeting to the Sun, a huge circle of glass solar panels that collect energy during the day and produce seemingly random light shows in the evening. Both of these attractions were really unique and interesting.

For dinner I visited a restaurant called Zadar-Jadera, where I sat outside in the courtyard and was served by extremely warm and friendly waiters. I had a squid ink risotto filled with various types of seafood, followed by a traditional monkfish stew with vegetables, evidently a popular dish here on Croatia's Dalmatian Coast. There was also a rich, dark chocolate cake. I left with a very positive impression of Zadar and wished I'd planned to spend more time there.

Greeting to the Sun.

Unfortunately, when I got back to the villa, my room was as hot as it had been earlier. I had to open the balcony doors, inviting numerous mosquitoes inside, just to be able to get the room cool enough so that I could sleep. At least the breakfast in the morning was nice and plentiful, but then I had a misunderstanding with my hostess, who said I couldn't pay for the room by credit card, so I had to go into town and find a bank to withdraw enough cash to pay her. I was sort of happy to see this place in my rear-view mirror.

I headed south once again, stopping in a couple of towns to take photos and have a refreshing swim at a beach before driving into Split. I'd been led to believe from my guesthouse's website that parking was provided, which was a major consideration in choosing this place. Split's Old City is largely a pedestrian-only zone and parking is difficult. However, when I got there, there was no parking lot. I called the guest-house and was told that someone would come out to meet me. Soon two young, boisterously friendly young women came out and stood in the street deliberating about whether we should unload my luggage there or find parking first.

My new friends ended up hopping into the car with me, directing me far up a hill where we drove around until we found a free, public parking space on the street. This meant a long downhill walk with my bag to reach the guesthouse, and I realized that if I wanted to go anywhere over the weekend, I'd have to find a parking spot again on my own. Not ideal, but I was too hot and tired to think about it as we descended the hill to the guesthouse. I then dragged my luggage up two flights of stairs to my room, giving me flashbacks to Dubrovnik. I shared with my hosts that the air conditioning at the prior night's lodging was so weak I almost died, and one of them laughed and said, "Here you will not die. You will live!" When my hosts left, I went straight for the air conditioner and sighed with relief as I was hit by an icy wind that felt like it came from the Arctic in February. Yes, for the next two nights I would live!

The guesthouse was a mere five-minute walk to the center of Split's Old Town, and the famous Diocletian's Palace, an elaborate ruin dating back to the Roman Empire. It now forms the heart of the city and is filled with trendy restaurants and shops and is populated by a combination of corny actors dressed in Roman costumes and talented groups of *a cappella* singers who wander the ruins and perform traditional *Klapa* or folk music. Outside the walls there are lovely green parks and gardens and an elegant promenade along the seafront, lined with more bars, restaurants, and shops. There were a lot of tourists, many from cruise ships docked offshore, but thankfully Split is more spread out than Dubrovnik, and didn't feel as overwhelmingly crowded.

An a cappella group performing in Split.

One of my favorite meals in Split was brunch at a place called Ciri Biri Bela. I sat outside on a beautiful stone terrace under the welcome shade of an umbrella and ordered an omelet with local cheese and sausages, delicious homemade bread, a salad, and for "dessert" I opted for "granny's fluffy pancakes", which were more like crepes and weren't all that fluffy but were absolutely delicious and topped with mixed berries and currants. The coffee was some of the best I'd had in Croatia, and the wait staff couldn't have been more welcoming.

As I dined, I wrestled with the logistics of how to spend my day and what to do with my car. I'd be leaving for the airport at 5:30AM the next morning and didn't relish the idea of dragging my bag uphill for fifteen minutes, so I wanted to move the car closer to my guesthouse. I also wanted to go to the beach that afternoon, so I decided to drive there, come back and find a closer parking space. I headed to Kasjuni Beach, a few miles west of the city center. It was another blisteringly hot day, and I longed to be in the water, but as I arrived at the beach, I realized I'd forgotten to my flip-flops. To get into the water I'd have to walk across scorching hot, rather sharp gravel and once in the water, I'd need to float because there were rocks and even sea urchins on the bottom that posed a threat to my unprotected feet.

I threw my towel onto the rocky beach as close to the water as I could, walked gingerly across the rocks, and awkwardly threw myself into the refreshingly cool water. The beach was crowded, but laid back and calm, and has a beautiful backdrop of towering limestone cliffs and lots of pine trees. Coincidently, when I got home and caught up on the latest season of TV's *Amazing Race*, half an episode showed contestants completing tasks at Kasjuni Beach in virtually the same spot where I'd been swimming!

I stayed at the beach for a few hours then returned to Split, stopping to fill up with gas so I wouldn't have to do so at 6AM. After circling the block only a couple of times, I found a seemingly free, open parking place right by my guesthouse. I've always had amazing parking karma, but this was almost too good to be true. I saw someone pulling out of a nearby space and asked her if the parking here was indeed free and she assured me it was. The next morning, I found that my car hadn't been towed or ticketed, and I navigated the quiet streets of the city out to the airport for my early morning flight.

The pristine coast of Croatia.

I'd been eager to explore Croatia after the brief taste I'd had of it on my cruise two years before and I was glad to have seen more of the country. But if I return, I'd do so at a cooler time of year, as the heat and humidity really killed me. The coastline is truly stunning, but I prefer the sandier beaches of Italy or Greece. The cost of food and lodgings in Croatia was as expensive as Western Europe but wasn't quite up to the standards I've found in other countries. Despite Dubrovnik's truly spectacular setting and beauty, the cruise ship hordes were probably the worst I've encountered anywhere in the world; I much preferred Split and Zadar and would urge anyone visiting the country to include those cities in their itinerary and think carefully about whether to actually stay within the walls of the Old City.

I must thank Croatia for one thing in particular: every time I travel in Europe, I lose about ten pounds in a month, because despite all the amazing foods I sample, I walk everywhere, and the pounds just fall off. On this trip the same thing happened, but I believe that at least half of those missing pounds were lost somewhere among the 4,343 stone stairs of Old Town Dubrovnik, and for that, I am grateful!

12.
Dippyplakadivvyplatakakapotomoose!
GREECE

Everyone appreciates the views on Santorini.

My first visit to Greece was in 2007 for a university trip with students and it became one of those destinations I longed to return to again and again. I led another student trip there a few years later, attended a number of conferences being held in Athens, and made it a point to spend some time in Greece any time I made a longer trip to Europe. While places like Olympia and Delphi on the Greek mainland were really interesting, and Athens has a few charms for a short stay, it is the Greek Islands that I really fell in love with. To date, I've been to Mykonos, Santorini, Rhodes, Symi, Milos, Corfu, Naxos, and Crete; all share commonalities that let you know you're in the Greek Islands, but each also has its own unique personality as well. For this chapter I'll share some stories about some of my favorites.

Santorini

If you have a bucket list of places you want to see, be sure that the island of Santorini is on it. If you don't have a bucket list, make one, then put Santorini at the top of it because in my opinion, it is among the most beautiful places on earth. It's easily accessible via a half-hour flight from Athens but, if possible, arrive by ferry, which rewards you with a stunning first impression of the island.

Santorini is semi-circular in shape, with a few other offshore islands completing the circle if you connect the dots. In the middle of the bay is an active volcanic island, with hardened lava flows entering the sea on all sides. Santorini was once a huge volcanic mountain, but about 3,600 years ago it erupted, sending a massive chunk of the island sliding into the sea and causing tsunamis on many a Mediterranean coastline. All that was left was a narrow, crescent-shaped rim protruding above the surface of the water. This eruption is thought to have inspired the legend of Atlantis, a once great city or continent that sunk beneath the sea. Whether this was Atlantis is debatable, but this disaster marked the beginning of the end for the advanced Minoan culture that had thrived in the Greek Islands and all but vanished after the eruption.

Except for a couple of small port areas, Santorini's major towns, Fira and Oia are perched precariously atop 1,200-foot cliffs on the crater rim and characterized by gleaming white houses, blue-domed Greek churches, and a few pastel-colored buildings thrown in for good measure. When seen from the sea, the towns look like white barnacles clinging to the rocks above. On my visits, I've always stayed in Fira at either the Hotel Kavalari or the Panorama Suites, which both terrace down the cliffside from the main street and offer views of the volcanic island and the bay that are nothing short of spectacular. Breakfasts are generous and delicious, and once you've grown accustomed to their Greek yogurt, there's no going back to what you find in supermarkets back home.

Oia from the sea and Fira after dark.

One well-hyped activity on Santorini is riding a donkey from the port up to Fira on a steep trail with multiple switchbacks. Many years ago, a group of students and I made this trip; we were a group of eighteen but were told that there were only six available donkeys, so some of us would need to wait. Six students hopped on their donkeys and went trotting up the trail; one donkey was temperamental and tried to buck its rider, so I was glad I'd waited. However, the tour company wasn't able to round up any additional donkeys, so after dropping off the folks at the top of the cliffs, they sent the same "recycled" donkeys back down for us. The second group of students left, and the donkeys seemed more mellow after their long climb. After another half hour, these same donkeys were back again, and it was my turn to ride.

I can't say I enjoyed the trip. The animals were obviously exhausted and sweating. I felt sorry for mine, but he immediately trotted out ahead of the group. Every so often he stopped to catch his breath and munch on some grass. I spoke softly to him while petting him, glad that he could get a little break. However, behind our group two men with big sticks were chasing the donkeys up the steep path, screaming "*Yalla Yalla!*", which is evidently an Arabic word used in Turkey and Greece meaning "Hurry up! Go!" They wouldn't let the poor animals rest and it was very unpleasant. Finally, not even halfway up the cliff, the men had us all dismount. I thought we were stopping to let the animals rest and drink water, but they just herded the animals back downhill again and left us to climb the rest of the way to the top on foot in the considerable heat and intense sun. It was not an experience I'd care to repeat!

There are a couple of archeological sites on Santorini; I once visited Akrotiri, sometimes referred to as the "Pompeii of the Aegean" and concluded that Pompeii had nothing to worry about if there was ever a competition. The second site is Ancient Thera, which is evidently a pale shadow of Akrotiri. On the trip with my students, I considered skipping the group tour one day and asked our tour guide if I'd be missing much by not seeing Ancient Thera. She replied, "If I never had to climb up that pile of rubble again, it would be fine with me!" That was all I needed to hear. Instead, a few of my students and I mutinied from the tour and went on a boat trip to the volcanic island in the bay. It was still March, but the weather was mild, and it was wonderful to be out on the water. The views of Oia and its mirror-like reflections on the calm sea were fantastic. We reached the volcanic island and had ninety minutes to hike up to the caldera and back. The sun was hot, there was no shade, and as is true in most volcanic locales, walking on the loose lava cinders was tiring, but the views of previous lava flows and the ground covered in a strange reddish-orange plant made for a surreal landscape. At the summit there were yellow sulfur deposits with steam vents emanating from them. Gathered at the crater, my students seemed far more interested in my impromptu lecture about what happened in the eruption 3,600 years ago than they'd been in class.

By the time we returned to the boat, we were hot and tired, so the opportunity to swim at some volcanic hot springs on the way back was exciting. The springs are located in a small cove inaccessible to our boat, so we were told we'd need to dive into the chilly Aegean and swim about thirty yards to reach the warm water. My student John, an ex-marine, tore off his shirt and dived into the water, swimming like a missile toward the springs. Next was Nick, a part-time lifeguard. He tore off his shirt, dived into the water and swam like a dolphin toward the springs. I was third, clambering down the ladder wearing a T-shirt to protect myself from the intense sun. I clumsily hopped into the cold water and dog-paddled after the guys. For a few seconds I really thought I'd made a bad decision, as the water was very cold, but the warm sun helped a lot. A couple minutes later, I looked back toward the boat to see a dozen of my female students leaping off the boat like a pack of deranged nymphs from Greek mythology, screaming bloody murder as they hit the frigid water.

Ultimately these were warm, rather than hot springs. The bottom was covered with mud and algae that didn't feel very inviting, but it was easy to float, and I bobbed happily. At one point I brushed up against some red rocks that stained the back of my bathing suit with rust-colored iron oxide, which I learned doesn't come out in the wash. My students said it looked as if I had an incontinence problem, which was not exactly the look I was going for as I toured the Greek Isles!

Back on the island, an experience not to be missed is the approximately seven-mile hike along the crater rim between Fira and Oia. I've made this journey every time I've visited Santorini; it's always challenging, but well worth the effort. The hike takes about three hours, depending upon your level of fitness and desire to stop along the way. Leaving from Fira, the first ninety minutes are relatively easy, despite being a gradual uphill climb. The trail takes you through some smaller villages and gives you spectacular views looking back toward Fira, its white-washed buildings gleaming in the sun, cobalt blue swimming pools seemingly hanging in mid-air and the even bluer domes of tiny Greek churches poking out everywhere. Below the city are a thousand feet of rugged volcanic cliffs, brown, olive green, and occasionally brick red that plunge into the deep blue sea. Gleaming white cruise ships are parked in the bay, with dozens of tiny shuttle boats pulling up alongside them to take passengers to the port, reminding me of puppies or piglets jockeying for position while suckling from the "mother ship." As you get farther away, the trail becomes rougher, demanding that you pay attention to your footing and often requiring you to make a full stop to soak in the never-ending vistas.

There is little shade along the way, and I recommend doing the trip later in the afternoon to avoid the intense sun and to experience the sunset once you reach Oia. This town is smaller and perhaps even more beautiful than Fira, with a wonderful array of shops and restaurants of its own. But beware that during the more touristy months, there's a mad rush to view sunset from one of the village's highest hills. It can really feel claustrophobic as you are pushed and pulled through the narrow streets by a river of aggressive, tank-topped tourists. Meanwhile, you must try not to step on stray dogs, cats, children, or the train of a bride's wedding gown; wedding parties tend to climb to the look-out point to get pictures taken.

The hike from Fira to Oia.

Santorini also features some stellar Greek cuisine. Noussa is my favorite restaurant in Fira. Located at the south end of town they serve up tomato fritters, bread with yogurt and beet spreads, grilled octopus, and giant prawns cooked in butter and white wine. Wash that down with some of Santorini's local white wine and you'll have a memorable dinner, especially if you're there for sunset. Another great restaurant outside of Oia is called Finikia's Place, which has an elegant but casual outdoor terrace. I remember a standout meal consisting of sweet red peppers stuffed with local cheese as an appetizer, followed by a dish resembling a Greek version of shepherd's pie, but made with tender and flavorful goat meat, eggplant, and a crunchy, browned yogurt crust topping.

I've found the Greeks to be warm and friendly, and most speak good English. If you try to memorize a few pleasantries, like *Kalimera* (Good Morning) or *Kalispera* (Good Afternoon), you'll be fine. Still, language misunderstandings can always occur and are often quite funny. One time I returned to my hotel to shower before dinner, but despite letting the faucet run for a long time, the water never got hot. I called the front desk and asked if there was any hot water and the front desk clerk asked, "Oh? You want hot water?" I repeated that yes, there was no hot water and I needed some. "OK, we'll send someone." I waited at least a half an hour, but because I needed to meet friends for dinner, I submitted to a cold sponge bath and shampoo. As I was getting dressed, there was a knock at the door. My host was standing there with a small teapot full of... hot water! The two of us laughed for a full five minutes when we realized the extent of our misunderstanding on the phone!

Sunset over the Aegean, Oia.

I also recall a wonderful evening when a group of students and I took a caravan of taxis from Fira to Oia. Our driver was very friendly, playing wonderful Greek music during the ride. When we arrived at Oia, he gave me his card and told me to call if I needed a ride back. Our group wandered Oia, taking way too many pictures, then purchasing some local white wine, cheese, and ham. We sat on a hillside overlooking town to watch the sunset, joined by three hilarious Australian tourists and a charming Serbian guy named Drasko who worked as a bartender in town. He left for a few minutes and returned with a couple bottles of the local Santorini white wine to share with us as the sun dropped like a ball into the sea. It was one of those golden travel moments when everything seemed to have a glow... perhaps enhanced by the wine.

Later I called my cab driver and he arrived with two other cabs behind him to accommodate our group. He shouted from the window, "Where is Matthew? He must ride again in MY cab!" I asked if he'd play the Greek music again and learned that it was a CD by a local artist. He turned up the volume, holding the radio mic up to the speaker so that students in the other two cabs could hear it too. I asked him where I might buy the CD, but he took it out of the player and gave it to me as a gift! He also invited me to join him and his family to hear this artist perform at a local venue the following weekend. Unfortunately, I couldn't take him up on the offer, as I was leaving the island the following day, but I was touched by his hospitality.

Milos

Whether you understand it or not, listening to Italian is like music to the ears; it has a wonderful rhythm and lilt that is almost melodic. The same, unfortunately cannot be said of Greek. At the risk of offending the Greeks and their proud heritage and language, listening to someone speaking Greek sounds to me like, "Dippy-plaka-divvy-plata-kakapoto-moose!" On a flight from Rome to Athens and then on to the tiny island of Milos, I began to hear less and less of my beloved Italian and more and more of what sounded like a made-up language from a *Saturday Night Live* skit. Basically, almost everything sounds like "Dippy-plaka-divvy-plata-kakapoto-moose!" But that's when they're speaking slowly and enunciating. It's more like: "Dippyplakadivvy-platakakapotomoose!" when they're speaking quickly. It really does make me chuckle when I listen to it.

After arriving on Milos in a propeller plane that was only slightly larger than a dragonfly, we exited onto the tarmac and were led to a small stone building that was labeled "terminal" even though it wasn't much larger than my apartment. We waited in this hot, stuffy little building for almost thirty minutes for our luggage. Some of my fellow passengers said they'd have been happy to have just grabbed their bag from the underbelly of the plane and dragged it in themselves! Eventually I was reunited with my bag, and then it was off to the tiny Greeka rental car office. No, that's not a typo; it was called Greeka! There I met Georgios, who assigned me a vehicle, described a few sights on the island, and showed me the route to my hotel on a map. As I was leaving, he said, "I'll see you soon!"

"When I return the car in two days?" I asked. He replied with, "No, I'll see you sooner. It's a small island and I live in Pollonia where your hotel is!" Georgios was not kidding. As I drove out to Pollonia, I thought I recognized him in the car behind me, and sure enough, he started flashing his lights and blowing the horn to say goodbye as I pulled into the Best Western Pollonia Hotel. There I met a desk clerk, also named Georgios, and after checking out my room, I set out to explore the town, which took me approximately six and a half minutes. The main street paralleled a crescent-shaped beach and harbor area, and was lined with a few restaurants, a bakery, a general store, a tiny church, and my hotel. I certainly wouldn't have to worry about getting lost!

For dinner I found an outside seat at a restaurant called Enalion and the food was fantastic. I had a colorful chickpea salad with sundried tomato, red pepper, feta cheese, onions, black olives, and basil. Then I ordered tomato fritters, a common appetizer on the Greek Islands, and for the main course I had octopus sautéed in honey and sweet local wine. I finished things off with another Greek Island favorite: Orange Pie. My waitress was named Georgia, making me wonder what the odds were that of the first three people I met on this island, two were named Giorgios and one, Georgia! Georgia and her father - I didn't get his name, but I suspect it was Georgios - owned the restaurant and she was a quick-witted, warm person who chatted with me and offered me samples of some wonderful after-dinner liqueurs. It was a pleasant evening, and I didn't exhaust myself walking back across the street to my hotel.

Orange pie; Georgia and her family.

The weather on Milos was strange. It rained overnight, but the wind must have kicked up a lot of dust or dirt because my car and all the others on the street looked like they'd been mud-bombed! The skies threatened rain most of the day and it was relatively cool, so not the best day for swimming. I had a breakfast of cake, coffee, and fresh-from-the-oven spinach pie at the bakery. A Greek Orthodox priest dressed in long black robes and a wonderfully puffy hat was dining there as well, greeting me with "Kalimera" and I subsequently ran into him around town several times that day; I wondered if his name might be Father Georgios.

After breakfast, I set off to explore some of the island's beaches. Like Santorini, Milos is volcanic and known for its colorful beaches and unusual rock formations. I drove along the western coast and waded at Sarakinko Beach, its rocky white shoreline resembling the surface of the moon - if the moon had an azure blue sea! I visited the colorful cliffside fishing village of Firopotomos, with an imposing white and blue church guarding the entrance to the harbor and then for lunch I headed inland to Plaka, the island's capital. I chose a lunch spot simply because goat was on the menu and hoped to re-experience a heavenly dish I'd tasted on Santorini. I ordered the goat in lemon sauce and received a plate consisting mostly of goat bones with lots of fat and gristle on them, drowning in a watery, vaguely lemony sauce. My French fries were soaking in this sauce as well, totally wet and virtually inedible. The waiter was pleasant enough, but when he collected my plate with about fifty mushy fries and a pile of goat bones still left on it, he asked if my meal was OK. I was honest, "Well, there was a lot of water; the fries were all wet." He shrugged and brought me the bill, but I sure felt better for having gotten that off my chest!

On the way back toward Pollonia I stopped at Papafragas Beach. The sun began to come out and I really wanted to swim, so I climbed down from the parking area to the entrance of a long, calm inlet. The water was chilly, but I managed to jump in and swam about the length of a city block to view the natural archways that the sea has created here. Just as I reached the mouth of the inlet, there was a loud clap of thunder very close to me, followed by flashes of lightning. I hadn't seen it from inside the inlet, but huge black clouds had rolled in and were bearing down on me quickly. What timing! I decided I'd better get back to shore quickly but found that the current was pushing me out; what had been a very easy paddle outbound became a very tough "salmon swimming upstream" situation inbound, and every crack of thunder increased my sense of urgency. I then realized that if I stayed close to one side of the inlet, instead of paddling down the middle, the current wasn't as strong, and I eventually made it back just fine. Of course, five minutes after I got out of the water and back to my car, the storm had already passed, and the sun popped out again.

Sarakinko Beach.

I walked to an open, sandier area and got back into the water, enjoying the sun on my face as I floated lazily. I looked down, marveling at how despite being in eight or nine feet of water, I could see the rippled sand on the bottom as clear as a bell. Then something moving directly beneath me caught my attention. I gasped as I saw a long, round white thing floating under me. Was it an octopus? A really big squid? A huge white jellyfish? Momentary panic was replaced by hysterical laughter when I realized that the round white thing lurking so close beneath me was actually my right thigh! Good Lord! I really needed to get more sun on these legs of mine!

I got back to town and felt like a local, waving to the Orthodox priest who was making his rounds and stopping to talk to Georgia who was out on the street. I asked if she could reserve a table for me that evening, telling her that I needed some good food after the horrendous lunch I'd had. She said, "I don't like to gossip, but I want to hear all of the details about your bad lunch and where you ate! Come at 8:30PM!"

I had another great meal and met Georgia's daughter and father. She brought me an after-dinner drink called a "submarine." Before she gave it to me, she cautiously asked how my blood sugar was. This was several years before I was actually diagnosed with diabetes, but perhaps this concoction helped lead me down that road. It was a sickeningly sweet, candy-like glob of some substance made from alcohol, stuck to the end of a spoon, and submerged in mineral water. I believe it must be the Greek cousin of Japanese mochi or Turkish Delight. It was not my favorite thing, but I didn't tell Georgia!

Overall, my visit to Milos reminded me of a Greek Island version of *Cheers*; a place where everybody knows your name, but that's because most people's names are some derivation of George!

Mykonos

My first impression of Mykonos was not positive. I stayed at a pretentious hotel in the main town and was turned off by the raucous nightlife and less than pristine beaches I encountered. Yet I kept hearing how wonderful Mykonos was, and it is perhaps the most accessible of all the Greek islands, so after some online research, I decided to return to Mykonos, but this time, in search of peace and quiet, I chose a hotel on the island's remote north coast, and that was a much better experience.

My hotel was the Mykonos Star, one of the most welcoming and tranquil places I've ever stayed. It's a little, cliff-top "village" of natural stone and white stucco surrounding an enormous azure swimming pool and overlooking the darker blue Aegean Sea below. The hotel manager was named Giorgios, perhaps an immigrant from the island of Milos! His late father had built the hotel, and the matriarch of the family, his mother Sia roamed the property walking her dog and wearing long black dresses on even the warmest of days. Olga the breakfast waitress was charming and treated me like a long-lost friend. The hotel was rather quiet, as it was still early in the season; the only other guests were a very reserved Indian couple and a group of three very funny gay Irishmen whose conversations were fun to eavesdrop on.

The Mykonos Star Hotel and the beach it overlooks.

Breakfast was a happy affair, with Olga laying out quite a spread each morning in the open-air dining area overlooking the pool and the sea. There were fresh fruits, warm spinach and cheese pies, cereals, homemade orange cake, eggs with bacon or ham, cheese, jam, yogurt with honey, and coffee, all of which were top-notch. My days were wonderfully lazy. Though it was uncharacteristically cool for this time of year, I still spent a lot of time in the gorgeous saltwater infinity pool, gazing out at the Aegean. The hotel is perched atop a cliff, and a short hike led to a pristine, mostly deserted beach where I swam in crystal-clear water, always alert for sightings of my eerie white thighs.

From the hotel it was a twenty-minute drive into Mykonos town, and I had a couple of dinners at outdoor restaurants along the harbor. One place, called Captain's was excellent and served up the freshest Greek salads and seafood possible. Unfortunately, another night I tried a place next door and didn't enjoy the experience nearly as much. I was seated outside near the entrance where a host, a man with a neatly trimmed beard, Jesus-length hair, and a deep tan tried to entice passersby to dine at the restaurant. He began a well-rehearsed, slightly smarmy pitch with, "We'd love for you to join us for dinner!" Then he described all of the fish preparations in painful detail and finished with, "We have outdoor tables so that you can dine *al fresco* this evening."

After hearing this about fifty times I was ready to throw a tomato fritter at him, but why waste a good fritter? Toward the end of my meal, this guy along with a woman wearing about eighty pounds of jewelry that I think was the manager, stood inches from my table and kept staring at me. Their message was clear that it was time for me to go to allow other people to dine *al fresco*. A man at the table beside me ordered dessert but made the mistake of going to the restroom. Like a vulture, the woman swept in, jewelry clinking like a crystal chandelier in a moderate earthquake and quickly cleared his table, but I stopped her before she seated a new party, explaining that my neighbor had ordered a dessert.

A far more interesting and rewarding dining experience awaited me at Kiki's Taverna, just over a hill from my hotel and overlooking a deserted stretch of beach. Kiki's is only open from 1:00 to 7:00PM and meats and seafood are cooked on an open grill. They don't accept reservations, and you can't put your name on a list and wander off; you must wait in line to get seated. One online reviewer said she'd broken this rule by going off to the beach for a while. She came back and pretended she'd been in the ladies' room, but Kiki busted her, saying he'd already checked there. "Back to the end of the line for you!" Another review likened Kiki to the "Soup Nazi" from *Seinfeld*. But the reviews all praised the amazing food, so I was intrigued if a little apprehensive!

I arrived thirty minutes before opening time and found about forty people already waiting in the hot sun. A large man wearing a purple and blue hibiscus aloha shirt introduced himself. "I am Kiki. I am sorry, but there is no room for you in the first seating. Next chance is 2:00." Disappointed, I walked to the beach debating whether I should stay, but as I trudged back up toward the restaurant, the first seating had begun. I jumped to the back of the line and ultimately five of us couldn't get in. However, there were now seats where we could wait in the shade and Kiki said we'd be the first parties seated as diners left. He also provided free, unlimited wine and cold water while we waited, so I grabbed a seat, shared some enjoyable conversation with the other folks waiting with me, and got a table about an hour later.

Within the next few minutes another thirty people showed up and Kiki carefully monitored who arrived and in what order but never wrote anything down. He just pointed at people saying, "You are first, you are second, you third..." I don't know how he kept track, but it was impressive because after the first few chairs were taken, people sat on steps or on the ground in no particular order, but there was no haggling and no cutting in line; Kiki kept it all under control!

When my table was ready, I was ushered into the open-air dining room. It felt like being in a large treehouse as it was built around a huge olive tree which shaded the entire room. The sea was visible out front, the temperature was comfortable, and the service was friendly and calm, with no pressure to hurry and make way for the ever-present crowd waiting outside. My waiter sent me to a room where a pleasant woman welcomed me and described a dozen available side dish options to accompany my main course, saying I could select any two. I chose a beet and green apple salad, and a sweet red pepper and feta salad, and was told they'd be brought to my table. For my meal I ordered grilled octopus. Before my first trip to Greece, I never would have imagined that octopus would be one of my favorite dishes, though I probably wouldn't order it in Bakersfield or Newark! I also ordered grilled chicken stuffed with feta and sun-dried tomatoes, not realizing what I was getting myself into.

The harbor at Mykonos Town.

The portions were enormous, even for a hearty appetite like mine! I knew that asking for "doggy bags" from a restaurant is a foreign concept to Europeans, but the food was so good, I didn't want to waste any of it. My waiter assured me that he'd be happy to pack my leftovers, and sure enough, when he delivered the bill, he brought out what looked like a small basket made entirely of foil, complete with a little handle to carry it by. It made a delicious dinner back at the hotel that evening. Kiki's was a unique experience and worth every minute of the wait to get in.

That night we had some wild weather, with several hours of wind, thunder, lightning, and torrential rain, making me wonder if Zeus was really pissed off about something. I love storms, so I enjoyed every minute of it, but at breakfast in the morning Sia greeted me and inquired about my reaction to the storm. I shocked her when I said, "Wasn't it beautiful!" Her face became a mask of horror and she gasped, "Beautiful? It was TERRIBLE! I hate storms. I was afraid all the night! Beautiful?" She walked away shaking her head and chuckling nervously.

The Greek Islands are breathtakingly beautiful, and I love the way I feel when I visit them. Life seems much simpler and more relaxed, revolving around the sea, the beach, wholesome and plentiful food, and a cold beer or two. There is a welcoming, small-town vibe that makes even the tourist feel a sense of belonging. Of all the places I've traveled, I think my mom would have been particularly fond of Greece. In my mind's eye I can picture her reading a good book on a secluded beach while nearby, I'd be frolicking in the sea, pretending to be Ulysses and fighting off a sea monster that ultimately turns out to be one of my pale thighs. I can just hear her uncontrollable laughter over that one.

13. An Episode of Star Trek or a Night in Reykjavik?

ICELAND

Morning on Iceland's remote eastern coast.

In June of 2008 I realized another of my travel dreams by capping off a stay in Europe with a visit to a place I'd always longed to visit: Iceland. I'd already been to Norway and Sweden; both were beautiful and offered many adventures, but Iceland seemed more exciting than its quieter Scandinavian neighbors to the east, especially given my fascination for volcanoes and hot springs. I arrived on a strangely timed flight from London at 11PM, but the skies were still light even at this hour. Once I checked in at my hotel I headed into downtown Reykjavik, which has a reputation as a wild place on weekend nights.

My friends think I watch way too much TV, and predictably, I'm going to make a *Star Trek* reference here. My love for *Star Trek* is something else I can blame on my mother, as she was a diehard "Trekkie" when the series first aired back in the 1960s, long before that term even came into popular use. And in typical *Star Trek* fashion, if we'd found ourselves in a parallel universe and she'd had her way, Mr. Spock would have been my stepfather. But I digress, so let me get back to *Star Trek* and how it relates to Iceland.

On an episode of the original series, the Enterprise crew visited a planet where citizens called themselves followers of a leader named Landru. They led their lives in a peaceful, trance-like state, greeting one another with the gentle phrase, "Hello, friend..." But every few days the peaceful demeanor of the populace was replaced by "festival," a time during which everyone went on a violent, drunken binge for the night. The next morning, peace was restored, the mess from the night before was cleaned up, and life resumed. The problem for the Enterprise crew was that these folks quickly sensed when they'd met someone who wasn't one of Landru's followers. They'd point their finger at the outsider, ominously declaring, "You are not of the body. You must be absorbed!"

Now, I know some of you are thinking, "What in hell does this have to do with Iceland?" Well, Reykjavik seems to have its own version of festival; it's called *Runtur*, a weekend ritual when the normally quiet, reserved Icelanders take to the bars or drink in the streets in a very cold version of Mardi Gras. Guidebooks described flying bottles and broken glass; I couldn't believe things got that extreme, but since it was close to midnight on a Saturday, I decided to check out Runtur for myself.

Along the main shopping street, cars were slowly cruising with their windows rolled down so passengers could chat with pedestrians. I parked in front of an upscale bar with a line of fifty well-dressed young couples waiting to get in. By 1AM there were hundreds of people in the streets; most of the women wore sexy gowns and high heels, while the men were in sport coats and ties. No one wore outer jackets or sweaters, despite the chilly temperatures. They traveled in packs, beers in hand, seemingly drunk but jovial. And then I heard it: the sounds of breaking glass. Every few minutes I heard or saw a beer or soda bottle being hurled into the street or onto an unpopulated stretch of sidewalk. They weren't being aimed at anyone, and the intention didn't seem aggressive, but woe to the person who happened to be in the wrong place at the wrong time without a helmet and a pair of safety goggles!

Downtown Reykjavik.

I left my car and leaned against the wall of a building, taking in this fascinating social scene (and thinking about that *Star Trek* episode) when I was approached by a man wearing a suit that made him look more like he was going to church in a rural town than to a swanky city nightclub. About my age, with a mop of blond hair and wire-rimmed glasses, he greeted me with, "Hello, friend! I am Olaf." My imagination raced; had he already determined that I wasn't a follower of Landru, not "of the body?" Was he wondering why I was simply watching "festival" instead of participating in it? Would Olaf's next words be, "You must be absorbed?" I wondered whether I should reach for my communicator and ask Scotty to beam me up!

At any rate, Olaf was a kind and amusing guy who'd been at a wedding party earlier that evening, but left to participate in Runtur; however, his friends complained that they were too tired and had bailed on him. As bottles were hurled around us, he assured me that no one gets hurt at *Runtur* and that it's all innocent mischief. We chatted for at least thirty minutes before he went off in search of a drink and wished me a good night. I was fading fast, so I returned to my car, thankful it hadn't been hit by any broken bottles, and got back to my hotel around 3AM.

I woke on Sunday morning, shaking off crazy dreams about *Star Trek* and broken glass, and set out to explore Reykjavik. It was drizzling and overcast, which may have contributed to my first impression of the city: depressing. It's a very gray city, though a few homes in the historic area are painted in colorful shades. I walked around the city center for two hours and was impressed that all the broken glass from last night's Runtur was gone. It actually made me wonder if I'd dreamed the whole thing. I had a waffle with rhubarb jam and a hot chocolate at a nice little cafe, but otherwise things were bleak. I visited Hallgrimskirkja, a famous church which was covered in scaffolding, but I rode the elevator to the bell tower for a nice view of the colorful houses in the historic area. I nearly had a heart attack and did experience temporary deafness when the bells of the church tower signaled that it was noon while I was in the enclosed tower just a few feet away.

I made one last stop along the waterfront to see a famous sculpture of a Viking ship called the Sun Voyager and had a fun chat with some visitors from the Czech Republic who wanted their picture taken with me because they thought I resembled martial arts star Chuck Norris. I was dubious but flattered and it made more sense than being called Rambo in Egypt!

Fields of lupine.

The landscape became dramatic immediately as soon as I left the city, with expansive fields of blue lupine stretching before me and soon, huge clouds of steam rising from fissures in the ground. Iceland is, of course, volcanic and straddles the Mid-Atlantic Ridge, a huge crack running down the middle of the Atlantic Ocean. Molten rock oozes from this fissure, gradually building an undersea, volcanic mountain range while pushing the Americas farther from Europe and Africa by an inch or two a year. Iceland is the only place along the Mid-Atlantic Ridge that is currently above sea level, and it's home to many active volcanoes.

I spent a night at the Frost and Fire Guesthouse in the town of Hverageroi. Please don't think the Icelandic place names were easily tripping off my tongue. I basically looked at the words, focused on a few letters and created my own names. Hverageroi became in my mind "Hurdy Gurdy", and the Myrdalsjokull Glacier became, "Murder Skull." This worked well for me until I had to refer to a place in a

220

conversation with someone; then it proved rather embarrassing! The guest house was charming, a row of small units sitting on a wildflower-covered hillside beside a river. Nearby, huge clouds of steam billowed from fissures and mineral pools of boiling water and mud. This geothermal power heated the guesthouse's swimming pool and fed two jacuzzi-like "hot pots." The air temperature was probably in the low forties, so it felt wonderful to soak in the warm waters. My room was brightly decorated in red, blue, and orange which sounds gaudy, but was actually very cheerful.

Around 5PM I set out for a famous waterfall called Gulfoss and the town of Geysir. It was cloudy and gray on the way to Gulfoss, but as I arrived, the sun broke through, creating a brilliant rainbow over the falls, a two-tiered, Niagara-like cascade that sent clouds of spray into the air. Nearby was the town of Geysir, reportedly the first place that the phenomenon we call a geyser was observed; the English word geyser is derived from this Icelandic town's name. The main geyser erupts about every seven minutes and put on quite a show for me. There were also colorful, bubbling mineral pools in the area to explore.

Iceland's spectacular, otherworldly scenery.

It was getting late as I started back toward the guesthouse. I feared I might not get dinner that night since this area was pretty desolate. Luckily, when I got back to "Hurdy Gurdy" I spotted an open restaurant in a strip mall. It didn't look like much, but there were no other options, so I went in and learned that I had five minutes to order before the kitchen closed. I ordered a lamb steak and fries and to my surprise, it was one of the most delicious meals of the whole trip. Back at the guesthouse I had an evening soak in the hot pot, then drifted off to the sound of the river outside all night. Of course, it never really felt like night; the sun set at 11:30PM, sunrise was around 2:30AM, and even between those times it remained quite light outside.

The next day, after a hearty breakfast of smoked salmon, cheese, eggs, warm bread, and strong coffee, I headed toward my next stop, Hof, 200 miles east via the Ring Road. The day was cool, but sunny, and the scenery was impressive all along the way. An odd thing about Iceland is that there are almost no trees. It seems that there were forests when the first Scandinavians discovered Iceland, but they cut them all down for timber, not realizing that because of the much harsher environment here, Icelandic trees grew far more slowly than those in Norway and Sweden. The forests never recovered. The upside of this is that the vistas are spectacular; you can literally see fifty miles in any direction, depending of course on the weather. There are immense fields of wild-flowers, wind and water-carved canyons, impossibly green hillsides, expanses of black lava fields covered in an olive-green moss, waterfalls everywhere, and huge glacier-capped, volcanic mountains floating like white islands in the sky off in the distance.

The village of Hof and its traditional turf church.

As I approached Hof, the sky looked threatening and there was an odd glow in the distance that looked like the area had been nuked. I gradually realized there was a strange rainbow hiding behind a hill and

I'd never seen anything like it before. I entered the storm and within a distance of maybe ten miles, I left a calm, sunny day for what felt like hurricane-strength winds, driving rain, and temperatures that dropped twenty degrees or more. I entered Hof, a collection of a dozen white farmhouses with red roofs and a traditional turf church, built mostly below the ground and covered with a sod roof for warmth. I looked for my guesthouse, Hof One according to the reservation voucher I received online but didn't see any place with that name. I hopped out of the car to knock on several doors, braving the wind and rain, only to be met by people who didn't speak English or knew nothing about the damp voucher I showed them. Then I noticed a branch of the Frost and Fire Guesthouse, went there for help, and found that my reservation was actually with them. This version of Frost and Fire wasn't as cute as the previous night and had no hot pools to soak in, but it was clean and painted in the same bright colors.

Jökulsárlón Iceberg Lagoon.

After a hot shower, some dry clothes, and a delicious lamb dinner, I left the guesthouse at 8PM driving twenty-five miles to the other side of the glacier to visit the Jökulsárlón Iceberg Lagoon. I learned that the bizarre weather I'd stumbled into was caused by the glaciers. When the wind blows across their surface, it sends rain, fog, and colder temperatures to the areas directly beneath. Once I left Hof, the storm stopped completely. The iceberg lagoon is a huge body of water at the mouth of one of the largest glaciers in Iceland; huge chunks of the glacier break off, filling the lagoon with gigantic floating icebergs of various shapes that slowly make their way toward the open sea. Birds were everywhere, dropping into the icy waters and coming up with fish in their beaks. It was one of the most stunning places I'd ever seen, and I had it all to myself. I stayed till almost 11PM, then headed back to Hof, where the storm was still raging, and I truly thought the wind would topple my car onto its side.

Morning at Jökulsárlón.

At Home in the World

It felt like another planet when I awoke to a sunny, calm morning and after filling up on warm bread and smoked salmon, I returned to Jökulsárlón, intending to take a boat trip on the lagoon. When I arrived, I saw noisy, extremely crowded motorboats that went to the middle of the lagoon and back, so instead I took a hike along the shore. It was a good decision; I was all alone and could enjoy the sounds of the lagoon. Seabirds screeched in the distance, but the sound of melting ice was incredible, like being immersed in a bowl of Rice Krispies as they snapped, crackled, and popped. Without warning a big iceberg was lifted by the current and began drifting out to sea, resembling a huge float in the Tournament of Roses Parade, but instead of waving beauty queens or celebrities, these "floats" were populated by dozens of birds. Seals barked and frolicked close to the shore. It was one of the most amazing hikes I've ever taken.

I'd signed up for a bird-watching excursion on the Ingolfshofoi Peninsula (in my mind I called it "In Golf Shoes"). Our guide was a farmer named Einar and he herded a group of about twenty-five of us into a giant hay wagon he pulled behind a huge tractor with tires the size of Volkswagen Bugs. We travelled about five miles across mudflats toward the ocean. As the hay wagon was dragged along, mud was being thrown up through the gaps between the planks of the hay wagon, which was of course exactly where I was sitting. We were subjected to bone-shattering jolts as we crossed streams, and anyone who didn't have back problems to start with would by the time this ride was over. The wind, which I might have described as a wind from hell except that it was way too cold to have come from there, picked up considerably, blowing black volcanic sand all over us, while my pants and shoes became covered with splashed mud. I actually laughed out loud as I thought, "It must really suck to be hay if this is your typical mode of transportation."

Einar finally stopped in a sandy area, led us to the top of a narrow, grassy promontory overlooking the ocean and described the scene below us. Far in the distance, across the expanse of black sand and mud we'd crossed, was the gigantic Vatnajokul glacier that lies atop a 6,000-foot active volcano.

In 1362, and again in 1727, this volcano erupted, instantly melting the vast glacier on top of it, causing what is referred to as a "glacial burst" that sent floodwaters down from the summit in all directions. These floods obliterated everything below. Imagine that for a distance of about fifty miles around the base of this mountain everything was washed away. This area was dubbed *Oraefi*, which literally translates as "wasteland," and the name fits. A minor glacial burst occurred in 1996 taking out parts of the Ring Road and some local farms, but thankfully the population in this area is less than 500 and no one was injured.

Oraefi and the famous hay wagon.

With the wasteland below us, Vatnajokul hovering in the sky in the distance, and gale force winds blowing from random directions, we followed Einar up the grassy summit to the bird sanctuary. He warned us that this was prime breeding season and some of the gull species we'd see become aggressive if you come too close to their nests. We were dive-bombed a few times by protective gulls, but we got to see a few nests of unhatched eggs, a hatchling that had likely only broken out of its shell an hour ago, and a couple of fluffy gull chicks being protected by their parents. We also saw some of the famous puffins, birds unique to Iceland that resemble small penguins. The wind was really fierce, and Einar had to warn some of our group to stay back from the cliff's edge, as the gusts were constantly shifting direction and could have easily blown them over the cliff without warning. Then it was back to the hay wagon, where I made sure to sit far away from the splattering mud. An unfortunate Dutch woman was seated where I'd been, and her mother, observing the mud splattering up from the floorboards all over her daughter, erupted into such violent convulsions of laughter that I seriously thought it might kill her. She actually made me laugh with her hearty guffaws as her good-natured daughter hung on for dear life and tried in vain to brush the mud balls off of her jeans! Yes indeed, it would suck to be hay.

Encrusted with mud and sand, I returned to the guesthouse for a shower, then set out again for some hiking in Skaftafell National Park. Later I drove to the far-eastern town of Hofn, not to be confused with Hof, where I was staying! Hofn is the lobster capital of Iceland, so I had to sample the local delicacy. Icelandic lobsters are much smaller than their Maine cousins and my dinner consisted of a platter of ten tails sauteed in white wine and butter sauce, served with rice and vegetables. For dessert I tried a local dairy product called *skyr*, somewhere between yogurt and ricotta cheese in taste and consistency; it was mixed with mandarin oranges and served atop a dark chocolate biscuit with a scoop of rhubarb sorbet. The food in Iceland was simply delicious.

The drive back from Hofn to Hof was among the most beautiful I've ever taken. The light at this time of the evening was amazingly sharp and accentuated all the colors: the green of the hills, the blue of the rivers and the sea, the gleaming white snowcaps of the glaciers, and the coal black lava rock. Sheep and goats wandered everywhere, scampering off the road as my car approached. The iconic Icelandic horses frolicked in fields along the road. Shorter than American horses and looking more like a Shetland pony, their distinctive characteristic is an amazingly long, lush mane, which would have been the envy of even *Charlie's Angels'*

Farrah Fawcett circa 1977. Beautiful music by Enya, Olivia Newton-John, and Sarah McLaughlin created a dreamy atmosphere that made me feel like I was floating among the clouds. It was a magical journey.

For my last full day in Iceland, I hit the road early and took a short hike at a beautiful canyon near Kirkjubaejarklaustur ("Kirk Bear Jerk" to me) where a river cuts through the lava rock to create amazing, column-shaped formations. I stopped for lunch on the coast at a restaurant called Fjorbordid ("Floorboards" in my dialect!), purported to serve Iceland's best *lobstersoup*, which is all one word in Icelandic. As a main course, it was served in a huge tureen that contained two and a half large bowls of creamy chowder with what seemed like a pound of lobster meat in it. It was served with delicious bread and spreads made from skyr, cucumber, tarragon, and honey.

An Icelandic horse; Kirkjubaejarklaustur.

I arrived in Reykjavik by mid-afternoon and the activity of a workday coupled with sunny weather made it seem brighter and more alive than it had on that prior rainy Sunday morning. Outdoor cafes were bustling, people were feeding the ducks and swans in the park, and I found the city much more appealing. I had an early dinner at a place called Icelandic Fish & Chips, known for organic food, fish dipped in a healthy barley and rye batter, and baked rather than fried chips.

I was the only customer at this early hour, and music was playing by Bjork, the quirky Icelandic pop singer, who, if you're not familiar with her, tends to shout, scream and make very strange sounds in some of her songs. While I was eating, a staff member began calling out the name Oliver, first loudly and sternly, and then with more urgency and panic in her voice. Before long she ran through the dining room and out into the streets, screaming the name over and over. My waitress ran to a window and scanned the block. I had no idea whether Oliver was a child or a runaway dog but was observing all this with great interest. And then I was startled by what sounded like a blood curdling scream. In my mind's eye, I envisioned that Oliver the run-away dog had just been found dead, but my waitress, who'd also momentarily looked concerned, was now laughing, and I couldn't fathom why until I realized that the blood curdling scream we'd just heard was only Bjork! I eventually learned that Oliver was the manager's son and had been playing hide and seek; I don't think I'd want to have been Oliver when his mother finally found him.

The Blue Lagoon.

After dinner, I drove an hour to Keflavik, near the airport and checked in at Motel Best, run by a big, bear-like man whose name, ironically was Gummi. In e-mail communications with him, I'd expressed concern about whether there was a wake-up service, since my flight out in the morning required me to be up by 5AM and he replied that to be safe he'd give me two alarm clocks. I'd made the reservation months ago, but to my amusement, Gummi actually handed me two alarm clocks at check-in.

My final stop was the Blue Lagoon, a famous man-made hot spring set amidst jagged black lava fields. Because of its heavy silica content, the water is an unearthly, milky-blue color against the black rocks. It's an amazing complex of pools, waterfalls, saunas, restaurants, and bars. I spent the evening soaking and though there were perhaps 100 people there, the lagoon is so vast it didn't feel crowded at all. I floated in the hot water, staring at the clouds and the blue skies and thought that if I had to leave Iceland, this was a unique and relaxing way to say goodbye.

Despite ranking Iceland among my favorite places I've ever visited, it took me fifteen years to return. In November 2022, as COVID restrictions lifted and international travel became possible again, I took advantage of cheap fares on a new Icelandic budget airline, Play and stopped in Reykjavik at the end of a longer European trip. I knew that Iceland in November would be a bit different fromwhat I'd experienced during my June visit back in 2008. Instead of twenty-one hours of light on summer days, sunrise in mid-November is at 10AM and sunset just after 4PM, so I'd have to squeeze my sightseeing into those few hours. I was also a little wary about weather and road conditions at this time of year since even in June I'd experienced some wild storms. I decided to play it safe and rented a large, 4 x 4 vehicle in case winds kicked up or roads turned icy. On my last visit I'd only explored the southern half of Iceland, but this time I was determined to drive the entire Ring Road, 825 miles in length to see what I'd missed.

Although I'd been skeptical, my Play Airlines flight from London to Reykjavik was surprisingly comfortable, and actually departed and arrived a bit ahead of schedule. I chuckled as I left the baggage claim area and saw a large sign with an arrow pointing out the door saying, "Exit to Iceland." In the shuttle to the car rental office, the driver was a quiet, low-key guy and I tried to strike up a conversation by asking about the strange statue in front of the airport terminal. It looked like a broken egg, with either a bird or some alien creature fighting its way out of the shell. Without cracking a smile, he replied, "I have no idea. I don't know if it is a bird leaving an egg or some abstract thing. It makes no sense to me. I have never known what it is." I later learned that the sculpture is called "Jet Nest" and represents an airliner breaking out of an egg, so I guess we were both on track with our general impressions. Still, it amused me that this man who'd driven past it multiple times each day had never been interested enough to figure out exactly what he was looking at.

Renting my car was unnerving. They gave me a Dacia Duster, which I'd never heard of before, and the poor beast had been through a lot, with over 100,000 miles on it and numerous scratches, dents, and pits. I was told to take photos of all this to protect myself from unfounded damage claims, which proved difficult because it was raining, I was trying not to get my phone wet, and the scratches and dents were barely visible in photos amidst raindrops and my own reflection on the car's surface. I finally gave up and put my faith in the fact that the car rental agent had obsessively photographed the damage. Within a mile of the office, as the windshield wipers kicked in, I noticed several big pits in the windshield that I hadn't noticed before, so I hurriedly took pictures of those too.

My destination for the night was a guesthouse called The Garage, two hours from the airport in a hamlet called Varmahlid. Along the way I stopped to take photos and when I got back into the car, the tire pressure light came on, not a welcome sight, since I was forty miles from the nearest town. I checked the tires, and one did look a bit low, so I drove slowly and with great caution until I reached the next town an hour later. I found a gas station with a self-service air pump, but then wondered what the correct tire pressure should be. I whipped out the trusty owner's manual for my Dacia and lo and behold, it was written entirely in Icelandic! The nerve! Had it been in any of the Romance languages or even German, I might have been able to decipher it, but Icelandic was totally Greek to me. I searched on Google for "Icelandic word for tires" and it came up as *dekk*. I looked up dekk in the owner's manual, was referred to Page 28 and there it was: PSI = 32. I put air in the low front tire, and with great relief, headed back out into the total darkness of 5PM.

I'd been advised to get dinner before arriving at the guesthouse, as there were no places to eat nearby, so I stopped at the highly rated Eldsto Art Café. I was craving fish and chips but noticed an appealing lamb stew on the menu too. The stew was served as a main course, and I knew it would be too much food and too expensive to order both. Then I noticed that the stew was offered on the children's menu, so I hesitantly asked the waitress if I could order that as an appetizer before my fish and chips. She thought this was a very clever idea, so I had a hearty, delicious turf and surf dinner that evening.

Lamb stew and fish and chips...

I got to The Garage, located on a sheep farm, around 8PM and met my hostess, Anna who showed me to my very cozy room, then invited me to come to the lobby and sample some cakes and cookies she bakes for guests each day. She also welcomed me to use the hot tub on a nearby hillside. It was drizzling and cold, but after grabbing some cake and cookies for later, I made a beeline for the hot tub. I soaked in the hot water, cool rain running down my face, and listened to the sound of a waterfall that tumbles down the mountain behind the farm. It was perfect, and I fell asleep early that night, well fed and extremely relaxed.

Iceland in the winter is a great place for those of us who would love to see sunrise but aren't morning people. I woke in pitch darkness at 8:30, had some cereal, strawberries, and milk I'd picked up the night before, and ventured out to have a look at my surroundings in the gray light of dawn at 9:30. The farm consists of several white buildings, completely dwarfed by the magnificent cliffs that loom behind it. Several waterfalls cascade down the cliff face, and the Atlantic Ocean is just across the road. One of the farm's sheep dogs immediately greeted me and after an extended petting session, faithfully followed me on a walk down to the ocean, sitting patiently whenever I paused to take a photo. As the sun rose, strange cloud formations created the illusion of what looked like the shadow of an ominous giant towering in the sky. It was beautiful, but also a little bit spooky.

An eerie sunrise; Skogafoss, southern Iceland.

From the farm I continued east but made a couple detours to visit some waterfalls, then a black sand beach called, Reynisfjara. From high above the coast, I saw huge black stacks of basalt rock jutting from the ocean, remnants of past volcanic eruptions. My car was buffeted by powerful wind gusts, and I recalled that the rental agent warned me that the most common way rental cars get damaged in Iceland is if someone opens a door without holding on to it, resulting in the door being bent completely backward by the wind! I reached a crowded parking lot and saw many people wandering the beach as huge waves, perhaps fifteen feet high, crashed to the shore. Signs warned of "sneaker waves" which do not resemble fashionable Adidas, but rather, are so named because they tend to sneak up without warning on careless people who turn their backs to the ocean. Evidently this beach has a history of people being washed quickly out into the Atlantic by such waves.

Unfortunately, as I started walking toward the beach, it began to rain heavily. I turned back, fighting the howling wind, and managed to open the car door without it blowing off. After a few minutes the squall subsided, so I tried again to get to the shore to take some photos. As soon as I got to the beach, the rain began again, harder than before, and the wind honestly felt like it was going to lift my 260-pound body and dash me against the rocks while the rain stung my face like a thousand bees. With great difficulty, I returned to the car, carefully pried open the door, hanging onto it for dear life, and collapsed into the driver's seat feeling as though I'd just been mugged, soaked to the skin, cold, and impressed by nature's incredible fury.

I stopped at The Soup Company, a popular eatery offering a selection of homemade soups and delicious bread in the nearby town of Vik. I ordered a curried seafood soup, and the friendly young woman waiting on me asked if I needed anything else. "Not unless you happen to have a towel back there!" I joked. My hair was soaked, raindrops were still running down my face as I described the scene at the beach, and she laughed. "Believe it or not, I heard that today it was pretty calm down at the black sand beach!" It couldn't imagine it being any wilder out there than what I'd experienced.

Many restaurants in Iceland allow free refills of soup, so I had two big bowls, packed with winter vegetables, fish, and shellfish. Though I was still wet, at least I started to feel warm inside. The waitress and I chatted a bit more; she shared that she was already feeling depressed by the shorter days and lack of light that winter brings. Perhaps it's not surprising that in places with prolonged hours of winter darkness, depression and alcoholism are more common. As I gazed out the window watching sheets of rain scour the parking lot, I wondered whether I'd be happy living in such a harsh environment.

It was almost sunset when I reached Jökulsárlón Iceberg Lagoon, one of the highlights of my first visit to Iceland. It was getting dark and there was a bitterly cold wind, so the area wasn't as inviting as I'd remembered it and compared to summer when there is likely more glacial melting, at this time of year there were very few icebergs floating past. The place was still impressive with small, crystalline chunks of glacial ice littering the shore, earning it the moniker "Diamond Beach" as the silvery ice sparkles like jewels against the black sand.

A return to Jökulsárlón and a "jewel" on Diamond Beach.

Leaving Jökulsárlón, an orange warning light appeared on my dash-board: Check Anti-Pollution System. Of course, I was miles from any town, and it was almost 7PM, so although I was nervous, the car seemed to run just fine, so I headed to my guesthouse for that night, a sheep farm outside Hofn. Compared to my prior night's lodgings, this place was much less impressive, but there was nothing else around for twenty miles in any direction, so I dined at their restaurant and turned in early.

The next morning I'd intended to search for a garage to have someone check the car, but when I started it up, no warning lights came on at all. I drove into Höfn without a problem, filled up with gas, and decided to press on since I had a six-hour drive to get to my next stop. Gas cost me well over $100, the equivalent of $9.25 a gallon. If winter's persistent darkness didn't get you down, these gas prices would!

The coastline of eastern Iceland is carved up by numerous fjords, so the Ring Road here winds back and forth aimlessly. Along stretches of open ocean, waves crashed violently against the shore, but along the sheltered fjords just a mile or so away, the water was placid and still. It took forever, but eventually the road turned inland and straightened out. I was now in a part of Iceland I hadn't seen before and was surprised by how devoid of civilization it was. The southern coast actually had a lot more traffic than I'd remembered from my prior trip, but on this section of highway I saw almost no other cars.

After a long day of driving, I arrived at Vogafjos Farm, located on the shore of Lake Myvatn in north-central Iceland. This area has several geothermal hot springs, but I'd read recent reviews that said the springs were barely lukewarm and not very clean, so I decided against a visit. Instead, I had a leisurely dinner at the farm's restaurant which featured a unique dining room: one wall is entirely glass and looks out on a barn full of cows. Guests who eat breakfast by 7:30AM can have their cereal while watching the cows being milked.

Lake Myvatn Reflections.

The dinner I had here was the most expensive of the trip but was truly delicious. The appetizer was lamb carpaccio, seasoned with horse-radish, beets, and rhubarb jam; it was a work of art visually and incredibly delicious. My main course was fish, arctic char, served with veggies, potatoes and most importantly, geysir bread, a dark rye steamed in a pot in geothermal areas; the cooking process makes the bread sweet and almost caramelized. If I had a geyser in my back yard, I'd make this bread every day! For dessert there was geysir bread ice cream, made by mixing breadcrumbs into a vanilla base. Rye bread ice cream? Only in Iceland!

After more geysir bread with breakfast I hit the road around 9AM in total darkness. Once the sun rose, it simply hung on the southern horizon at a very low angle, even at noon. The journey westward from Lake Myvatn along the Ring Road was gorgeous, leading over and around several snowcapped mountains, then along the idyllic shores of Eyjafjordur Fjord near the city of Akureyri. I passed many ranches where adorable Icelandic horses grazed amidst pastoral backdrops of mountains and lakes. It was another beautiful drive.

Eyjafjordur Fjord.

Leaving my luggage at my hotel near Saurbaer (Sour bear?) in western Iceland, I rushed to nearby Hvammsvik Hot Springs for a 4PM reservation. A relatively new spa built along the shores of a fjord, it's a collection of eight geothermally heated pools of varying temperatures, a sauna, changing rooms, and a restaurant. To prevent overcrowding, patrons must make a reservation. You may stay as long as you like, but at least there's a limited number of people arriving at any one time. There were only a dozen people there when I arrived, and for much of the time

I had an entire pool to myself. The air was brisk, but I sat contentedly in the hot water, watching the sunset and then stars gradually appearing. It was the first night without clouds or rain and I wondered if I'd have a chance to see the Northern Lights.

I could have soaked all night, but hunger eventually drove me to shower, dress, and visit the restaurant, where I dined on seafood soup, and an absolutely scrumptious open-faced sandwich of warm smoked salmon on rye bread with an apple salad. As I drove back to my hotel, the sky was dark and filled with twinkling stars. I pulled off the road high on the cliffs above the fjord, cut the lights and waited for my eyes to adjust to the darkness. And then I saw them: the Aurora Borealis or Northern Lights! I'd seen them only once before a few years ago in Finland, north of the Arctic Circle and they looked like vivid green curtains shimmering across the sky. The ones I saw here in Iceland were fainter, more subtle whitish bands that could almost have been mistaken for clouds reflecting lights from below except there were no lights anywhere. I watched them arch across the sky for a few minutes until clouds moved in, rain started, and the show was over. Still, I was grateful I'd had at least a glimpse of them again.

I was tense on the ninety-minute drive back to the airport the next morning. As I was driving back to the hotel the night before, another engine warning light came on: Check Fuel Injectors. That light went out but was replaced by the Anti-Pollution System warning again. Good Lord! I seriously wondered if I'd get this car back to the airport, but we made it. The rental car agent momentarily questioned some damage on the vehicle, but quickly found a photo of the scratches he'd taken before I left. I told him about the various warning lights, but he shrugged it off. "These cars are always having electrical problems!" And I was worried?

Iceland and I have now forged a deeper relationship. Although it's a place that I find captivating, it may not hold universal appeal for every traveler. It's cold, rugged, wild, and a bit intimidating, even in summer and like the rest of Scandinavia, it's very expensive. However, the people are friendly, the food is fresh and delicious, and the scenery often defies description. It's a place that feels isolated from the rest of the world, and I suppose that depending on one's perspective, that could be a good or a bad thing. For me, it was a breath – or perhaps a hurricane force wind – of fresh air. Iceland left me with unforgettable memories of hearty soup and warm bread on a stormy day, cool air on my face as my body soaked in warm thermal waters, and otherworldly vistas that seem to stretch to the very ends of the earth.

Another unique Icelandic vista.

14. Feeling at Home in the World

Feeling at home in my favorite city, Venice.

Allora... as I assembled this collection of travel tales, I often found myself thinking, "I can't believe I've actually done all these things!" It was difficult to decide which stories to share and which to leave out lest this book be 1,000 pages long. I'd have liked to describe driving up endless mountain switchbacks into the Andes of Ecuador, feeling that I'd reached the very top of the world, only to gasp as a break in the clouds revealed peaks towering much farther above me. I could have shared my surprise at falling so in love with Budapest, Hungary, a place that hadn't previously been on my travel radar. Probably one of the peak experiences of my life was watching the yellowish-green curtain of the Northern Lights undulating above me in Lapland, Finland on a frigid November night. I could speak endlessly about time spent in great cities like Paris, Berlin, Amsterdam, and Barcelona. And I could easily write another entire book about my adventures during the countless road trips I've taken across the United States or my intense love for the Hawaiian Islands. Maybe if this book is well received, I'll come up with Volume II.

The Northern Lights over Finland; the grandeur of Budapest.

I've often wondered how my life might have been different had my mom lived a long, healthy life. Would she have shared some of these adventures with me or would she have preferred to stay closer to home in her little cottage on the coast of Maine, waiting for me to return and share my stories with her? I know she'd have loved the California of the 1970s, and that one visit to Hawaii might have convinced her to abandon the idea of living in Maine in favor of a modest condo on Maui. I don't think she ever traveled outside the United States except to hop over the Canadian border at Niagara Falls and when I was a child we never really thought much about international travel. Given her personality and tastes, I'm certain she'd have adored Great Britain, Australia, and New Zealand, and while she might have been intimidated by the language issues, I think she'd also have loved France, Italy, and Greece as much as I do. I know that visiting the Biblical sites I saw in Israel would have meant the world to her. It makes me sad that she never got to experience such things, but I do take comfort in knowing that I was able to take advantage of the opportunity to do them for us.

It's been three years since I retired, and I don't miss the daily grind of academia at all, but I do miss teaching and being in the classroom. So in this closing chapter, I decided to share some topics I used to discuss in the Psychology of Travel course I taught for several years and some of the things I've observed during all my travels. If the stories I've shared have inspired you to pursue your own travel adventures, then I hope that some of the things I discuss here will be useful and of interest.

Where Should I Go? - Choosing a Destination

You know yourself better than anyone, so when you consider where to go on your next vacation, think about what would make you happiest or what you're most comfortable with. Research on travel destinations differentiates between "authentic" vs. "staged" destinations. An authentic destination is one that's attractive for its own intrinsic qualities: you may have dreamed all your life of hiking the Grand Canyon, experiencing a city like Paris or Venice, or seeing the pyramids of Egypt firsthand (despite my warnings!). Staged destinations, in contrast, are places created exclusively for the purpose of attracting tourists and catering to visitors: Disneyland, Universal Studios, luxury resorts, Dubai or the Las Vegas Strip. Typically, experienced travelers prefer authentic destinations, while those with less experience prefer the staged ones. To my horror I've actually heard people say they don't need to see Paris or Venice because they've been to the Paris or Venetian Resorts in Las Vegas. Oh well, that means shorter lines for me to get my croissant and *café au lait* in the real Paris or my cone of gelato in the real Venice.

Similarly, less confident travelers or those who plan to visit a place with a very foreign culture or where a foreign language is spoken may prefer structured group tours or cruises, while more independent travelers tend to want to explore on their own. If you haven't figured it out already, I'm definitely in the latter category here; I find cruise ships and group tours too confining and prefer to chart my own course and set my own pace. There's no judgment call here as to which type of travel is "better" – it's a matter of personal taste. The point is that you're likely to have a better experience if you choose the type of travel or the destination that best matches your needs. That being said, I do think that it's healthy to at least make an attempt to challenge yourself to try and experience things that may be outside your comfort zone, as you may find that really rewarding.

Your motivations for travel should also be considered when thinking about a travel destination. Research identifies a number of basic motives for travel: Social (visiting family or friends or strengthening bonds with loved ones in a new setting); Play (seeking entertainment or recreational opportunities); Escape (reducing stress, relaxing, breaking from your routine); Nature Seeking (getting away from the urban environment to experience the natural world); and Growth or Challenge (learning about a place or culture or testing yourself in some way). Obviously, some of these may overlap and more than one of these motivations may apply to you, but whichever ones are most relevant should guide your destination choice. If you want to experience a foreign culture, you'll likely be disappointed with a stay at a staged resort destination that ensures you'll never come into contact with local people. If you need to rest and relax, a trip to a national park, a beach, or a quiet rural area would accomplish that better than a week in New York City or Rome. It's not exactly earth-shattering science, but in general the more closely a destination meets your own needs and objectives for travel, the more likely you are to enjoy the experience.

Don't be Afraid to Travel Alone!

Many people are amazed at how much traveling I've done on my own, but if I'd waited until other people were willing or able to join me, I'd never have experienced all the adventures I've had. We're all different regarding how comfortable we are being alone, and I'm on the far end of the spectrum in terms of being OK on my own. While I'd have liked to have shared more of my travels with companions, I will say that I'd much rather travel by myself than with someone with whom I'm not compatible.

Back in 1986, my friend Joyce and I spent a few days together in England; she was doing study abroad and I visited her there on what was my first trip to Europe. We quickly learned that our ideas of a rewarding day of travel differed considerably. She loved museums and read every caption on every exhibit. If time permitted, she'd run out for some fast food so she could get back to the museum and continue to see every last square inch of it. My idea of a good day was a casual stroll through the museum to see a few exhibits that interested me, then a leisurely lunch or afternoon tea, some people-watching at an outdoor café, and browsing some shops looking for a nice Scottish wool sweater. I suggested we get a boat and try punting on the Thames River; Joyce thought that would be dangerous. I wanted to rent a car and visit Stonehenge; she wasn't comfortable with the way people drove. After two days of being exasperated with one another we parted ways; she had other museums to scour, and I wandered off to Scotland in search of the ultimate tea and scones. Thankfully, our friendship endured and we actually travel well together these days.

I strongly suggest that if you do travel with other people, even someone you know quite well, you might want to split up and take time to pursue your own interests for a day or even an afternoon. One of you might go for a swim, a hike, or a bike ride while the other goes shopping or visits a museum; at the end of the day when you meet up for dinner, you'll have lots of experiences to share. And if you do travel alone, one benefit is that you're more likely to meet people and talk to fellow tourists and locals than if you're traveling with others. These days you can use the internet to find and contact people who share a common hobby with you like art, music, or cooking and arrange to meet them in the places you're traveling to. You could also connect with groups into hiking, jogging, biking, or various sports. Several of the deep friendships I've made in my travels started by making Internet connections before my trip and then meeting these folks for coffee or dinner in a public place once I arrived.

From Being a Tourist to Becoming a Traveler

Another issue discussed in the psychological research on travel is the distinction between being a "tourist" versus a "traveler." Tourists tend to seek out rather superficial travel experiences, seeing the major sights, staying in comfortable chain hotels, eating familiar foods, and barely scratching the surface in cultivating a deeper understanding of the places they're visiting. Travelers desire a more immersive experience, wanting to make connections with locals, to stay at an apartment or a B&B in a less-touristy area, to shop for groceries, try local cuisine, and learn something about the language or culture. While some people are content with the experience of being a tourist, I think many people strive to be more of a traveler but may be unsure how best to accomplish that. I have some suggestions for you if you're one of those individuals.

Get Off That Phone!

I always elicited eye rolls from my students when I'd preach about the importance of putting down their phones and interacting with the world around them. As a social psychologist and someone who lived in a time when we weren't "on call" twenty-four hours a day, I know that our obsession with texting and staring at our phones is having detrimental impacts on our mental and emotional health and our social interactions. I think this same issue is also relevant to getting the most out of a travel experience.

Without a doubt, having a phone, coupled with the availability of Internet access in even the most remote locations means that today's traveler can - and is often expected to - stay in touch with those "back home" to an unprecedented extent. Posting your latest photos on Instagram or Facebook is a great way to share your travel experiences with loved ones, but I'd urge you to keep that to a minimum and only check in once every day or two. While frequent interactions with those back home may be comforting and posting your latest photos online may elicit some ego-boosting "likes" on social media, it becomes harder to disengage from home and fully appreciate the place you're visiting. I've seen students on some of the study abroad trips I've led who spent hours on their phones chatting with friends and posting pictures. Meanwhile they were ignoring the sights and sounds of Paris or Rome that were happening all around them. So many of the wonderful experiences I described in my travel stories happened because I actually acknowledged and spoke to the people around me.

Embrace the Place!

When I travel, I try to blend in and feel a part of the places I visit. For me, music is a big part of that. When I'm driving across the deserts of Arizona or Utah, I listen to playlists of Native American music and traditional cowboy ballads. Anywhere south of the Mason-Dixon Line, I need to hear Country-Western; on Maui I listen exclusively to Hawaiian artists, and as I mentioned earlier, my rental car radio is always tuned to Radio Italia as I explore the Italian countryside. I know I'm an odd duck, but I just can't imagine listening to the Beach Boys in Tuscany or Bruce Springsteen on a Greek island. Listening to music appropriate to the setting helps me to get more in touch with the place I'm visiting.

As I've said before, I also think it's important to try and learn at least a few helpful words or phrases in the language of the country you're visiting. It will help you get your needs met, but just as importantly, you'll win over the locals with even a small amount of effort. I recall learning the word *Piacere*, which Italians use as a way of saying, "it's a pleasure" when meeting someone. During my next visit I tried it out for a spin at a big dinner party when I was meeting a friend's extended family. People smiled and nodded in approval, turned to one another, and made remarks to the effect of, "Aw, look! He knows about *piacere!*" I even remember getting a few claps of applause for uttering one little word!

Similarly, even if you're not terribly adventurous, try and at least sample some of the local cuisine of the places you visit, though you have my permission to avoid mochi and Turkish delight. When dining at restaurants I like to ask my servers about typical dishes of that region or what they'd recommend, and this has led to some wonderful culinary experiences. I discovered that unusual combinations like pizza topped with pears and gorgonzola cheese in Italy or pasta with chicken livers, brie and fresh figs in France were dishes I still remember years later.

Don't Overpack!

Nothing can spoil a trip faster than being burdened by too much luggage. I once read that before a trip you should pack everything you intend to take with you, then walk around the block with it a few times. If you find this tiring or cumbersome, you've definitely overpacked! Consider the throngs of tourists you'll have to maneuver through, and either excessive summer sun, heat, and humidity or freezing winter cold, snow, or rain. You may need to drag your luggage onto buses or trains, and up hills or stairways. Too much luggage is a recipe for travel disaster! I'm not immune to overpacking. I bring a pair of jeans and a warm shirt with me to Hawaii every single time I go "in case it gets chilly one night" and then curse myself, because I have never, ever needed them and they took up space and added weight to my bag. Remember, you can always wash clothes or buy some new ones, and you can find pretty much anything else you might need in the vast majority of places you will visit.

On a trip with some of my students, I met Danny, Steph, and Katie at the airport in Rome. As they exited Customs, Danny had a single backpack, but the women each had suitcases that weighed more than they did and were almost as tall as they were. I was mortified and wondered how we'd ever maneuver on the Metro or the streets of the city with all this. As I tried to lead the way out of the airport, they stopped me and said, "Wait, we have more bags!" I thought they were kidding, but the women ran back to baggage claim and returned with two smaller bags each. Danny just stood there shaking his head, muttering, "I'm not helping you carry any of this!" I agreed with him; I was younger then, but I could barely lift those bags, never mind carry them for any distance. How we got to our hotel is a blessedly repressed memory, but ultimately, the women were forced to pack up more than half of what they'd brought and have it shipped back to the U.S. at considerable expense because they couldn't take all this luggage on our flight from Italy to Greece at the end of the week. Travel light!

Don't try to do it all!

I think something that many of us are guilty of is trying to see and do too many things when we travel. It's understandable that if you've spent a lot of money to travel somewhere and aren't sure you'll ever get back there, you'd have a list of things you want to see and do, but if your days are packed solidly with a list of attractions and no time to let it all soak in, you're likely in for a far less enjoyable trip. A marathon of visits to tombs and temples like I experienced in Egypt, countless hours spent in museums, or touring twenty-seven cathedrals as you cross Europe is exhausting. Think more like a traveler than a tourist; take time to slow down and enjoy the place.

Be Nice!

At the risk of sounding like a cross between a nursery schoolteacher and a pastor, try to be kind and patient with the people you encounter in your travels. I view myself as an ambassador for my country when I travel and strive to make a positive impression. The old adage, "You catch more flies with honey than with vinegar" really has some merit. I recall arriving at an airport in Germany to find that my flight home to the U.S. had been cancelled, so I trudged to the customer service line, dreading what I assumed would be a nightmarish experience. The man in front of me in line was to have been on my canceled flight, and he screamed obscenities at the airline staff, argued with everything they said, and demanded to be compensated for his inconvenience. I stepped up to the adjacent window, handed the agent my itinerary and simply asked in a quiet voice, "Can you please help me get home today?" I ended up being re-routed and placed on a flight that actually got me home two hours earlier than my original flight. As I walked off with my new ticket, the man at the other window was getting nowhere, literally.

Avoid comparing the things you're experiencing in your host country to "how it is back home." A popular restaurant in Italy's Cinque Terre region that is open for breakfast has posted a sign on the front counter: "We do not serve eggs! Please don't ask. This is Italy! Eat our food!" I've overheard patrons challenging such a policy, indignantly asserting that the establishment should cater to them. Such demands aren't typically well received. Be aware of some of those cultural norms I mentioned back in Chapter 9 and try to modulate things like your style of dress, how loudly you speak, or your use of obscenities to conform to what's expected in the places you're visiting. I cringe when I witness a group of tourists invade a small, quiet restaurant dressed in revealing beachwear, uttering curse words in loud voices that are impossible for other diners to ignore, and acting as if they own the place.

Feeling More at Home in the World

Some folks don't adapt well or easily to visiting places where things are a lot different from what they're used to, and this can be an even more serious issue on longer trips. Students doing a semester abroad, business travelers spending significant amounts of time in another country, or people taking a multi-week trip may be particularly susceptible to home-sickness or a sort of culture shock due to the stresses of communicating in a foreign language or adjusting to local customs or different cuisines. Even though I thrive on travel, I haven't been immune from experiencing some of these feelings on some of my longer trips; my language struggles in Japan or my struggle to cope with the aggressive vendors in Egypt are a couple of personal examples.

If you're on a lengthy trip and/or are someone who is less comfortable with throwing yourself head-first into a new place or culture, there are definitely things you can do to make yourself feel more at home during your trip. For example, if you're in a country where you don't know the language and are feeling isolated, see if there's an English language channel on the TV in your room and watch a familiar show. Once during a lengthy stay in Paris, I found it strangely reassuring to be in front of the TV at 4:30PM each weekday to catch an episode of MTV's *Road Rules* that aired in English with French subtitles. It wasn't even a show I liked or cared about, but it was nice to at least hear English being spoken once a day and with the help of the subtitles, I actually learned a little French! I also watched a few episodes of *La Petite Maison dans la Prairie* ('Little House on the Prairie") that were dubbed into

French. Because I knew every episode by heart, the fact that the Ingalls family was conversing in French didn't really matter, and I took some comfort in time spent with Pa and Laura Ingalls.

If you become tired of the local cuisine, plan a meal of more familiar food. Hard as it is to imagine, after a few weeks of pasta and pizza in Italy, I started craving a good old fashioned American burger and fries, and after a little research online I satisfied that craving when I found a restaurant specializing in "American cuisine." After several days in Germany and the Czech Republic on a trip with students, I recall them excitedly running toward the first McDonald's they saw when we arrived in Prague, seemingly desperate for a taste of home. To their credit, they at least experimented with fried brie sticks instead of regular fries to accompany their Big Macs. Such little tastes of home are like a touchstone, allowing you to continue exploring the place you're visiting while staving off any pangs of homesickness.

Another way to feel more at home no matter where you are is to continue to pursue hobbies or activities that are part of your everyday life. If you're someone who likes to walk, jog, do crossword puzzles, meditate, or play golf, make time to enjoy these familiar activities in whatever place you're visiting. And if you're going to be in a place for several days or weeks, seek out a café or restaurant you like and go there a few times. You'll be comforted by its familiarity, the staff will begin to recognize you, and you may develop a sense of belonging that will make you feel a bit like a local. One of my fondest memories of Rome didn't occur at the Trevi Fountain or the Colosseum. It was at a neighborhood laundromat where the proprietress kindly showed me how to use the machines and chatted with me as I washed my clothes one afternoon. A couple weeks later I passed through Rome again and returned to the laundromat. Not only did she treat me like an old friend, but she enlisted my help when a group of Australian tourists who spoke no Italian were trying to explain to her how they wanted their clothes washed and dried. It was actually a lot of fun, and she playfully offered me a job as a translator if I ever decided to move to Rome!

Making Lemonade Out of Lemons

Travel doesn't always go smoothly, or as my friend Brent said, "The sun doesn't always shine in Tuscany." There are flight delays and cancellations, as well as train and bus strikes. Tourist attractions can be crowded, requiring long waits in line and hotels in real life don't always look like they do on their websites. Worse, you might have an accident, become the victim of a crime, or experience a medical issue while traveling. I've already shared my tales of colliding with the kangaroo in Australia and dealing with my injury during "the camel incident" in Egypt, but there have been many others!

There was the time I accidently drove into a pedestrian zone in a small town in southern France; as I hurriedly tried to back up, I hit a metal pole and destroyed one of the tires on my rental car. Local teens swarmed around me and to my amazement, banded together to change the tire for me! I left my hotel in Stockholm, Sweden early on a Sunday morning to drive to the airport and discovered that my rental car was locked inside a parking structure that I'd been assured was open twenty-four hours a day. No one could be contacted to help me get it out, so I had to notify the rental company where the car was, leave the keys at the hotel desk, and hail a cab to the airport, almost causing me to miss my flight! I've been pickpocketed on the Paris Metro once, and on Rome's Metro twice, requiring credit cards to be canceled and replacements sent to my hotel. Even more exciting was heading to the Rome airport by train and falling victim to an elaborate hoax that involved a well-dressed man spilling an oatmeal-like substance all over me as he walked past my seat. As he "helped" me clean it off with the dozens of napkins he suspiciously just happened to be carrying with him, someone in the row behind me stealthily lifted my briefcase with my laptop inside right off the seat beside me while I was being distracted. Airport police shook their heads in disgust when I reported the incident but said that this little caper plays out dozens of times every day. Luckily my passport and wallet were in my pocket, so at least I was able to fly home that day!

Probably the most frightening travel experience I've ever had also occurred in Italy, which is a testament to how wonderful Italy is; I still love it despite the mishaps I've experienced there! During one of my visits, I rapidly lost sight in one eye due to a ruptured blood vessel in the retina and ended up in an emergency room at a hospital in Livorno, Italy one Sunday morning. A soft-spoken surgeon and empathic nurse, neither of whom spoke English, opened an otherwise empty optometry ward, and performed laser surgery on my eye as my English-speaking cab driver stayed with me to help translate and offer moral support! My vision was saved, and I've been told by many eye doctors since that this surgeon did flawless work. Amazingly, I was not even charged for the surgery because I was a tourist. *Grazie, Italia!*

Now, don't let this litany of horror stories dissuade you from taking your dream trip. Any of these things could have just as easily happened to me a mile from home, and as disturbing as some of them were, they ultimately ended up on a positive note. As is true for life in general, all we can do is prepare for things as best as we can, try to keep our wits about us when things do go awry, and rely on the kindness of the many good people that surround us to help us cope, no matter where we are. Hard as it may be, try to find the humor in whatever happens to you. Sometimes in the midst of crises either great or small I've thought to myself, "This is going to be a great story to tell when I get home."

One relatively trivial example to illustrate this was when I stumbled upon an adorable, authentic-looking restaurant in Paris' *Rive Gauche* or Left Bank neighborhood. I got a window seat and ordered a three-course lunch. My first course was onion soup, which is to France as pasta is to Italy... how can you go wrong? Alas, this was a dreadful bowl of tepid water with half an onion in it and a greasy residue floating on top. I couldn't even finish it. My entrée was a steak that could easily have replaced the worn sole of someone's shoe and was accompanied by some soggy French fries. As I choked this down, dozens of tourists, lured by the restaurant's charming façade, stopped to peruse the menu on display in front of the window a few feet from where I was sitting. Not wanting to incur the wrath of the owner and my waiter who were hovering nearby, I subtly attempted to get these potential diners' attention and establish eye contact. When I'd succeed, I'd shake my head "no" while grimacing or gritting my teeth, or I'd use my hands to make a motion as if to shoo them away, a non-verbal message of "Run! Save yourselves!" In one case I ran a finger across my throat and shook my head "no" emphatically. Some people looked at me quizzically and my odd behavior perhaps scared them off, to their benefit. Others got the message, burst out laughing, gave me a wave of thanks and moved on down the street. My dessert was awful too. It was a terrible and expensive meal and very disappointing, but I have to say, I had a blast trying to save others from my fate, it actually ended up being a fond memory, and it still makes me laugh to think about it today.

My Travel Addiction Today

So here I am, a few years into retirement with lots of spare time on my hands but not quite the financial means to do all the things I'd like to do. Still, I look for ways to feed my travel addiction and make it affordable. I've made several road trips around the U.S. in the last couple of years, and of course, while the COVID nightmare definitely cramped my style in terms of international travel for a while, the world has opened up again and continues to call to me.

I'm often asked, "Are there places you still want to see that you haven't been to yet?" It takes me some time to come up with an answer, which tells me that I've done a pretty good job of crossing things off my bucket list. One of my biggest regrets is that when I traveled to Ecuador for a conference, I had the chance to visit the Galapagos Islands for a few days. I'd already taken time away from teaching my classes to attend the conference, and though my colleagues encouraged me to do it, my conscience wouldn't allow me to take the extra time away that I'd have needed for the Galapagos tour. Damn my conscience! I've seen photos by people who've been there, and I now realize what a huge mistake I made!

I'd also like to visit Peru to see the Inca site Machu Picchu or the strange "alien landing strip" carvings into the Nazca Plains, though I'm not sure I could make these trips at my age or in my current physical condition. After watching forty-plus seasons of *Survivor* I'd love to see more of the Pacific Island nations featured on the show, like Fiji or Palau, hoping that they'd be more exciting than Tahiti and that I wouldn't have to build my own shelter or risk being voted off the island by the locals. A visit to see the mysterious stone statues on Chile's Easter

Island would be awesome, and islands like the Seychelles or the Maldives in the Indian Ocean look very appealing. Closer to home, I have yet to visit the Caribbean and think I'd enjoy island hopping and relaxing on some quiet, pristine beaches, even though that sounds like a retirement cliché. More exotic trips I'd like to make would be a wildlife safari somewhere in Africa, or an excursion to Antarctica. Maybe I just need to save my money and book a seat to Mars on Elon Musk's proposed Starship spacecraft, in which case the sky would truly be the limit.

Italy's Dolomiti and Hawaii's Lanikai Beach.

If there's any downside to my travel addiction, it's that I'm torn between a desire to see new places while wanting to return to those I love. When I do visit a place that I'm not so fond of, it's actually a relief to be able to say, "I'm glad I've seen this, but I don't need to come back here again." Unfortunately, the places that have elicited this reaction are few and far between compared to the places that I long to return to. Of those, Italy and Hawaii are probably the biggest "offenders," two vastly different places, literally on opposite sides of the globe from one another, yet they both haunt me on an almost daily basis. Like a reverse form of homesickness, my longing to return to them is almost painful.

Why Travel?

As I was finishing this book, my friend Daniel asked a question that seemed simple, yet it stumped me: "Why do you travel?" I couldn't come up with an immediate reply and pondered the question for several days. As I've already explained, my mom instilled a sense of adventure and love of exploration in me, and I think media influence also fed my desire to see with my own eyes the places that television brought into my living room each week. As I think is true for many young people, travel represented a way to break away from the place where I was raised and see what else the world had to offer. After the loss of my mom and with no immediate family, nothing was tying me down. I had childhood friends who'd never been out of the state or had no knowledge of or curiosity about geography, and I didn't want to be like them. So, some of my early wanderlust was fueled by a desire to escape the provincialism that was so common in my hometown.

Utah's Bryce Canyon; Lava flow, Hawaii.

After giving it some more thought, I identified a number of reasons why travel has been and remains so important to me. It allows me to see natural wonders that can't be experienced close to home: hiking through the colorful, otherworldly formations of Utah's Bryce Canyon, seeing a glacier close-up, watching the northern lights dancing overhead, listening to the deafening silence of the desert, witnessing an ongoing volcanic eruption, or floating on a pristine aqua sea. These experiences are worth the financial costs, the hours of travel, or the strenuous hikes I've endured to reach them.

Similarly, I travel to see wildlife in its natural environment and my encounters with whales, manta rays, penguins, manatees, alligators, pelicans, moose, elk, and even black bears (from the relative safety of my car) have been spiritual experiences for me.

Travel transforms history from dry textbook passages into engaging, real-life adventures like walking amongst the ruins of Pompeii and Herculaneum, Petra, the Acropolis in Athens, and yes, even the pyramids of Egypt. It provides the opportunity to visualize, remember, and contemplate events from our past, like what happened on the beaches of Normandy or on the battlefields of Gettysburg. It can take the form of a pilgrimage to pay homage to victims of horrors that occurred in places like Auschwitz, Hiroshima, or Ground Zero.

Moose in Maine, meeting a Florida manatee; Canadian black bear.

Travel is humbling and forces me to at least consider other ways of living beyond my own limited experience: a city where the streets are canals and the buses, police cars, ambulances, and garbage trucks are all boats; places where people still live in tents and make dinner over a fire or bake bread over a volcanic steam vent; regions where there is intense poverty, yet those living in such conditions are more generous, and seemingly more carefree and content than at least half the people I know back home. It's provided me with the chance to talk to people who lead wildly different lives or have had vastly different experiences than me, only to discover how similar we really are when it comes to the most important things in life.

I've never been fond of goodbyes and perhaps that's why I've struggled a bit with how to end this book. I hope the travel memoirs I've shared here have amused, enlightened, or inspired you in some way. Our lives are ultimately all travel stories, journeys filled with joy, pain, laughter, tears, wonder, fear, boredom, adventure, routine, and uncertainty. Life truly is a mystery ride; we never know how long it will last or where it will take us, but getting the most out of the journey itself is really the whole point. On my own mystery ride, I intend to continue to dream of new destinations, to always take the scenic route, to stop and appreciate the treasures I find along the way, to keep my seat belt buckled, to watch out for that random kangaroo that could drop out of the sky into my path at any moment, and to enjoy every single minute of it all. I wish the same for each and every one of you.

About the Author

Matt Davis is a Professor Emeritus of Psychology from Dominican University of California. His research on how people view their risk from natural hazards led to numerous international speaking engagements and an appearance in the 2006 television documentary, *Could It Happen Here?*

An avid traveler (travel addict?), he has visited 35 countries and made over 50 coast-to-coast road trips across the USA. His website, www.mattathomeintheworld.com showcases his travel writing and photography and has attracted thousands of visitors from over two dozen nations.

After living in San Francisco for 30 years, Matt retired from a career of grading student assignments and attending endless faculty meetings in 2020 and recently returned to his hometown of New Bedford, Massachusetts.

Whether traveling or not, his passions include great food, a variety of musical genres, classic television shows, hiking, and being at or in the ocean. Matt is enjoying retirement and finally found the time to assemble a collection of some of his favorite travel stories into the book that he always hoped to publish.

Made in the USA
Columbia, SC
24 October 2023

24904215R00147